Text Ana
in Trans

Amsterdamer Publikationen zur Sprache und Literatur

in Verbindung mit

Peter Boerner, Bloomington; Hugo Dyserinck, Aachen;
Ferdinand van Ingen, Amsterdam; Friedrich Maurer†,
Freiburg; Oskar Reichmann, Heidelberg

herausgegeben von

Cola Minis†
und
Arend Quak

94

Text Analysis in Translation

Theory, Methodology, and Didactic Application of a Model for Translation-Oriented Text Analysis

Second Edition

Christiane Nord

Amsterdam - New York, NY 2005

Translated from the German by Christiane Nord and Penelope Sparrow

Textanalyse und Übersetzen: theoretische Grundlagen, Methode und
didaktische Anwendung einer übersetzungsrelevanten Textanalyse.
- Heidelberg: Groos, 1988

The paper on which this book is printed meets the requirements of "ISO
9706:1994, Information and documentation - Paper for documents -
Requirements for permanence".

ISBN: 90-420-1808-9
©Editions Rodopi B.V., Amsterdam - New York, NY 2005
Printed in the Netherlands

Contents

Preface VIII
Preface to the second edition IX
I. INTRODUCTION: The need for text analysis in translation 1
II. A MODEL FOR TRANSLATION-ORIENTED
    TEXT ANALYSIS 5
1. Theoretical principles 5
    1.1. Translatological foundations 5
        1.1.1. Factors and constituents of the translation process 5
        1.1.2. The role of the initiator 9
        1.1.3. The role of the translator 11
    1.2. Text-linguistic foundations...13
        1.2.1. The text as a communicative interaction 13
        1.2.2. The process of text reception 17
        1.2.3. Text typologies 19
2. The role and function of source-text analysis..........................25
    2.1. Possible relationships between source text and target text 25
        2.1.1. Fidelity   liberty   equivalence 25
        2.1.2. Skopos and intertextual coherence 27
        2.1.3. Intercultural cooperation 30
        2.1.4. Functionality plus loyalty 31
    2.2. Phases of the translation process 34
        2.2.1. The two-phase model 34
        2.2.2. The three-phase model 35
        2.2.3. The looping model 36
3. Factors of source-text analysis 41
    3.0. General considerations 41
    3.1. Extratextual factors 43
        3.1.0. Basic notions 43
        3.1.1. Sender 47
        3.1.2. Sender s intention 53
        3.1.3. Audience 57
        3.1.4. Medium/channel 62
        3.1.5. Place of communication 67
        3.1.6. Time of communication 70
        3.1.7. Motive for communication 74
        3.1.8. Text function 77
        3.1.9. The interdependence of extratextual factors 83

3.2. Intratextual factors 87
   3.2.0. Basic notions 87
   3.2.1. Subject matter 93
   3.2.2. Content 98
   3.2.3. Presuppositions 105
   3.2.4. Text composition 110
   3.2.5. Non-verbal elements 118
   3.2.6. Lexis 122
   3.2.7. Sentence structure 129
   3.2.8. Suprasegmental features 131
   3.2.9. The interdependence of intratextual factors 139

3.3. Effect 143
4. Applications of the model in translator training 155

4.0. General considerations 155

4.1. Planning the training process 161
   4.1.0. Fundamentals 161
   4.1.1. Selecting texts for translation classes 162
   4.1.2. Grading the difficulty of translation tasks 165
   4.1.3. Grading the difficulty of translation texts 172

4.2. Classifying translation problems 174

4.3. Testing transfer competence 177

4.4. Assessing translation quality 179
   4.4.0. Forms and functions of translation criticism 179
   4.4.1. Translation criticism vs. translation comparison 181
   4.4.2. A didactic model of translation criticism 182
   4.4.3. Defining translation errors 186
   4.4.4. Evaluating translation tasks 188

5. Sample texts 191

5.0. General considerations 191

5.1. Text 1: The relationship between intention and function –
   Alejo Carpentier: "Acerca de la historicidad de Víctor
   Hugues" 192
   5.1.0. Text 192
   5.1.1. Analysis of extratextual factors 193
   *5.1.2. The postscript   Acerca de la historicidad de Victor
   Hugues* 194
   5.1.3. The reflection of the extratextual factors in the text .195
   5.1.4. Analysis of intratextual factors 197
   5.1.5. Analysis of effect 200

5.1.6. Translation criticism 201
5.1.7. Conclusions and suggested translations 217

5.2. Text 2: The relationship between subject matter, text
     structure and effect – Miguel de Unamuno: "Niebla" 223
5.2.0. Text 223
5.2.1. Analysis of extratextual factors 223
5.2.2. The beginning of a text as a key to its interpretation 224
5.2.3. Some considerations on ironic intention 225
5.2.4. Analysis of text structure 227
5.2.5. Translation criticism 234
5.2.6. Conclusions and suggested translations 240

5.3. Text 3: The relationship between text function and receiver
     orientation – Tourist information text "Spezialitäten"........243
5.3.0. Text 243
5.3.1. Analysis of extratextual factors 243
5.3.2. The relevance of audience orientation 244
5.3.3. Analysis of intratextual factors 244
5.3.4. Translation criticism 250
5.3.5. Conclusions 256

III. FINAL CONSIDERATIONS 257

IV. Index of translation problems 263

V. Index of examples 264

VI. References 265

Preface

For more than twenty years I have been teaching courses in translation at the Institut für Übersetzer und Dolmetscher at the University of Heidelberg. In this book – the result of my "lifelong" attempt to teach translation on a systematic basis – I hope that I have come up with a methodology which will provide students with a "tool" for preparing translations not only for the classroom but also perhaps later in their professional life, and which may also serve as a stimulus for further research in the field of translation teaching.

I am deeply indebted to the several generations of students who, through their cooperation and constructive criticism in class, have contributed to the development of this model of translation-oriented text analysis, a model which may serve as a starting point for the systematic basis I am striving after.

This book was first published in German in 1988 and now, with the help of my friend Penelope Sparrow, I have produced an English version for English-speaking students, teachers, and translators. It is a translation that conforms to my concept of "functionality plus loyalty", which means that we have adapted the text, especially the examples and sample texts, to what we expect to be the needs of the new addressees, yet at the same time preserving the pedagogical intention of the original. Where there were no official translations of the German quotations available in English, these have been translated by the author.

My thanks go to Dr. Arend Quak of the Instituut voor Oudgermanistiek at Amsterdam University and to Fred van der Zee, who were instrumental in making it possible for this book to be published by Rodopi. I would also like to thank all those who, with their criticism, suggestions, advice, interest and understanding have helped me to complete this project, especially Klaus Berger, Hans J. Vermeer, Heidrun Gerzymisch-Arbogast, Joanna Best, and Penelope and Michael Sparrow.

Needless to say, I have only myself to blame for those inadequacies which are still present in the text.

Heidelberg, January 1991

Christiane Nord

Preface to the second edition

Almost 15 years after its publication and in spite of having been out of print for a number of years, *Text Analysis in Translation* still seems to be rather widely used in translator training institutions all over the world. Letters (or rather e-mails, nowadays) from students and colleagues in Africa, Asia or Latin America tell me that they need the book for their research projects or theses and cannot get hold of it anywhere. They have convinced me that a new edition would be worth a bit of extra work.

For although the basic structure and contents continue to be "functional" with regard to the needs and wishes of its readers, the book had to be polished up a little. First, with regard to terminology. At the beginning of the nineties, translation studies had only just started to develop the concepts and terms that may be considered rather well-defined today. Second, with regard to references. To make the book more reader-friendly for an English-speaking audience, I have cut down the number of references to articles or books written in German, which seemed imperative in a scholarly book when I first elaborated the methodology of pre-translational text analysis. To compensate for this reduction, references to more recent studies in the field have been added, which clearly indicate present trends and tendencies in the area of text analysis in translation.

Last, but not least, gender was not yet an issue when Penelope and I worked on our translation, but it is now. Therefore, I have taken great care to establish an equilibrium of masculine and feminine pronouns and to avoid any reference to the translator as a male person (except in quotations, which have been left unchanged). It is not a secret that there are more female than male translators in the profession.

My thanks go, again, to Mr. Fred van der Zee, who jumped at the idea of publishing a revised edition when I timidly ventured to ask him about the possibilities of a re-print.

Heidelberg, April 2005

Christiane Nord

I. INTRODUCTION: The need for text analysis in translation

Most writers on translation theory agree that before embarking upon any translation the translator should analyse the text comprehensively, since this appears to be the only way of ensuring that the source text (ST) has been wholly and correctly understood. Various proposals have been put forward as to how such an analysis should be carried out and how particular translation problems might best be dealt with. These tend, however, to be based on models of text analysis which have been developed in other fields of study, such as that of literary studies, of text or discourse linguistics (e.g. de Beaugrande & Dressler 1981), or even in the field of theology.

But what is right for the literary scholar, the text linguist or the theologian is not necessarily right for the translator: different purposes require different approaches. Translation-oriented text analysis should not only ensure full comprehension and correct interpretation of the text or explain its linguistic and textual structures and their relationship with the system and norms of the source language (SL). It should also provide a reliable foundation for each and every decision which the translator has to make in a particular translation process. For this purpose, it must be integrated into an overall concept of translation that will serve as a permanent frame of reference for the translator.

What is needed is a model of source-text analysis which is applicable to all text types and text specimens, and which can be used in any translation task that may arise. Such a model should enable translators to understand the function of the elements or features observed in the content and structure of the source text. On the basis of this functional concept they can then choose the translation strategies suitable for the intended purpose of the particular translation they are working on.

In my view, it should be possible to produce a model of translation-oriented text analysis without reference to the specific characteristics of the source or target languages. It should not depend on the translator's level of competence (i.e. on whether he or she is a professional or a trainee) and should be valid for both directions, i.e. translating into as well as out of the translator's native language. The model thus produced can then serve as a general theoretical framework for translation studies, translator training, and translation practice. The translator who has been trained to work with the model using one particular language-and-culture pair as a basis should also be in a position to apply it to other language-and-culture pairs, given the necessary linguistic and cultural proficiency.

The model should therefore be (a) general enough to be applicable to any text and (b) specific enough to take account of as many generalizable translation problems as possible. Specific intercultural or interlingual problems or difficulties, depending on the level of competence of the translator or the direction of the translation process, can then be introduced into the corresponding slots of the model. The model we are striving to produce, then, is largely concerned with the language-independent aspects of culture, communication and translation.

Such a model of translation-oriented text analysis could be of use not only to the students and teachers in translator training but also to the professional translator. It would be useful for trainee translators at Schools or Faculties for Translating and Interpreting or at similar institutions, since it would enable them to justify their translational decisions, to systematize translation problems, and to understand translational behaviour conventions more clearly. In translator training, teachers all too often have to rely on their intuition, on their own professional experience or academic research, on trial and error, imagination and luck. If they don't merely want to show their students "how it is done", then this model may provide them with a more objective frame of reference for their translational choices. For these teachers, the model can, among other things, provide some criteria for the classification of texts for translation classes and some guidelines for assessing the quality of a translation. Finally, it could be of interest to professional translators. For even if they are convinced that they have found the best and most efficient translation strategies for their particular (usually highly specialized) field of work, they may get some new ideas (e.g. how to defend their own translations or how to justify their judgement in translation quality control).

This book is intended to be a practical aid in teaching professional translation. It is for this reason that the analysis of literary texts and the specific problems of literary translation have not been given top priority. However, if a model for text analysis is meant to be applicable to all types of text, it does make sense to take the most complex text type as a starting point. All the factors involved in the "simpler" texts will also be found here. I have therefore included a considerable number of examples taken from the field of literature.

This study has a secondary purpose that may also prove to be relevant to translation teaching. It tries to establish where translation studies can draw upon the theories and methods of related disciplines, such as linguistics and literary criticism, etc. In an area of academic studies that only recently discovered the importance of scientific research – translation studies are now part of the examination syllabus at almost all training institutions – it seems worthwhile examining the relationship between translation theory (or "translatology") and philology (comprising linguistics and literary studies). Although it is impossible to present a definitive study, several examples will serve to clarify where, and to what extent, philological methods can contribute to providing solutions to translation problems.

Part 1 of the study presents the theoretical principles on which the model of translation-oriented text analysis is based, and surveys the various concepts of translation theory and text linguistics. Part 2 describes the role and scope of source-text analysis in the translation process and explains why the model is relevant to translation. Part 3 presents a detailed study of the extratextual and intratextual factors and their interaction in the text. Part 4 discusses the applications of the model in translator training. The book concludes with the practical analysis of a number of texts and their translations (Part 5), taking into account various text types and several languages.

SOME ABBREVIATIONS

ST   source text
TT   target text
SL   source language
TL   target language
SC   source culture
TC   target culture
TRL translator, translation

II. A MODEL FOR TRANSLATION-ORIENTED TEXT ANALYSIS

1. Theoretical principles

In order to establish the theoretical framework for the translation-oriented model of text analysis I shall first discuss those principles of translation theory which determine my concept of translation. The term "translation" here covers oral translation, i.e. interpreting, as well as written translation. Secondly, I shall deal with the text-linguistic principles which provide the basis for the model.

1.1. Translatological foundations

After a short description of the general conditions and constituents of the setting in which translation takes place I shall proceed to a more detailed analysis of the roles of the "initiator" and the translator since they are the most important factors in the production of a translation.

1.1.1. *Factors and constituents of the translation process*
My concept of translation is basically functional[1], and it is this notion of function that is the overriding criterion for the model of the translation process[2] depicted below (see Fig. 1 and Fig. 3).

---

[1] The functional approach to translation was first suggested by Reiss ([1971]2000: 92ff.), when she included the "special function of a translation" as an additional category in her model of translation criticism – a category which was to replace the normal criteria of equivalence-based critique in those (special) cases where the target text was intended for a purpose different from that of the source text. This point of view is also expressed by Reiss 1976a. From 1978 onward, both Reiss and particularly Vermeer have frequently postulated that as a general rule it must be the intended purpose of the TT that determines translation methods and strategies, and not the function of the ST. In 1978, Vermeer formulated this postulate as the *skopos* rule ([1978]1983: 54), which later on was to become the main component of his general translation theory (*Skopostheorie*, cf. Reiss & Vermeer 1984). Holz-Mänttäri, too, regards the target function as the core of "product specification", as she calls the description of properties and features required of the target text (1984a: 114).

[2] In order to make a distinction between the setting of the translation process, i.e. the totality of factors and constituents connected with the making of a translation (*Translationsvorgang*, cf. Nord 1988a: 283), and the translation process in the narrower sense, i.e. the procedure that leads from ST analysis to TT production, I shall refer to the former as the "process of intercultural text transfer". In either case, however, my concept of process must not be confused with the psycholinguistic notion of "what is going on in the translator's mind", which is studied empirically on the basis of think-aloud protocols (TAP, cf. Kußmaul 1995: 5ff., among others).

A translation process is usually initiated by a customer or "initiator" (INI.), approaching a translator (TRL) because they need a certain target text (TT) for a particular target addressee or receiver (TT-R)[3]. It might also happen that it is precisely the initiator who wants to understand in the target language (TL) a certain source text (ST) written in a source language (SL) by an SL author or text producer (ST-P) or transmitted by a source-language sender (ST-S) under the particular conditions of the source culture (SC).

It seems sensible to make a methodological distinction between the text producer (ST-P), who actually produces the text, and the sender (S), who transmits a text in order to convey a certain message. Senders using a text written by themselves can be considered to be both text producer and sender in one. Therefore, they are responsible for every feature of the formulation, and I prefer to call them "authors" instead of senders or text producers. However, if an expert on text production (e.g. a ghost-writer) is asked to write a text for somebody else, a discrepancy may occur between the sender's intention and its realization by the text producer. The sender may also allow the text producer a certain scope of stylistic creativity, which may then be reflected in the style even though it does not depend directly on the sender's intention (see below, ch. 1.1.3., and example 3.1.1./1).

Once the process of intercultural text transfer has been initiated, the translator may be regarded as the actual receiver of the ST, even though he or she would not normally be one of the addressees. As a general rule, texts are not produced just in order to be translated but to fulfil certain communicative purposes for a specified SL audience.

Example 1.1.1./1
a) In the translation of a business letter, the ST receiver is clearly identifiable from both the address and the salutation formula. b) A text specified as a "children's book" is intended for a group of addressees of a certain age. c) A translator who has to translate a literary text from another period in history, often has to resort to text-analytical methods in order to determine the conditions of its reception. In such a case, it may even be necessary to distinguish between the "original" reception in the author's time and reception in the translator's time.

Although not normally taking an active part in the process of intercultural text transfer (except in the special case of interpreting), the ST addressees are an important factor in the ST situation in that the lin-

---

[3] The distinction between addressee and receiver is discussed in detail in Nord 2000: 196.

guistic and stylistic features of the ST may have been chosen according to what the text producer thinks they expect. Moreover, it may be part of the translation skopos to "imitate" the effects of the original ST reception (see below, ch. 3.1.8.c).

For these reasons I have included ST reception as a second track in the diagram depicting the process of intercultural text transfer.

The essential factors and constituents of the process of intercultural text transfer are, then, in chronological order: ST producer, ST sender, source text, ST receiver, initiator, translator, target text, TT receiver. These are communicative roles which can, in practice, be represented by one and the same individual. For example, the ST author himself, the TT receiver, or even the translator can act as the initiator of a translation.

Example 1.1.1./2
a) A German medical professor has to give a lecture at an international conference, where the official language will be English. She knows sufficient English to be able to read out an English text, but not enough to write her lecture in English. So she writes a German text and asks a translator to put it into English (ST-P = I = TT-S). b) A translator produces a translation in order to submit it as an example of her work on applying for a job (TRL = I). c) A copywriter asks for the translation of a foreign advertisement in order to gain an impression of the marketing strategies used in other countries (TT-R = I). d) A Latin American author living in exile in France translates his own novel from Spanish into French (ST-P = I = TRL).

In addition to these essential constituents we also have to consider a number of non-essential constituents. In the diagram (Fig. 1) I have left empty spaces or slots [X] to account for any additional persons or institutions which may be involved in a particular process of intercultural text transfer.

Example 1.1.1./3
a) An advertising agency orders the ST from a copywriter (ST-P), specifying certain requirements for a later translation (X = advertising agency). b) The final layout of the TT is assigned to a text designer, so that the translator need not bother about this (X = text designer). c) Before being sent to print, the TT is revised by an expert who adapts the text to the firm's own terminology (X = expert).

Interpreting is a special form of translation, because the situation requires the presence of the ST receiver (ST–R) as well as of the translator and the TT receiver (TT–R). Since interpreting is a form of face-to-face communication, both the sender and the receiver are present – as is shown in the usual models of communication – together with the translator in the role of TT producer. All the participants communicate in the same place at the same time using the same medium, and the function of the text is the same for all of them except the translator. However, what is different is the cultural background of the ST-S and the ST-R on the one hand, and the TT-R, on the other.

The translation of written texts usually takes place in a different type of situation. Even though the medium by which the text is transmitted may remain the same, the ST sender and the ST and TT receivers are separated in time and space and their communication is a "one-way communication", which does not permit immediate feedback. Moreover, written texts can exist outside their original situation and can therefore be applied to new situations – a procedure which may change their function(s) altogether. One such new situation is translation. In order to find out whether the text is suitable for the new situation in the target culture, the translator has to take into consideration the factors and constituents of the original situation.

> **Being culture-bound communicative signs, both the source and the target text are determined by the communicative situation in which they serve to convey a message.**

Since in written communication sender and receiver are usually separated in time and space, we have to make a distinction between the situation of text production and that of text reception both in the source and the target culture (SC, TC). In SC, we have to differentiate between the original reception and the translator's reception, except in those cases where the original text is produced specifically as a source text, i.e. for translation only. As these texts have no SC addressee, the SC reception track of the model will then be assigned zero.

Example 1.1.1./4
Texts intended for advertising abroad, business letters, and tourist information leaflets may have no receivers in the source culture, but only in the target culture. In these cases, the translator will be the only actual ST receiver.

Accordingly, the diagram representing the process of intercultural text transfer shows an ST situation (SIT-S) and a TT situation (SIT-T), both of which are divided into a text-production and a text-reception part. In written translation, ST reception and TT production by the translator usually coincide in time and place, whereas in interpreting it is the whole of SIT-S and the whole of SIT-T which form the one communicative situation.

Figure 1: The process of intercultural text transfer (1)

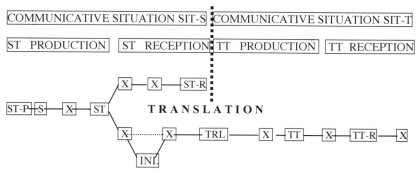

As illustrated above by the examples under 1.1.1./2, the initiator (INI) need not necessarily be part of SIT-S, but may also be part of SIT-T. This is why (INI) appears "lowered" in the diagram; it is only the *function* of (INI) that fits into this particular slot.

1.1.2. The role of the initiator

In the process of intercultural text transfer depicted above, the initiator plays a crucial role. Apart from being an individual (unless, of course, the role of initiator is taken by the translator, the TT receiver, etc.) having his or her own personal characteristics, the initiator is the factor that starts the process and determines its course.

The process of intercultural text transfer is started because the initiator wants a particular communicative instrument: the target text. This implies that the initiator wants the translation for a certain purpose. The reception of the target text by the initiator or any other person the target text is passed on to depends on this purpose. It is this purpose that determines the requirements to be met by the translation.

> **Example 1.1.2./1**
> a) An American physicist asks for a translation of some Russian technical literature to find out about the latest state of scientific research in Russia. b) A German company wants to present their products or make an offer to a Spanish salesperson. c) By having a French novel translated into English, a British publisher wants to launch a bestseller on the market. d) A language teacher wants to find out by means of a translation task whether the students can tell the difference between the functions of a gerund and a present participle in English.

If the translation is to be suitable for a certain purpose, it must fulfil certain requirements, which are defined by the translating instructions

or translation brief[4]. They consist of a (explicit or implicit) definition
of the prospective target situation, which I shall call the "skopos" of
the target text ("TT skopos"). Not being experts on translation, initiators are often unable to formulate the brief themselves. They might
simply say, for example: "Would you please translate this text into
Russian?" However, they certainly have it in mind because they know
what purpose they want the translation for. In this case it is the translator, as an expert in the target culture, who converts the information
provided by the initiator about the prospective TT situation into a
practicable definition of the TT skopos.

The main point about the functional approach is the following.
It is not the source text as such, or its effect on the ST receiver, or the
function assigned to it by the author, that operates the translation process, as is postulated by equivalence-based translation theory, but the
intended function or skopos of the target text as determined by the initiator's needs. This point of view corresponds to Vermeer's *Skopostheorie* (Reiss & Vermeer 1984: 95ff.)[5].

Although the initiator is the one who actually defines the TT
skopos (even if he or she may not be able to formulate the brief), the
responsibility for the translation will always rest with the translator. It
is the translator alone who has the competence to decide whether the
translation which the initiator asks for can actually be produced on the
basis of the given source text and, if so, how, i.e. by which procedures
and techniques, this should best be done. After all, it is the translator,
and not the initiator, who is the expert on translation (see below, ch.
2.2.3.).

---

[4] The German term *Übersetzungsauftrag* (cf. Nord 1986a) literally translates as
"translation assignment". In English, I would prefer to speak of "translating instructions" when the term is intended to highlight the pedagogical aspect, and of "translation brief" where the focus of attention is on professional aspects (cf. Nord 1997a:
30).

[5] Reiss & Vermeer (1984) maintain that it is the translator who fixes the translation
skopos. It is certainly true that certain types of transfer situations are conventionally
linked with certain TT skopoi. In these cases, the translator can often infer the translating instructions from the situation and, if necessary, come to an agreement with
the initiator. But in principle, the TT skopos is still subject to the initiator's decision
and not to the discretion of the translator. It is the initiator, after all, who judges in
the end whether or not the translation meets his or her needs.

> **The function of the target text is not arrived at automatically from an analysis of the source text, but is pragmatically defined by the purpose of the intercultural text transfer.**

As text function is determined by the situation in which the text serves as an instrument of communication (cf. Nord 1992b), the translation brief should contain as much information as possible about the situational factors of the prospective TT reception, such as the addressee(s) or possible receivers, time and place of reception, intended medium, etc.

As pointed out by Reiss & Vermeer (1984: 101), the information about the addressees (socio-cultural background, expectations towards the text, the extent to which they may be influenced, etc.) is of particular importance. The more unequivocal and definite the description of the TT addressee, the easier it is for translators to make their decisions in the course of the translation process. The translator therefore should insist on being provided with as many details as possible.

In view of this strict orientation towards the addressees, it may well be that translators are in possession of more detailed information about "their" addressee(s) than the author, whose readers may be found not only in the source culture but, in the case of a later translation, also in the respective target culture(s).

> **Example 1.1.2./2**
> A Latin American novelist and Nobel prize winner may write a new novel not only for a national audience but also with foreign readers in mind, if he or she expects the book to be translated later. The translator who renders the novel into German will not normally have to take into consideration any French or Italian readers.

1.1.3. The role of the translator

In the diagram representing the process of intercultural text transfer (Figure 1), the translator (TRL) occupies the central position. Being a receiver of the source text as well as the producer of the target text, TRL takes part in both the ST situation (SIT-S) and the TT situation (SIT-T). Nevertheless, translators are no ordinary participants in the communication process. In their function as translators they do not actually belong to the group of receivers addressed by the ST sender in an ordinary communicative situation. This also applies when the ST has been produced for translation only, i.e. for the target audience. From the sender's point of view, the translator may be compared with a ghost-writer who produces a text at the request, and for the use, of somebody else.

Translators are a very special kind of receiver not only from the sender's point of view but also because they receive the text in a very peculiar situation. They do not read it for their own purposes (i.e., in order to be informed or amused or to find out how to use a new machine). Unlike a professor who reads a certain book in order to prepare her lecture, or a literary critic who reads a particular novel in order to be able to write a review of it, translators have no "personal need" to read the text, so to speak. They read the ST instead of the initiator, or some other receiver who belongs to a target culture which may be quite different from the source culture. After reading the text, the translator is going to convey to them, by means of the translation, a certain piece of information from or about the source text.

> The translator s reception (i.e. the way s/he receives the text) is determined by the communicative needs of the initiator or the TT addressees.

In practice, translators usually receive the brief or instructions (or infer them from the situation) before they start reading the ST. Therefore, the reception process will inevitably be influenced by this knowledge, even though they may do their best to approach the text in as unbiassed a way as possible. Moreover, like the literary critic or the linguist, the professional translator will never read a text that has to be translated in a naïve or intuitive manner, but will aim for a critical, comprehensive, translation-oriented analysis.

Professional translators read every new ST in the light of their experience as critical readers and translators. This experience forms a framework into which they integrate the findings of each new ST reception. In translator training we therefore have to set up the basic structure for such a framework.

Last but not least, the reception of a text is determined by the receiver's particular competences. The translator-as-receiver is (ideally) bi-cultural, which means s/he has a perfect command of both the source and the target culture (including language), and possesses a transfer competence, which comprises the skills of text reception, text production, and the use of translation tools, as well as the ability to "synchronize" ST reception and TT production (cf. Wilss 1977: 626). Their command of the source culture (SC) must enable them to reconstruct the possible reactions of an ST receiver (in case the TT skopos requires an "imitation" of the ST functions by the target text), whereas their command of the target culture (TC) allows them to anticipate the possible reactions of a TT receiver and thereby verify the functional adequacy of the translation they produce.

The particular situation in which translators have to simulate a communicative situation that is determined not by their own but by somebody else's needs and purposes brings about the special conditions of TT production.

> **The translator is not the sender of the ST message but a text-producer in the target culture who adopts somebody else s intention in order to produce a communicative instrument for the target culture, or a target-culture document of a source-culture communication.**[6]

1.2. Text-linguistic foundations

In this chapter I will outline the theoretical principles behind the model of text analysis by means of a few basic concepts, thus defining my text-linguistic starting point.

1.2.1. The text as a communicative interaction

Experience shows (as is illustrated in Fig. 1) that translation takes place within the framework of a communicative situation and on the basis of linguistic units which I have up to now, rather intuitively, called "texts": source text (ST) and target text (TT).

Unlike other communicative situations, intercultural text transfer is special in that two cultures (including languages) are involved and that the message transmitted between the sender (here: ST-S) or text producer (here: ST-P) and the receiver (here: TT-R) is formulated using the elements of not one, but two codes (cf. Kallmeyer et al. 1980: 12). Moreover, the act of intercultural text transfer seems to some extent to be "broken" by the intervention of the initiator and the translator. Nevertheless, both the source and the target text are texts, each embedded in a communicative situation and thus part of a com-

---

[6] Cf. chapter 3.1.8c and for more details Nord 1997c, where I have tried to work out a functional translation typology. The two main translation types are (according to their function) *documentary* and *instrumental* translation.

municative act or interaction. De Beaugrande & Dressler (1981: 3) refer to the text as a "communicative occurrence".

An essential prerequisite for such a communicative occurrence
is, first of all, the existence of a situation, i.e. "that sub-set of non-linguistic events which are clearly relevant to the identification of the
linguistic feature(s)" (Crystal & Davy 1969: 11). It is, or can be, fixed
in time and space and comprises at least two participants who are able
and willing to communicate with each other for a certain purpose and
by means of a text. The text is transmitted via a suitable channel or
medium and (ideally!) will have the function of fulfilling the intended
communicative purpose. The communicative act-in-situation provides
the framework in which the text has its place. The text can only be understood and analysed within and in relation to the framework of the
communicative act-in-situation.

The "text-centred notions" of textuality (de Beaugrande &
Dressler 1981: 7), especially those of coherence and cohesion and the
procedures for obtaining them (such as recurrence, parallelism, paraphrase, pro-forms, anaphora, cataphora), refer to structural features. In
an action-oriented concept of textuality, these features only gain relevance against the background of situation and function, as shown in
the following examples.

Example 1.2.1./1
The first traces of translation date from 3000 BC. The children broke my valuable Chinese vase. Contributions should be sent to the foreign correspondents
listed below. The last word ended in a long bleat, so like a sheep that Alice
quite started.

Example 1.2.1./2
There is nobody who is not fascinated by her song. Our singer is called Jose-
phine. Song is a word of four letters. Singers love using pathetic words. (Adapted from the example quoted by Dressler 1973: 7).

Example 1.2.1./3
It is well known that cats are more intelligent than dogs. For example, three
out of four motorists die of heart diseases before they are fifty. Another example is the commonly observed ability of dolphins to understand human speech.
In conclusion I should like to emphasize that whereas girls learn mathematics
quickly, boys learn mathematics equally quickly (Graustein & Thiele 1981:
7).

In the first example there is neither cohesion nor coherence between
the sentences that have been taken at random from various texts I happened to have at hand. The other two examples show certain features
of cohesion (recurrence, substitutions, anaphoric and cataphoric ele-

ments), but semantic coherence is not found in them either. According to purely text-linguistic criteria, the three examples would have to be regarded as non-texts. There may be situations, however, where even these non-texts will have to be accepted as texts. For instance, in an absurd drama the author might have played with the lack of semantic coherence in order to produce a certain effect on the audience.

De Beaugrande & Dressler have taken these aspects into consideration by supplementing the text-centred notions of cohesion, coherence and informativity with the user-centred notions of intentionality and acceptability as "speaker and hearer attitudes" (1981: 79), and the "social" factors of situationality and intertextuality (cf. also de Beaugrande 1980: 19f.). In a similar way, the German text linguist Schmidt regards intentionality, communicativity and/or partner-orientation as "irreducible characteristics of language as a social medium of verbal interaction" (1976: 22, my translation).

If textuality is no longer considered a mere structural property of an utterance, but primarily a feature of its use in communication, the concept of text on which my model of translation-oriented text analysis will be based has to include both the structural and the pragmatic-situational aspects. Furthermore, this should not be seen as being purely an addition, but as a form of mutual interdependence of both aspects.[7] In accordance with Schmidt I therefore distinguish between

> (a) *textuality* as a structural feature of socio-communicative (and, as such, also linguistic) acts of or between the participants of communication; and
> (b) *texts* as the concrete realizations of the structural feature "textuality" in a particular medium of communication.
> According to this definition, texts are always sets of linguistic signs in a socio-communicative function, which means that they are texts-in-function embedded within the framework of communicative actions. As such they are generally defined and definable by both linguistic and social criteria (Schmidt 1976: 145, my translation).

Consequently, the distinction between text and non-text must be based on the criterion of communicative function, a criterion which is of par-

---

[7] The interdependence between situational and structural aspects shows up very clearly when we consider those intratextual features that can only be interpreted in regard to their relationship with the extratextual conditions of the communicative situation, such as deictic expressions (e.g. *today* or *here* or lexical items referring to the participants in the communicative act like *I*, *you*, *dear colleagues*). This relationship is referred to as "exophoric reference" by Halliday & Hasan (1976: 18), who point out that it is coherence, not cohesion, which is brought about by such elements.

ticular relevance in intercultural communication. It is not always possible for a text as a whole to be assigned to any one single function. This applies to the so-called "complex text types" (Reiss & Vermeer 1984: 180) or to frame texts including embedded texts belonging to different text types. In these cases, situation and function have to be analysed separately for each of the embedded texts or text sections (paragraphs, chapters, etc.).

For the translator, the semantic and syntactic structural features of the text-in-function are important not as an evidence that the utterance in question actually is a text, but as a means of analysing its meaning, both in the sense of denotation (i.e. reference to extralinguistic reality) and connotation (i.e. reference to language use and style).

There is yet another aspect which has to be taken into account for a translation-oriented concept of textuality. It is mentioned implicitly in the definition given by Kallmeyer et al.: "A text is the totality of communicative signals used in a communicative interaction" (1980: 45, my translation). Communicative signals need not always consist of linguistic elements alone, but these may also be complemented or accompanied by non-linguistic or non-verbal means, such as intonation, facial expressions, or gestures in face-to-face communication, or by illustrations, layout, a company logo, etc. in written communication. In some texts, non-verbal elements may be of even greater importance than verbal elements, as is the case in comic strips.[8] In the translation process, the translator may occasionally find it necessary to change non-verbal into verbal elements, or vice versa (see below, ch. 3.2.5.).

> **A text is a communicative action which can be realized by a combination of verbal and non-verbal means.**

If we consider the text to be a communicative action, it is clear that in text analysis the dimensions of the communicative situation as well as the participants in the communicative act must be the prime factors. In

---

[8] However, not every form of non-verbal communication can be regarded as a text. To include other forms of non-verbal communication which are not complementary to verbal communication would mean, as Gülich & Raible (1977: 33f.) rightly comment, that playing chess or feeding a baby would have to be considered a "text" as well. Moreover, non-verbal text elements cannot always be regarded as message transmitters that exist independent of the verbal elements of the text or at least serve to support the message or as an orientation for the reader. They may very well be mere conventional text markers with little or no meaning at all. The analyst has to check from case to case whether or not the non-verbal elements of the text in question carry any communicative intentions.

a translation-oriented analysis, we will first analyse these factors and their function in the ST situation and then compare them with the corresponding factors in the (prospective) TT situation, since the target text, too, like the source text, will be embedded in a communicative interaction which determines its reception.

1.2.2. The process of text reception

If a text is to be regarded as a combination of communicative signals within a communicative situation, as has been described above, we can analyse text function from either the producer's or the receiver's point of view. This is true, at least, of written communication where the situation of text production is quite different from that of text reception. Where text production is concerned, we are mainly interested in the intention which the author is trying to realize by means of the text. It is this intention that determines the strategies of text production (such as elaboration of the subject matter, choice of stylistic devices or non-verbal elements etc.) and thus has a strong influence on text function. As Vermeer aptly puts it:

> If the sender wants to communicate, he attunes himself to the receiver's personality, or, to be more precise, he adapts himself to the role which he expects the receiver to expect of him. This includes the judgement which the sender has of the receiver (Vermeer 1972: 133, my translation).

Let us now look at how text function can be analysed from the receiver's point of view. It may seem to be stating the obvious to say that good will is not always a guarantee of good results. It can all too often happen that the sender's intention has not been realized successfully in the text (especially if the sender is not the text producer). Receivers cannot therefore always assume that what they infer from the text is actually the sender's intention. However, even if the sender's intention has been realized unambiguously in the text, receivers may read the text with an intention (or rather, an expectation) of their own, which may be entirely different from that of the sender.

> **The reception of a text depends on the individual expectations of the receivers, which are determined by the situation in which they receive the text as well as by their social background, their world knowledge, and/or their communicative needs.**

The sender's intention and the receiver's expectation may be identical, but they need not necessarily coincide nor even be compatible.

The consequences of these considerations for translation are as follows. If the translator has no knowledge of the situation in which the ST production occurred, and cannot ask the sender or producer of the text for information, because they are either dead (in the case of old texts) or not traceable, she has to rely on conjecture. Therefore, for any ST production which took place in the past under particular circumstances and cannot be repeated under the same circumstances, we cannot claim "scientific verification" at least where written texts are concerned, though perhaps not in an interpreting situation.

Text reception, however, has to be seen in a different light. The translator is a real ST receiver with source-culture competence, even though this is by chance and not the intention of the sender. Moreover, the translator is a "critical receiver" (see above, ch. 1.1.3.), who is aiming at least to achieve an objective, conscientious, and verifiable comprehension of the source text. Translators receive the text on various levels: (a) on the level of SC-competent receivers (in their own TRL situation), (b) on that of an analyst who puts her or himself in the situation of both the intended ST receivers and possible real ST receivers, and (c) from the standpoint of a TC-competent receiver, reading the ST "through the eyes" of the intended TT audience and trying to put her or himself in their shoes as well. As House (1981a: 196f.) puts it, the translator has to "place a cultural filter between ST and TT; he has to, as it were, view ST through the glasses of a target culture member".

According to the dynamic view of the text we have adopted, a text does not "have" a function; a function can only be assigned to the text by the receiver in the act of reception.

> **As a product of the author's intention, the text remains provisional until it is actually received. It is the reception that completes the communicative situation and defines the function of the text. We may say that the text as a communicative act is completed by the receiver.**

This leads to the conclusion that a text can be used in as many functions as there are receivers of it. We have all seen how one and the same person at different times in his or her life may "read" the same text in quite different ways. If that person is a translator, s/he would certainly have produced different translations. It is "the individual re-

ceiver R at the time t with his individual and social history of reception that receives the message M. R's individual and social circumstances are part of the reception", as Vermeer points out (1979: 70, my
translation).

In view of this concept of text reception it may seem pointless
to consider the possibility of matching one translation with one particular source text, or even offering any criteria for an optimum translation. If reception is absolutely dependent on individual conditions,
there will be no chance whatsoever of finding evaluation standards
which will take into account every single reception process.

The only way to overcome this problem is, in my opinion, first
to control ST reception by a strict model of analysis which covers all
the relevant text features or elements, and, second, to control TT production by stringent "translating instructions" which clearly define the
(prospective) function of the target text. With this function in mind,
the translator can then find arguments for ruling out one solution or
giving preference to another so that the variety of possible translations
is reduced on the basis of functional criteria. Only then will it become
possible to justify the comparison of various translations of one source
text (provided they have been translated for the same TT function) and
to succeed in achieving a comparative assessment of translations,
which is needed, for example, in translator training.

1.2.3. Text typologies
a. The importance of communicative function
Communicative function is not only the fundamental constitutive feature of texts but it also determines the strategies of text production.
For translators, this view has two consequences. From a retrospective
angle, they try in their ST analysis to verify their expectation regarding text function, which has been built up by situational clues, or (if
there is no extratextual information about the setting of the text) to
correlate the structural features of the ST with possible text functions
and thus make inferences about the communicative situation. From a
prospective angle, on the other hand, they have to check each ST element as to whether it can fulfil the intended TT function as it stands or
whether it has to be adapted, since the structural properties of any
target text have to be adjusted to the function it is intended to have for
the target-culture receiver.

As structural text features are normally polyfunctional, the relation-ship between text function and text structure is rarely 1:1. As a general rule, a text with a particular function is characterized by a combination or "configuration" of features, which can be constituted by both extra-textual (i.e. pragmatic) and intratextual (semantic, syntactic, and styl-istic) elements.

This idea can be useful as a starting point for a systematic clas-sification of text groups, classes, genres, or types according to certain common features or feature combinations, where the relation between a particular configuration of features and a particular text function is culture-specific.

German linguists and translation scholars (cf. Lux 1981 or Reiss & Vermeer 1984, for example) usually distinguish between text type (*Texttyp*), which is a *functional* classification (e.g. informative vs. expressive vs. persuasive texts or descriptive vs. narrative vs. argu-mentative texts), and text class (*Textsorte*), a category that refers to the occurrence of texts in standard situations (e.g. weather report, prayer, folk-ballad, operating instructions). English-speaking authors often seem to use the term text type for both classifications (cf. de Beaugrande 1980: 197, de Beaugrande & Dressler 1981: 183ff., or House 1981a: 35)[9], as the following definition given by de Beau-grande (1980: 197) clearly shows:

> A text type is a distinctive configuration of relational dominances obtaining between or among elements of (1) the surface text; (2) the textual world; (3) stored knowledge patterns; and (4) a situation of occurrence.

This means that as certain kinds of text seem to be used repeatedly in certain situations with more or less the same function or functions, these texts have acquired conventional forms that have sometimes even been raised to the status of social norms, the observance of which is expected by the participants in the communication process, whereas non-observance may be penalized. Thus, text-type conven-tions and norms play an important part both in text production (be-cause authors have to comply with the conventions if they want to succeed in realizing their communicative intentions) and text recep-

---

[9] More recently, the use of the term *genre* has been extended to non-literary texts, es-pecially in translation studies. Hatim & Mason (1992: 241) define *genre* as "[c]on-ventional forms of texts associated with particular types of social occasion (e.g. the sonnet, the cooking recipe, etc.)". I will therefore use *genre* to translate the German term *Textsorte*.

tion (because the receiver may infer the author's intentions from the conventional form of the text).[10]

Example 1.2.3./1

All instructing texts, such as operating instructions, directions for use or recipes, are characterized by a typical syntactic structure. In English, it is the imperative ("melt the butter on a medium heat"); in Spanish, it is the traditional impersonal construction ("se mondan y lavan las patatas"), which, however, is now often replaced by an infinitive ("mondar y lavar las patatas"), and in German, infinitives are used almost exclusively ("Fischfilet säubern, säuern, salzen"), whereas old recipes made use of the subjunctive mode ("Man nehme drei Eier...").

Not only do text-type norms vary from one culture to another, but they are also subject to historical change, as shown in example 1.2.3./1. Certain genres that are very common today did not exist in former times (e.g. radio news or advertisements), whereas others, which were quite commonplace centuries ago (e.g. magic spells or heroic poems), have changed function or become obsolete altogether.

> **Genre conventions are not universal, but linked to a certain culture at a certain time.**

b. Literary vs. non-literary conventions

It is interesting that the notion of genre norms is applied mainly to non-literary texts, such as recipes or directions for use, as it is these texts that in the social practice of appropriate behaviour and role-playing seem to develop rather rigid forms. Therefore, their realization in the form of individual texts is merely a reproduction of existing models.

In the field of literary texts conventional elements are not so frequent as in the field of non-literary texts. Designations such as "novel", "short story", or "anecdote" may, however, indicate that the texts belonging to one of these genres are expected to possess certain common features. Literary genres are often differentiated by special fea-

---

[10]In view of these considerations the classification of translations (i.e. target texts) as a genre, which is suggested by Dressler (1975: 253f.), does not seem to be justified, although it is certainly true that in the practice of professional translation, target texts are often recognized – unfortunately! – by certain common features, such as "manifestations of interlanguage" (cf. Toury [1978]1980: 74), which are in fact due to the specific (transfer) situation in which they have been produced. I can only assume that Dressler starts out from a different notion of genre. If the genre is determined by text function, it seems clear that the function of a text will rarely be exclusively that of being a translation.

tures of subject matter or content (anecdote vs. joke), extension (novel vs. short story) or by their affiliation to a literary era (novella vs. short story), as well as by certain stylistic properties. Nevertheless, a literary text usually has to be regarded as the result of an individual creative process. Its (artistic) significance lies precisely in the fact that it does *not* reproduce existing text models (in that case it would be regarded as epigonic), but represents an original innovation.[11]

c. Translation-oriented text typologies

If in ST analysis the translator finds the text characterized by a strict observance of text-type conventions, s/he can be fairly certain that individual stylistic features which have their own particular effect on the receiver do not play an important part. If, on the other hand, the TT skopos requires the target text to conform strictly to target-cultural genre conventions, the translator will be justified in "neglecting" the conventional linguistic and stylistic properties of the source text in the process of analysis.

In order to be able to find out which text features are conventional and which are not, the translator needs comprehensive (intralingual or contrastive) descriptions of genre conventions. Recently, corpus-based genre comparisons have become a rather popular object of students' masters or doctoral theses.

The translator, of course, is particularly interested in those typologies which claim to be "translation-oriented", even though their approach is of a rather general nature. As early as 1971 Katharina Reiss published the first translation-oriented text typology, which was slightly modified (especially with regard to terminology) in 1976 (cf. Reiss 1971, 1976a). On the basis of Bühler's *organon model* of language functions (cf. Bühler 1934), Reiss made a distinction between informative texts (e.g. news or scientific articles), expressive texts (e.g. works of literature), appellative or operative texts (e.g. advertisements), and subsidiary or audio-medial texts (e.g. songs or radio plays, whose realization involves media other than print). This fourth category was abandoned in later works. Reiss & Vermeer (1984) also refer to Reiss' functional text typology, stressing the view that by assigning

---

[11]Another criterion to differentiate between literary and non-literary texts is the relationship between the text and "reality". Harweg (1974: 108) calls the distinction between fictional and non-fictional texts a "fundamental opposition" for text typology. For translation, this distinction gains relevance in regard to text presuppositions (cf. ch. 3.2.3.b).

the source text to one of these text types the translator can decide on the hierarchy of equivalence postulates which has to be observed in TT production. This points to the fact that a typology which is intended to be a basis for translation strategy will only make sense if the TT skopos requires "equivalence" (in the sense of text-type analogy) between source and target texts.

Equivalence is also Koller's starting point (1979: 187ff.). On the one hand, he severely criticizes Reiss' text typology, but on the other, he has no convincing alternative to offer. Instead of one typology, he presents five, his criteria being language function (following Bühler, as Reiss does), content, style, formal-aesthetic characteristics, and the pragmatic aspect of receiver orientation. This method of classifying every text according to five categories, each of which follows different criteria, makes it very difficult to set up any systematic guidelines for translation.

In their translation-relevant typology of German and French texts (note the language-pair specific orientation), Matt et al. (1978) also start from the postulate of equivalence. However, they do not classify texts according to the predominant text function, but according to the number of relevant text functions (e.g. bifunctional or trifunctional texts). This approach, which is adopted by Thiel (1980) as well, implies a hierarchy of categories: first, the level of text type with the relevant functions (e.g. evaluating text with the functions of representation and evaluation), second, a subcategory specified according to the typical social relationship between sender and receiver, and third, the text type (Thiel's sample text is a "political commentary").

What is important in this last typology is that, taking into account the polyfunctionality of texts, both Matt et al. and Thiel abandon the idea of assigning texts clearly and unequivocally to any one text type. Instead, they develop a detailed model of analysis based on verifiable factors. In my opinion, the assignment of a text to a particular type or genre cannot bring about the "ingenious" solution for its translation. Rather I would suggest the following procedure.

> **By means of a comprehensive model of text analysis which takes into account intratextual as well as extratextual factors the translator can establish the function-in-culture of a source text. This is then compared with the (prospective) function-in-culture of the target text required by the initiator, identifying and isolating those ST elements which have to be preserved or adapted in translation.**

Inasfar as they can contribute to achieving this aim, the afore-mentioned and some other approaches to text classification and typology will be taken into account in our model of translation-oriented text analysis.

2. The role and function of source-text analysis

As we have seen, then, source-text analysis can have various functions and varying degrees of relevance in the translation process. The following chapter deals with the consequences which the different concepts of translation have on the role and function of ST analysis (cf. Nord 1986a).

2.1. Possible relationships between source and target text

2.1.1. Fidelity - liberty - equivalence

A translation is normally expected to render "faithfully" all the relevant features of the source text. It is a fairly common assumption, and also one often held by linguists and literary critics, even, that the concept of faithfulness or "fidelity" can be equated with "equivalence", as is illustrated by Königs' statement that "aiming at equivalence is implicit in the very definition of translating or translation" (Königs 1983a: 6, my translation). Here, equivalence means "the greatest possible correspondence between source text and target text".

This rather unreflected equation of translation and equivalence appears to be responsible for the deplorable fact that the eternal discussions about faithfulness or liberty in translation have got us absolutely nowhere. The line between fidelity (being faithful) and servility (being too faithful) on the one hand, and liberty (being free) and libertinage (being too free, i.e. adapting or "even" paraphrasing) on the other, is drawn according to the criterion that a "too faithful" or "too free" version is not equivalent and therefore cannot be regarded as a translation proper. Even Benjamin's attempt (1972: 20) to proclaim "the law of fidelity in liberty" as the principle of his concept of translation (in which the word was the prime element for the translator) failed to bring about any clarification of the problem.

The concept of equivalence is one of the most ambiguous concepts in translation studies, and consequently has been interpreted in very different ways. Equivalence implies that various requirements have to be met on all text ranks. The claim that ST and TT should have the "same" function and be addressed to the "same" receiver illustrates the pragmatic aspect of the concept, whereas the demand that the TT should "imitate", "reflect" or "mirror" the ST or "show its beauty" points to the intratextual factors of content and form. The interpretation of equivalence as identity of "meaning", "value" or "effect" suggests that the target text should reproduce the interdepen-

dence of intratextual (content-oriented and form-oriented) and extratextual (situational and, above all, receiver-oriented) factors which is
characteristic of the source text.

The concept of equivalence has been questioned ever since it
was first established. From Nida's formulation of "dynamic equivalence" (Nida 1964) it is a long and tortuous path via Koller's specification of denotative, connotative, text-normative, pragmatic and formal equivalence (1979: 187ff., cf. also Koller 1995) to Neubert's
"text-bound equivalence" (1984: 68 and 1986: 87ff.), which the translator constantly has to strive after and which may compensate for non-
equivalent translations on lower ranks (e.g. at the level of words and
phrases).

In my experience, however, sporadic redefinitions do not solve
the problem of the inherent "fuzziness" of the concept (Snell-Hornby
1986a: 16). Equivalence continues to be equated with fidelity, and
translations continue to be evaluated according to this "fuzzy" criterion. Target texts which do not comply with the standard of equivalence are, on principle, ruled out of the sphere of translation proper.
Thus, word-for-word translations and literal translations (cf. Wilss
1982: 87f.) or philological translations (in the terminology of Reiss
1985) are not accepted as translations in the strict sense of the word
because they "too faithfully" reproduce certain features of the original.
On the other hand, adaptations, free renderings and paraphrases are
regarded as equally unacceptable because they take "too many liber-
ties" with the source text.

Within the framework of such a translation concept, source-text
analysis is supposed to provide the only legitimate foundation for the
determination of equivalence. This, in my opinion, is a demand that
source-text analysis is unable to meet. Even for the production of an
equivalent target text, it is impossible not to take into account the
particular requirements of the prospective target situation. Once these
have been elicited and contrasted with the characteristics of the
source-text situation, which have been gained from ST analysis, then
the production of an equivalent or "functionally equivalent" target text
may be one out of several possible translation purposes.

Functional equivalence between source and target text is not the
"normal" skopos of a translation, but an exceptional case in which the
factor "change of functions" is assigned zero.

2.1.2. Skopos and intertextual coherence

In a functional view of translation, equivalence between source and target text is regarded as being subordinate to all possible translation *skopoi* and not as a translation principle that is valid "once and for all" (cf. Reiss & Vermeer 1984: 146f.). In Vermeer's *Skopostheorie* the skopos of a translation is determined by the function which the target text is intended to fulfil. *Skopostheorie* is part of a "general theory of translation" which was first presented by Vermeer in 1978 and hinges on the so-called *skopos rule* with its sociological sub-rule.

> Human interaction (and as its subcategory: translation) is determined by its purpose (*skopos*), and therefore it is a function [in the mathematical sense of "being dependent on", C.N.] of its purpose: IA (Trl) = f(Sk). (...) The purpose can be described as a function of the receiver: Sc = f(R). (Vermeer [1978]1983: 54, my translation).

In this theory, too, the starting point for a translation is a text (as part of a "world continuum", according to Vermeer) written in the language S (= SL), which has to be translated into a language T (= TL) in such a way that it becomes part of a world continuum which can be interpreted by the receiver as "coherent with his situation" (Vermeer [1978]1983: 57). The relationship between source text and target text can supposedly be described using the term of "coherence" (in Vermeer's terms, intertextual coherence = fidelity).

The demand for fidelity, however, is subordinate to the skopos rule. If the skopos demands a change of function, the required standard will no longer be intertextual coherence with the source text, but adequacy or appropriateness with regard to the skopos (cf. Reiss & Vermeer 1984: 139).

According to the concept described in chapter 1.2.1., each text has its place in a configuration of particular, interdependent elements (= factors), whose constellation determines its function. If only one element is changed, the constellation of the other elements within the configuration will inevitably change as well. In any translation (even in the most traditional sense of the word) which is intended to allow people to communicate across a cultural and linguistic barrier, at least one element is different every time, and that is the receiver. Even if the TT receiver were the very image of the ST receiver in sex, age, education, social background etc., there would be one difference, namely that they are bound into diverse linguistic and cultural communities (cf. Nord 1992b).

It follows that, having grown up in another culture, the TT receiver has a different knowledge of the world, a different way of life, a different perspective on things, and a different "text experience" in the light of which the target text is read. All those factors affect the way in which receivers handle a text. That may mean, for example, that the target reader is not familiar with the subject matter, which in the source text is dealt with in a special terminology that is supposed to be well-known to the ST addressees or vice versa, as illustrated by the following example.

Example 2.1.2./1
The Spanish paperback edition of the textbook *Filosofías de la educación* ("Philosophies of Education"), Barcelona 1979, by the Catalan Marxist priest Octavi Fullat is addressed, as the author makes clear in his preface, both to students of academic training in the educational sciences and to interested parents who are looking for an educational concept. The German version of this book, *Philosophische Grundlagen der Erziehung* ("Philosophical Principles of Education"), Stuttgart 1982, is – to judge from its presentation and price – certainly not addressed to German parents interested in educational concepts, but to university students only. In view of the abundance of existing textbooks, German students of educational sciences are accustomed to a more "scientific" character (in content and form) than this book can offer. As the translator could not possibly "rewrite" the content of the book, she had to adjust the form (particularly where the text-type conventions were concerned) to the standards expected by the TT receivers (= students, not parents). This affected, for example, the form of bibliographical references.

This adjustment or "adaptation" of the source text to target-culture standards is a procedure that is part of the daily routine of every professional translator. We could make a methodological distinction between translation (in the narrower sense of the word) and adaptation but I doubt whether this will get us any further. I would prefer to include the feature of adaptation into the concept of translation in order to make people (i.e. the users and initiators of translations!) understand what translation is really about. If an occasion actually does arise where all the factors have to remain unchanged (for example, in the translation of an internal communication to the staff members of an international company who are supposed to be equally familiar with the subject matter and with the respective source and target cultures), the feature of adaptation can be assigned zero in this particular translation process.

Contrary to what bilingual dictionaries seem to suggest, there is no such thing as an "ordinary" TL equivalent for a linguistic and/or

cultural unit in the ST; the "extra-ordinary" case is what constantly
occurs in the practice of translation.

Example 2.1.2./2

In the amusing history book *Otra historia de España* by Fernando Díaz Plaja,
we find the following sentence in the chapter on the case history of the Spanish Civil War: "No había un solo ministro comunista en el gobierno de la Re-
pública en julio de 1936, dirigido por un miembro de la Izquierda Republica-
na, o partido de Azaña, llamado Casares Quiroga." The "ordinary" equivalent
for *partido de Azaña* would be "Azaña Party", but this unofficial name of the
party (which is officially called the "Republican Left-Wing Party") is only of
interest to TT receivers if there is anything they can associate with the name
of the party founder. The culture-specific knowledge possessed by the ST
receiver (and not by the TT receiver) produces an immediate response as soon
as the name Azaña is mentioned. In view of the (intended) TT function, the
translator has to decide whether to expand the text by providing more information about Azaña or to replace the allusion by the official party name.

One of the objections frequently put forward is that translation in the
strict sense of the word only allows adaptations which would not be
necessary in intralingual communication. Example 2.1.2./2 shows that
this argument is not valid since the same comprehension problems
could arise for a young Spanish (or Latin American, for that matter!)
reader today.

As I have said, in a skopos-oriented translation the observance
of the skopos is performed prior to intertextual coherence with the
source text. However, whenever intertextual coherence is compatible
with the skopos, then this is what the translator should aim for. This
compatibility will show up in text analysis.

Compatibility of an intended TT function with the given ST depends upon whether all the elements required for TT production can
be provided by the source text or whether possible deficiencies in the
ST can be compensated for by the translator's background knowledge
and transfer competence. Transfer competence comprises, as has been
mentioned before, the ability to use the appropriate information
sources and tools. In the case of the example given above, this means
that the background information about the party founder Manuel
Azaña, which is implied in the ST as a presupposition or "pre-information", can (and must) be obtained by the translator if required by
the TT skopos.

Thus, the number of ST-provided elements plus the translator's
background knowledge must not be smaller than the number of TT-
required elements. If "compatibility control" shows that the informa-

tion provided by the ST is not sufficient for the production of a TT that meets the requirements of the initiator, and that it cannot be supplemented from the translator's background knowledge, then translation will not be possible unless additional material is provided or the TT skopos is modified (according to prior agreement with the initiator).

Example 2.1.2./3
The labelling on a bottle of medicine produced and sold in the United Kingdom is inadequate as a source text for the production of the patient package insert required for any drug sold on the German market. The form and content of such inserts are stipulated in the corresponding law, which requires certain pieces of information not given on British packaging (cf. Hönig & Kußmaul 1982: 46ff.). As this information is not normally part of her background knowledge, the translator would have to draw the initiator's attention to the problem and ask for additional material. Spanish medicines are provided with leaflets that contain even more information than that required under German law. There is no problem here with a translation into German.

2.1.3. Intercultural cooperation

Taking a functional approach to translation as a starting point, too, Justa Holz-Mänttäri has developed her theory and method of "intercultural cooperation". She avoids using the term *translation* in order to get away from the traditional concepts and unreflected expectations connected with the word. She defines intercultural cooperation as "the process of producing a certain kind of message transmitter, which is utilized in superordinate configurations of activities in order to coordinate actional and communicative cooperations" (Holz-Mänttäri 1984a: 17, my translation).

Although Holz-Mänttäri's model of intercultural cooperation includes a "source text" and even a kind of source-text analysis, which she calls "analysis of construction and function" (cf. 1984a: 139ff.), the quoted definition does raise one or two questions. What is the source text's actual part in the process? Or, more to the point, does this model need a source text at all?

Example 2.1.3./1
A translator receives operating instructions written in English that are full of mistakes and errors (perhaps a translation from Japanese), which she is required to translate into German. Instead of translating the faulty source text and thereby running the risk of producing a non-functional text (and of being regarded as incompetent by the initiator), the translator asks an engineer to explain to her how the machine works and afterwards writes operating instructions in German with due regard to genre conventions.

In our example, the initiator gets what is needed: perfectly functional operating instructions in German for the machine in question. The assignment has been fulfilled to satisfaction. The problem is that, in my opinion, this is not a translation, but a different kind of intercultural operation, which certainly overcomes a cultural barrier (between the English initiator and his/her German customers) – but the text that is produced is not based on an existing source text. If the engineer has given the explanation in English, the TT production requires a bicultural competence, as opposed to a "transfer" competence, and if the engineer has given the explanation in German, only a text-producing competence in the target culture (including language) is called for.

Holz-Mänttäri claims that, where translation is concerned, "intercultural cooperation" is a generic term.

> Intercultural cooperation can therefore be regarded as a combination, on the one hand, of the action concept of "translation" for the translation expert, and, on the other, the cooperation pattern "customer + translation expert" for the customer and the translator and all members of the community (Holz-Mänttäri 1984a: 42f., my translation).

According to my concept of translation, which is doubtless conditioned by the conventional concept of translation I have grown up with (cf. Nord 1991), a TT production that is not based on, or bound to, a given source text (whatever the specification of this being "based on" or "bound to" may be) cannot be called a translation, even though the conditions under which the text is produced may be similar to a translating situation.[12]

2.1.4. Functionality plus loyalty

The decision on what may or may not be considered a translation is based on the prevailing concept of the relationship between situation and text. Holz-Mänttäri views the text as a mere tool for the realization of communicative functions. It has no intrinsic value, is totally subordinate to its purpose, and its sole raison d'être is to meet the requirements of the situation. The text is so inextricably linked with its purpose that there appears to be no other responsibility whatsoever and absolute freedom as regards the source text. The translator, here,

---

[12]This idea has been elaborated in Nord (1997a: 18), where a distinction is made between "translational action with a source text" (e.g. translating or interpreting) and "translational action without a source text" (e.g. cross-cultural consulting or cross-cultural technical writing).

is unilaterally committed to the target situation. In my view, however, there can be no process of "translation" without a source text.

> **Translation is the production of a functional target text maintaining a relationship with a given source text that is specified according to the intended or demanded function of the target text (translation skopos). Translation allows a communicative act to take place which because of existing linguistic and cultural barriers would not have been possible without it.**

Translation is always realized for a target situation with its determining factors (receiver, time and place of reception, etc.), in which the target text is supposed to fulfil a certain function which can and, indeed, must be specified in advance. As the target receivers have to rely on the functionality of the target text, the translator is bound to maintain a certain loyalty towards them.

Functionality is the most important criterion for a translation, but certainly not the only one. In my definition I have stated that there has to be a certain relationship between the source and the target text. The quality and quantity of this relationship are specified by the translation skopos and provide the criteria for the decision as to which elements of the ST-in-situation can be "preserved" and which may, or must, be "adapted" to the target situation (facultative vs. compulsory adaptation). In addition to the compatibility between TT-required and ST-provided material (cf. ch. 2.1.2), we have to postulate a compatibility between ST intention and TT functions, if translation is to be possible at all.

Translation therefore depends on the compatibility of the TT skopos with the given source text, a compatibility whose definition is culture-specific. In our culture it implies loyalty towards the ST author or sender at least in those cases where the ST sender also "signs" as TT sender. The translator is expected not to falsify the author's intention.

According to this view, the translator is committed bilaterally to the source text as well as to the target-text situation, and is responsible to both the ST sender (or the initiator if s/he is also the sender) and the TT receiver. This responsibility is what I call "loyalty". Loyalty is a moral principle indispensable in the relationships between human beings, who are partners in a communication process, whereas fidelity is a rather technical relationship between two texts (cf. Nord 1989, 1991, 2001a, 2002).

With regard to example 2.1.3./1 this means that in the case of an unsuitable source text translators must ask for additional material or refuse to translate the text. However, they might then offer the initiator their services as text producers in the target culture, operating with a different brief.

Within the framework of the concept "functionality plus loyalty" translators can focus on particular ST aspects (for example, syntactic structures in a word-for-word translation), and disregard others, if this is required by the TT skopos. However, in such cases they would be obliged, in view of their loyalty towards the ST sender, to specify exactly which ST aspects have been taken into account and which have been neglected.

Depending on the percentage of preserved ST elements, different forms or "grades" of translation can be arranged on a scale extending from extreme fidelity at one end to extreme liberty at the other. This is illustrated in Figure 2, where the formal aspect is taken as an example.

Figure 2: Preservation and adaptation in translation

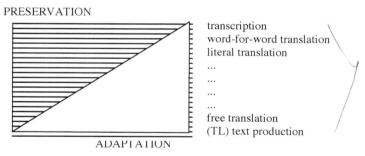

PRESERVATION

transcription
word-for-word translation
literal translation
...
...
...
...
free translation
(TL) text production

ADAPTATION

The limits of translation are represented by transcription or transliteration, in which 100 per cent of the ST surface elements are preserved, and free text production (in the target culture), in which none of the ST surface elements are preserved. Between these two poles we find several forms of translation, which are characterized by different percentages of adaptation, depending on the translation skopos.

Similar diagrams might be drawn for other ST aspects as well, such as content, function, effect, etc.

According to this concept, it is the task of source-text analysis first to control compatibility and then to find out which ST elements can be preserved and which have to be adapted so as to comply with the translation skopos.

2.2. Phases of the translation process

Now, where does source-text analysis with its particular functions fit into the translation process?

In translation studies, the translation process is usually represented either in a two-phase or in a three-phase model. After a short explanation of these two models I shall present my own view of the translation process which I call "looping model". In my opinion translation is not a linear, progressive process leading from a starting point S (= ST) to a target point T (= TT), but a circular, basically recursive process comprising an indefinite number of feedback loops, in which it is possible and even advisable to return to earlier stages of the analysis.

2.2.1. The two-phase model
This model represents translation as a process consisting of two chronologically sequential phases, namely analysis (in other terminologies, decoding or comprehension phase) and synthesis (encoding, reconstruction or reverbalization phase). In the first phase, the translator reads the source text, analysing all its relevant aspects (Wilss 1982: 80 speaks of the "SLT identification step"). In the second phase, the ST meaning or sense is reverbalized in the target language. This means that by using meaning and sense as a tertium comparationis, the translator chooses the corresponding TL signs to match the SL signs.

Wilss considers the two-phase model to be more "concise" than the three-phase model, which contains transfer as a third phase inserted between analysis and synthesis. In his opinion, the two-phase model "brings out more clearly the double R1/S2 function of the translator", i.e. his role as ST receiver and TT sender, and "depicts the activity of the translator in a more true-to-life way" (Wilss 1982: 80). Perhaps he is thinking here of simultaneous interpreting. In this special form of translation, situational factors (e.g. time, place, medium) are identical for the ST producer, the translator, and the TT receiver, and most translating operations have to be automatized as far as possible for time reasons, so it may actually seem as if there is no space left for the "transfer" as such between ST reception and TT production. In my opinion, however, the transfer phase has merely been reduced here to a minimum of time by automatization, but it has not disappeared altogether.

The two-phase model is based on the assumption that translating is a code-switching operation (cf. Wilss 1977: 626) on a sign-for-sign basis. But this only applies to "habitualized or partly habitualized translating procedures", as Wilss puts it, e.g. the interlingual substitution of formulaic expressions, such as *No entry*, *Zutritt verboten*, *Prohibido entrar*, *Défense d entrer* etc., or to strictly conventionalized genres, such as weather reports. The two-phase model wrongly suggests that a receptive proficiency in the source language and a productive command of the target language are all a translator needs.

2.2.2. The three-phase model

The intermediate phase for transfer operations, which is not present in the two-phase model, is inserted between the comprehension phase and the reconstruction phase in the three-phase model, so that the translation process is divided into three steps analysis (decoding, comprehension phase), transfer (transcoding), and synthesis (recoding).

> That is to say, the translator first analyzes the message of the SOURCE language into its simplest and structurally clearest forms, transfers it at this level, and then restructures it to the level of the RECEPTOR language which is most appropriate for the audience which he intends to reach (Nida 1975: 79f.).

As in the two-phase model, the first step in the three-phase model is the comprehension phase with a detailed analysis of the grammatical, semantic, and stylistic elements of the text, which ensures that the translator grasps the full (denotative and connotative) meaning of the information given both explicitly and implicitly in the text.

In the second phase, the "meaning of the received message" is related to the "intention of the target message", as Zimnjaja (1977: 72) puts it, and transferred into TL either on the basis of an equivalence relationship between lexical items or, if the text function is to be changed, according to the TT function. This is where transfer competence comes into play, since the translator has to devise a kind of translation "plan" or "strategy".

The third phase in the three-phase model is the same as the second in the two-phase model. The transferred ST items are restructured into a target text which conforms to the needs of the TT receiver.

The three-phase model is based on the idea that the aim of translation is "the realization of verbal communication between people who speak different languages" (Komissarov 1977: 46, my translation). It therefore seems contradictory to maintain that the translator can be both ST receiver and TT sender at one and the same time. In a verbal communication between a ST author and a TT receiver, the ST author does not give up his or her role of sender, and the translator is a text producer following the sender's instructions.

2.2.3. The looping model

The three-phase model seems to come much closer to the reality of professional translation than the two-phase model. Both models, however, start out from the hypothesis that, since the ST has a certain function attached to it which must be transferred to the target situation, it is source-text analysis alone that provides the transfer criteria. According to this model, every ST is supposed to carry its own translation brief telling the translator how it should be transferred.

As described in chapter 1.2., however, text function is established in and by the communicative situation, and this applies to both the source and the target text. Accordingly, there is no such thing as a source text with a text-immanent function. Rather, we have to assume a greater or smaller variety of different ST versions each with a different function. Since the translator is only one of many possible ST receivers (and not really a typical one at that), her or his opinion on the source-text function cannot be regarded as being definitive. What s/he focusses on as one function of the ST need not necessarily be *the* function of the ST (cf. Vermeer [1979]1983: 72f.).

The approach to this problem suggested by Reiss & Vermeer (1984) is more convincing. In their opinion, the target text represents an "offer of information" about the offer of information supplied by the source text. Or, to be more precise, the translator offers information on certain aspects of the ST-in-situation, according to the TT skopos fixed by the initiator.

So, the three-phase model cannot be regarded as a satisfactory representation of the translation process either, because it does not take account of the translation brief formulated by the initiator (possibly in cooperation with the translator). The brief is the only means of checking the results of the translator's ST reception and subordinating them to a higher criterion.

Therefore we have to extend the diagrammatic representation of inter-cultural text transfer presented in Figure 1 as follows (see Figures 3 and 4). The first step (I prefer to speak of steps rather than phases) in the translation process is the analysis and/or interpretation of the TT skopos, i.e. of those factors that are relevant for the realization of a certain purpose by the TT in a given situation SIT-T. It would be useful to operationalize the TT skopos in such a way that its importance for the processing of the various ST elements and aspects is apparent (see below, ch. 4.0.c).

The second step is the analysis of the source text, which is divided into two parts. Whereas in the first part of ST analysis, the translator only needs to get a general idea on whether the material provided by the source text is compatible (C) with the requirements stated in the brief, the second part may require a detailed and comprehensive analysis of all ranks of the text, focussing the attention on those text elements that according to the TT skopos are of particular importance for the production of the target text.

Example 2.2.3./1
A report by an eyewitness of the "soft revolution" in the former GDR on November 9th, 1989, has been recorded on tape and subsequently transcribed. An American journalist asks for a translation of the transcript because s/he wants to use the information for a book on the political changes in Eastern Europe in 1989. In view of this intended TT function, the translator will pay special attention to any information explicitly or implicitly contained in the report, neglecting, however, the features of spontaneous, informal speech and the rhetorical clichés used by the eyewitness to impress the interviewer, as these are of secondary importance for the journalist's purpose. However, if the transcript is to be translated for publication in an American newspaper as an "eyewitness report", the features of spontaneous and emotional speech are of particular interest because they will signal the genre "eyewitness report" to the readers.

After finishing the ST analysis, the translator is able to pinpoint the translation-relevant ST elements or features, which are then, where necessary, adapted to the TT skopos and matched with the corresponding TL elements. The translator has to decide which of the potentially appropriate TL elements will be suitable for the intended TT function. The final structuring of the target text is the last step, which closes the circle. If the translator has succeeded in producing a functional text conforming to the initiator's needs, the target text will be congruent with the TT skopos.

Figure 3: The process of intercultural text transfer (2)

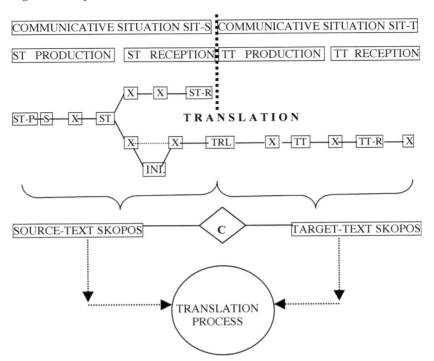

Figure 3 is the continuation of Figure 1 and shows all the phases and constituents involved in translation, whereas Figure 4 represents the actual translation process based on the looping model described above. The latter is closely linked to the person of the translator, who is the central figure in the process of intercultural text transfer. It starts, after the initiator has fixed the TT skopos (target situation and TT function), at the top of the circle with the analysis and, if necessary, the interpretation of the translation brief and proceeds in an anti-clockwise direction until the production of a TT which fits into the (prospective) target situation.

The circular path of the translation process contains a number of smaller circular movements or "loops" that keep recurring between ST situation and ST, between TT situation and TT, between the individual steps of analysis, and between ST analysis and TT synthesis. This means that at each step forward the translator "looks back" on the factors already analysed, and every piece of knowledge gained in the

course of the process of analysis and comprehension may be confirmed or corrected by later findings.

Figure 4: The translation process

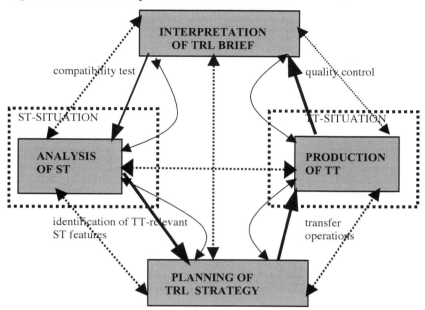

Levý compares this process with a strategic game:

> ...since the process of translating has the form of a GAME WITH COM-
> PLETE INFORMATION – a game in which every succeeding move is influ-
> enced by the knowledge of previous decisions and by the situation which re-
> sulted from them (e.g., chess, but not card games) (Levý 1967: 1172).

The interpretation of translation as a circular process can therefore be
regarded as an analogy to a modern hermeneutical concept (cf.
Gadamer 1972: 250ff.), in which the "circle of comprehension" is a
metaphor for the "interdependence of the movements of tradition and
the movement of the interpreter" (Gadamer, ib.: 277, my translation).

3. The factors of source-text analyis

3.0. General considerations

Let us restate, then, that communicative function is the decisive criterion for textuality, to which the semantic and syntactic features of the text are subordinate. Utterances lacking semantic coherence as well as utterances without the necessary formal and syntactic properties of cohesion are considered "texts" by their receivers as soon as they fulfil a communicative function. In professional translation, source texts are very often defective, and yet they have a communicative function, which they normally fulfil, and, what is more, they have to be translated. Like any other receiver, translators will recognize the defects and compensate for them, both in the comprehension and in the transfer phase, by their competence of text reception and their general knowledge of the world.

Thus, the factors of the communicative situation in which the source text is used are of decisive importance for text analysis because they determine its communicative function. I call these factors "extratextual" or "external" factors (as opposed to the "intratextual" or "internal" factors relating to the text itself, including its non-verbal elements). Extratextual factors may, of course, be mentioned, i.e. "verbalized", in the text, and in this case we speak of "metacommunicative utterances". The interplay between extratextual and intratextual factors can be conveniently expressed in the following set of "WH-questions", based on the so-called New Rhetoric formula. Depending on their relationship to either the communicative situation or the text itself, these questions can be assigned to the extratextual or intratextual factors of analysis.

Who transmits	*On what subject matter*
to whom	*does s/he say*
what for	*what*
by which medium	*(what not)*
where	*in what order*
when	*using which non-verbal elements*
why	*in which words*
a text	*in what kind of sentences*
with what function?	*in which tone*
	to what effect?[13]

---

[13]Traceable back to the 2nd century B.C., when the Stoic Hermagoras of Temnos coined the formula "quis quid quando ubi cur quem ad modum quibus adminiculis", which was framed in a hexameter verse by Matthew of Vendôme in 1170 ("Quis quid ubi quibus auxiliis cur quomodo quando?", this formula was introduced into

Extratextual factors are analysed by enquiring about the author or sender of the text (who?), the sender's intention (what for?), the audience the text is directed at (to whom?), the medium or channel the text is communicated by (by which medium?), the place (where?) and time (when?) of text production and text reception, and the motive (why?) for communication. The sum total of information obtained about these seven extratextual factors may provide an answer to the last question, which concerns the function the text can achieve (with what function?).

Intratextual factors are analysed by enquiring about the subject matter the text deals with (on what subject matter?), the information or content presented in the text (what?), the knowledge presuppositions made by the author (what not?), the composition or construction of the text (in what order?), the non-linguistic or paralinguistic elements accompanying the text (using which non-verbal elements?), the lexical characteristics (in which words?) and syntactic structures (in what kind of sentences?) found in the text, and the suprasegmental features of intonation and prosody (in which tone?).

The extratextual factors are analysed before reading the text, simply by observing the situation in which the text is used. In this way, the receivers build up a certain expectation as to the intratextual characteristics of the text, but it is only when, through reading, they compare this expectation with the actual features of the text that they experience the particular effect the text has on them. The last question (to what effect?) therefore refers to a global or holistic concept, which comprises the interdependence or interplay of extratextual and intratextual factors.

Since the situation normally precedes textual communication and determines the use of intratextual procedures, it seems natural to start with the analysis of the external factors although, in view of re-

American New Rhetoric by Harold Dwight Lasswell in 1948 ("Who says what in which channel to whom with what effect?"). Later on, Mentrup (1982: 9) adopted it in an amplified form as "universal pragmatic chain" ("Who does what when where why how for whom what for with what effect?") for lexicological and text-typological studies. Reiss (1984), Bühler (1984), and Hönig (1986) have discussed its applicability to translation-oriented text analysis. I have interpreted the questions with regard to their relevance to translation, partly in a more restrictive, and partly in a slightly different sense. The specification of intratextual factors anticipated in this chapter will be justified in detail in ch. 3.2.0. One distinction I should like to stress is that between sender's intention ("what for"), text function ("with what function"), and text effect ("to what effect").

cursiveness and circularity, the order of the analytical steps is not a constituent of the model. In written communication, the situation is often documented in the "text environment" (i.e. title and/or bibliographical references, such as name of author, place and year of publication, number of copies, etc.). This is what is usually called a "top down" analysis. If no information on the external factors can be inferred from the text environment (for example, in the case of old texts whose original situation of production and/or reception is uncertain or unknown), the analysis of internal features, again in a recursive procedure, can yield information from which the translator is able to make fairly reliable conjectures about the situation the text was used in.[14] The latter procedure is referred to as a "bottom-up" analysis.

The application of the model will show that normally both procedures have to be combined, demonstrating once more the recursive character of the model.

In the following chapters, I am going to examine the extratextual dimensions and then go on to the intratextual dimensions of translation-oriented text analysis. I shall conclude with a diagrammatic representation of the interdependence of all the factors, illustrated by means of a sample text.

However, in order to show the state-of-the-art position on translation-relevant text analysis in the German-speaking area, each chapter begins with a short review of the main publications I have drawn on.

3.1. Extratextual factors

3.1.0. Basic notions
a. State of the art
Basically, the situational factors (in particular sender and sender's intention, receiver, and text function) are taken into account by all the authors, although they are not always dealt with in great detail. Reiss (1974a, 1980a), for example, stresses the importance of text type and text function, whereas Koller (1979) limits the pragmatic aspect to the characteristics of the receiver. Wilss (1977) points to the relevance of

---

[14]Under the general question 'Apart from the message communicated, what other kind of information does the utterance give us?'. Crystal & Davy (1969: 81f.) list a catalogue of thirteen sub-questions such as: "Does it tell us which specific person used it? " (Individuality); "Does it tell us where in the country he is from? (Regional dialect)"; "Does it tell us which social class he belongs to? (Class dialect)", etc.

"the relationship between sender and receiver" and the "social role" of the two participants, and Thiel (1974b, 1978a) underlines the relevance of the "knowledge presuppositions" with respect to the receiver.

The factors of the communicative situation (which in the narrower sense of the word refers to place and time and occasionally to the motive for communication) are for the most part not discussed in detail, but subsumed under the concept of "situative presuppositions". This concept usually comprises not only the features of the given communicative situation of the ST but also the characteristics of the communicative background of sender and receiver (cf. Reiss 1974a).

Sender and intention are usually dealt with as belonging to one dimension. I have decided to treat them as separate factors in my model because their effects on the internal factors can be clearly distinguished. On the one hand, several texts or, indeed, all texts written by the same author may exhibit certain idiosyncratic features – irrespective of his or her intention – which depend on the sender's biography (sex, age, geographical origin and social background, level of education, etc.). On the other hand, various senders may want to realize the same intention in their texts by using the same or a similar means of expression. The distinction is relevant for translation because – at least in non-literary texts – idiosyncratic features are often less important to the TT receiver than intentional features, although they may cause more comprehension difficulties for the translator.

Just as we have to take the author's intention into consideration, so we have to account for the expectation with which the audience reads or "receives" the text. If there is no extratextual information about the expectations of the addressed audience, it may be difficult for the translator to reconstruct them – the greater his/her temporal and spatial or cultural distance from the original communicative situation, the more difficult the task will be (cf. Nord 2000). Nevertheless, it is essential for the translator to try and analyse the expectations of the ST receiver, since they have to be contrasted with those of the TT receiver. It does not seem practical, however, to treat the receivers' expectations as a completely different factor because they are inextricably linked with the receiver's personality.

b. External versus internal situation

In classifying the situational factors as "extratextual factors" I have to make the following fundamental qualification. When referring to "situation" I mean the real situation in which the text is used as a means of communication, and not any imaginary setting of a story in a fictional text). The characteristics of a person who speaks in a fictional text do not belong to the dimension of sender, as I understand it, but have to be regarded as an intratextual factor which is analysed in connection with the internal dimension of "content". It is the author of the text who has to be regarded as "producer" of the fictitious utterance, whereas the fictitious speaker is a "secondary sender" (S').[15]

This qualification also applies to the so-called complex text types (Reiss & Vermeer 1984: 180), where a text of a certain genre is embedded into a frame text belonging to another genre. Complex text types occur not only in fiction, but also in non-fiction. For example, in newspaper reports authors often cite remarks made by third persons in literal quotations in order to show that they do not share the speaker's opinion. In this case, the sender of the quoted utterance is not identical with the sender of the frame text.

Example 3.1.0./1
After King Juan Carlos of Spain had received an honorary doctorate from New York University, the journalist who commented on the event in a Spanish newspaper quoted verbatim parts of the King's speech of thanks. For the translation of the quotation, the King has to be regarded as sender, whereas for the translation of the framing newspaper report, the journalist is the sender (and author). The formulation of the two texts has to conform to the different situations and positions of the two senders.

For both fictional and non-fictional complex texts it is advisable to analyse the constituent texts separately according to the principle of recursiveness. The necessary information on the situational factors of the embedded text is usually given within the frame text.

c. A systematic framework for external analysis
If we want to encompass the whole situation of a text by means of a model that will serve for the analysis of any text with any possible translation skopos, we must ask the following fundamental question:

---

[15]Reiss (1984) illustrates the interrogative "Who?" with the fictitious letter-writer Judy from Jean Webster's novel *Daddy Long-Legs*. But Judy is neither the sender of the novel nor the author of the letters; both have been written by Jean Webster herself, who lets the fictitious person Judy act – and write letters – according to her – Jean Webster's – own intention. Within the (fictitious) situation of correspondence, Judy is, in fact, the author of the letters, but this is an "internal situation" which must not be confused with the "real" communicative situation. In another article where she uses the same example, Reiss correctly refers to Judy as "secondary sender" who acts in an "internal communicative situation" (1980b).

What information on the various factors may be relevant to translation?

Neubert ([1968]1981: 60) regards "age, origin, social environment, education etc." as relevant information about the language user.
Vermeer ([1974b]1983: 23) in a matrix relates attitude, status, role,
strategy, behaviour and activity of the participants of communication
to the corresponding features of the type of situation in order to fur-
nish evidence of the conformist or deviant behaviour of the participants. Schmidt (cf. 1976: 104) lists the following data: (a) socio-eco-
nomic conditions (role, status, economic situation), (b) socio-cultural
and cognitive-intellectual conditions (text and world knowledge, education, experience, models of reality), and (c) biographical-psychical
conditions (individual competences and dispositions, present biographical situation, plans, intentions). Gülich & Raible (1977: 28) even
regard "hoarseness, cheerfulness, unhappiness" and the picture that
speaker and hearer have of each other as factors which may influence
the communicative act.

This list is in no way complete, but it clearly shows that the situation or world of a text cannot be analysed by a mere compilation of
informational details. We have to find the categories by which we
conceive the world, which will apply equally to the world of a text,
i.e. to its historical situation.

"The facts in logical space are the world", Ludwig Wittgenstein
says in his *Tractatus* (1955: 31, 1.13), and this means that "facts" are
produced through logic binding together the totality of relationships
("world"). This applies to the situation of a text as well.

> (a) The basic categories of any historical situation are time and space. The ca-
> tegory of time also comprises the historic conception a world has of itself. The
> first fundamental aspect of analysis will therefore be the temporal and spatial
> dimension of the situation.
> (b) The situation of a text is always a part of human culture. The second fun-
> damental aspect of analysis therefore has to refer to the culture-specific fea-
> tures of the situation.
> (c) In its world, the text has a function which establishes its textuality. The
> third fundamental aspect therefore comprises the relationship between situa-
> tion and communicative function of the text

The communicative function of a text has to be considered within the
framework of the transcultural, possibly universal, communicative
functions of language in general (cf. Reiss & Vermeer 1984: 150).

According to the models of Bühler (1934) and Jakobson (1960)[16], we find four basic functions of communication: (a) the referential (also denotative or cognitive) function, focussed on the referent or context referred to by the text, (b) the expressive or emotive function, focussed on the sender, the sender's emotions or attitude towards the referent, (c) the operative (also appellative, conative, persuasive or vocative) function, focussed on the orientation of the text towards the receiver, and (d) the phatic function, serving primarily "to establish, to prolong, or to discontinue communication between sender and receiver, to check whether the channel works, to attract the attention of the interlocutor or to confirm his continued attention" (Jakobson 1960: 355). As I see it, the phatic function is also responsible for the development of the social relationship between sender and receiver (cf. Nord 2003: 4 et pass.)

Apart from space, time, and culture, it is the influence of these basic functions[17] that constitutes the "world" of a text. They will therefore form the systematic framework for the range of possible questions which can be asked regarding the situational factors of our analytical model (see the standard or model questions in the "checklist" at the end of each chapter). In order to illustrate the interdependence of factors and dimensions, the last question will always refer to the expectations raised by the analysis of the factor in question.

3.1.1. Sender
a. Sender vs. text producer

In Figure 1 and Figure 2, I have separated the roles of sender and text producer (cf. ch. 1.1.1.). Although in many cases these two roles are combined in one persona (e.g. in the case of literary works, textbooks,

---

[16]Bühler's three main functions of language (representation, expression, and appeal) were supplemented by Jakobson's phatic, poetic, and metalingual function. As I understand it, the metalingual function can be regarded as a sub-function of representation or referential function (the object of reference being language in general or a specific language), and the poetic function as a means of supporting the expressive or appellative-operative function (Jakobson speaks of conative function). Therefore it is, in my view, only the phatic function (i.e. the "set towards the contact medium", which serves to establish, to prolong or to discontinue communication, cf. Jakobson 1960: 355) that is really lacking in Bühler's model, and consequently in the text typologies based on Bühler, such as the one presented by Reiss (1971).

[17]Apart from using it in my translation classes (cf. also Nord 2001c, 2001d) I have applied the four-function model to the analysis and intercultural comparison of titles and headings (Nord 1995), to the analysis of Bible translation (Nord 2002), and to the comparison of general style conventions in Spanish and German (Nord 2003).

or newspaper commentaries, which are normally signed by an author's name), the distinction seems to be highly relevant to a translation-oriented text analysis.[18]

Many texts do not bear any author's name at all. These are usually non-literary texts for practical use, such as advertisements, laws or statutes, or operating instructions. Nevertheless, there has to be a sender who, even if not named explicitly, can be identified implicitly. For example, the sender of an advertisement is usually the company selling the product, and the sender of statutes is normally the legislative body of a state. The fact that no text producer is named in these cases leads to the conclusion that either they are not relevant as a person or – as is the case with certain genres – they do not wish to be known.

If a text bears the name of both sender and text producer (cf. example 3.1.1./1), the latter usually plays a secondary role because s/he is not expected to introduce any communicative intention of her or his own into the text.

The sender of a text is the person (or institution, etc.) who uses the text in order to convey a certain message to somebody else and/or to produce a certain effect[19], whereas the text producer writes the text according to the instructions of the sender, and complies with the rules and norms of text production valid in the respective language and culture. The formal design of the text, such as the layout, may be assigned to another expert, and in some cases, the text is presented to the public by yet another person (e.g. a news reader or an actor).

Example 3.1.1./1
The imprint on the back of a tourist information brochure of the city of Munich reads as follows: "Edited by the Tourist Information Office of Munich (...). Text: Helmut Gerstner." The Tourist Information Office, which intends to inform the visitors and to promote the beauties of the town, is the sender of the text. Mr Gerstner is the text producer, and he is the person responsible for the stylistic features of the text, but not for the sender's intention. The im-

---

[18]This distinction is not made by the authors whose articles on translation-relevant text analysis have been consulted. Reiss speaks of the author or writer (1974a, 1980a) or of the sender (1984), Thiel and Wilss generally speak of the sender, Bühler of the author; Cartellieri (1979) refers to the person emitting the text as "originator" and does not specify whether this means the text producer or the sender.

[19]The sender must not be confused with the medium. If a report signed by an author's name is published in a magazine, then it is not the editor of the magazine, but the author who has to be regarded as sender, because s/he is the one who wants to communicate her or his impressions to the reader. S/he could have published the article just as easily using any other medium.

prints on the English, French, and Spanish versions of the brochure contain
the same information, which in this case is obviously wrong. Although the
Tourist Information Office is the sender of these texts, too, it is the respective
translators who have to be regarded as text producers. Their names ought to be
mentioned in addition to, or instead of, that of Helmut Gerstner.

As is shown by the example, it is usually the text environment (imprint, reference, bibliography, etc.) that yields information as to whether or not the sender and the text producer are different persons. If the
author's name is the only one given, s/he can normally be assumed to
be the text producer. However, this cannot be regarded as a hard and
fast rule, as is illustrated by the following example.

Example 3.1.1./2

In her book *Estudio sobre el cuento español contemporáneo* (Madrid 1973),
Erna Brandenberger has included the short story "Pecado de omisión" by the
Spanish author Ana María Matute to give an example of a certain type of plot
which she calls a "fast moving story". For the German version of the book,
Brandenberger (as sender and translator in one person) has translated the story
into German with the intention of showing the typical features of a fast moving story. If the same story is published in a collection of modern Spanish
short stories, however, it is the author herself who acts as sender, and in translation it would be her intention that determines translation strategies.

The situation of a translator can be compared with that of the text producer. Although they have to follow the instructions of the sender or
initiator and have to comply with the norms and rules of the target language and culture, they are usually allowed a certain scope in which to
give free rein to their own stylistic creativity and preferences, if they
so wish. On the other hand, they may decide to stick to stylistic features of the source text as long as their imitation does not infringe the
text norms and conventions of the target culture.

Another aspect of sender pragmatics is the question as to whether a text has one or more than one sender (monologue vs. dialogue,
question/answer, discussion, exchange of roles between sender and
receiver, etc.). If there is more than one sender, the corresponding data
have to be analysed for each of them[20].

---

[20]This question is discussed by Crystal & Davy (1969: 69f.) under the heading of par-
ticipation in discourse. They lay particular stress on the distinction between speech
and writing, admitting, however, that dialogue is not limited to spoken language,
since there are various forms of dialogue (such as filling in and returning forms, exchanges of letters, etc.) in written language as well.

b. What to find out about the sender

What information about the sender is relevant to translation? Reiss points to "the author's influence on the formulation of the text" (1974a); Wilss (1977) and Thiel (1978a) stress the relationship to the receiver and the "social role", whereas Cartellieri is interested in the "particular sociological environment" (1979). Since the "role" is defined by the situation and not by the person, I prefer to deal with this aspect in connection with the dimension of intention (cf. below, ch. 3.1.2.). Along with Vermeer ([1974a]1983: 3) I would like to distinguish between role and status (the sender's personality as part of a cultural, linguistic, and communicative community). Within the framework established by time, space, culture and the basic functions of communication, what I regard as being relevant to translation is all data which may throw light on the sender's intention, on the addressed audience with their cultural background, on the place and time of, and the motive for, text production, as well as any information on the predictable intratextual features (such as idiosyncrasies, regional and social dialect, temporal features, knowledge presuppositions, etc.).[21]

Example 3.1.1./3
a) If a text is written in Spanish, it may be vital for comprehension to know whether the author is from Spain or Latin America, since a large number of words are used with different meanings in European and American Spanish. Even if a Peruvian like Mario Vargas Llosa writes in a Spanish newspaper for Spanish readers, he can be expected to use americanisms. b) In a Spanish edition of Cuban short stories (*Narrativa cubana de la revolución*, Madrid 1971), certain cubanisms are explained to the Spanish readers in footnotes, e.g., *duro*: "moneda de un peso cubano" (which was then a five peseta coin in Spain!), or *ñeques*: "sorpresas, golpes imprevistos". For the translator, these footnotes may be important not only in the comprehension phase, but also – if the TT skopos requires the preservation of the effect the book has on the European

---

[21]An exhaustive catalogue of questions would be impossible. I shall therefore only list a few examples: Where does the sender come from? (This question points, for example, to the dimensions of receiver and space, and to the probability of regional dialect.) When did s/he live or write? (This question may throw some light on the motive for, or time of, text production, the historical variety of language used, a possible limitation to epoch-specific text types.) Which particular events have influenced her or his thinking and emotional development? (From this question we may draw some conclusions as to the sender's intention or favourite subject matters.) What kind of education did s/he receive? (This question may lead the reader to expect, for example, a social dialect used in the text.) What is the sender's profession, is s/he an expert in the subject dealt with in the text? (This question may point to a preferred medium or text function.) What is the sender's status in society? What kind of receiver does s/he normally address? etc. etc.

Spanish-speaking reader – in the transfer phase. c) The Portuguese eclogue *Crisfal* can be ascribed either to Cristovão Falcãos or to Bernadim Ribeiro. In the first case, the text has to be interpreted literally as a naturalistic poem, while in the second case, it must be regarded as an allegory. As Kayser points out, "the words may have a completely different impact if they come from an author who really was put into prison for his love, who really was separated from his lady, and whose lady really was forced to stay in the cloister of Lorvão" (Kayser 1962: 36, my translation).

c. How to obtain information about the sender

How can the translation-relevant information about the sender (or the text producer) be obtained? The first clues are provided by the text environment (imprints, blurbs, preface or epilogue, footnotes, etc.). The author's name may already carry further information which either belongs to the receiver's or translator's general background knowledge or can, if necessary, be obtained. The name of a writer usually evokes some knowledge of their literary classification, artistic intentions, favourite subject matters, usual addressees, status, etc.; similarly, the name of a politician evokes his or her political standpoint, function or position, public image, etc. Since this is culture-specific knowledge, which belongs to what Fourquet (1973: 114) calls the "hinterland" of the text, it cannot be presumed that it is shared by the target receiver. Therefore, the translator has to consider whether the TT receiver might lack information. Whenever such a lack interferes with text comprehension, it should be compensated for by some additional piece of information given in the target text or in the TT environment.

Example 3.1.1./4
If ex-Prime Minister Edward Heath writes an editorial in a British newspaper, British readers will immediately know what political party the author belongs to. If the text is translated and published in the German weekly paper DIE ZEIT, many German readers may not be able to "classify" the author as easily. If, however, the classification is relevant for the comprehension and/ or interpretation of the article, the information has to be supplied in a few introductory lines or even in the text itself, if possible.

Further information about the sender may be provided by other factors of the communicative situation (either individually or as a combination of several factors). There may be clear and unambiguous information, which I call "data" (see Figure 5), or there may be hints (Figure 5: "clues") which may allow the necessary information to be inferred. If the analyst knows, for instance, by which medium, at what time, and for which function a text has been published (local newspaper of the day X, death announcement), s/he is able to tell who the sender may be (relatives, employer, or friends of the dead person). The place of publication points to the origin of the sender or possible origin, if the language is spoken in various countries (Great Britain – United States – Australia – India; Portugal – Brazil; Spain – Latin America – Bolivia), and the medium can throw light on the possible status of the sender (specialized journal – expert; newspaper – journalist), etc.

Sometimes it may even be possible to ask the sender in person, or a person related to him or her.

Another source of information is the text itself. If the text environment does not provide the necessary details, the analyst has to look for internal hints about the characteristics of the sender. The use of a certain regional or class dialect may reveal the (geographical or social) origin of the text producer (although not necessarily that of the sender, if they are not the same person), and the use of obsolete forms may tell the analyst that the text producer probably lived in another age. These questions, however, can only be answered after completing the intratextual analysis.

d. Checklist

The following questions may help to find out the relevant information about the sender:

1. Who is the sender of the text?

2. Is the sender identical with the text producer? If not, who is the text producer and what is his/her position with regard to the sender? Is s/he subject to the sender's instructions? Is s/he an expert in text production or an expert on the subject?

3. What information about the sender (e.g. age, geographical and social origin, education, status, relationship to the subject matter, etc.) can be obtained from the text environment? Is there any other information that is presupposed to be part of the receiver's general background knowledge? Can the sender or any person related to him or her be asked for more details?

4. What clues as to the characteristics of the sender can be inferred from other situational factors (medium, place, time, motive, function)?

5. What conclusions can be drawn from the data and clues obtained about the sender with regard to

(a) other extratextual dimensions (intention, receiver, medium, place, time, occasion, function) and

(b) the intratextual features?

3.1.2. Sender s intention

a. The difference between intention, function, and effect

In order to ascertain the dimension of intention we have to ask what function the sender intends the text to fulfil, and what effect on the receiver s/he wants to achieve by transmitting the text. It may seem difficult to distinguish the concept of intention from that of function and effect. Bühler (1984), for example, equates "author's intention" with "purpose and effect". As I understand it, however, the three concepts are three different viewpoints of one and the same aspect of communication. The intention is defined from the viewpoint of the sender, who wants to achieve a certain purpose with the text. But the best of intentions does not guarantee that the result conforms to the intended purpose. It is the receiver who "completes" the communicative action by receiving (i.e. using) the text in a certain function, which is the result of the configuration or constellation of all the situational factors (including the intention of the sender and the receiver's own expectations based on his/her knowledge of the situation). The question "What is S aiming at with the text?" can therefore not be assigned to the factor of text function, as is done by Wilss (1977), but belongs to the dimension of intention.

Text function is defined "externally", before the receiver has actually read the text, whereas the effect the text has on the receiver can only be judged after reception. It is, so to speak, the result of the reception and encompasses both external and internal factors.

It is true that certain genres are conventionally associated with certain intentions, but these need not necessarily be realized in the communicative situation. Some ancient genres, for example, such as magic spells or epic poems, are received today in a function which differs considerably from that intended by the original sender.

Ideally, the three factors of intention, function and effect are congruent, which means that the function intended by the sender (= intention) is also assigned to the text by the receiver, who experiences exactly the effect conventionally associated with this function. Methodologically, the three factors have to be distinguished because their separate analysis allows for a different treatment (preservation, change, adaptation) in the translation process. If the intention has to be preserved in translation, we must often be prepared for a change in function and/or effect.

The intention of the sender is of particular importance to the translator because it determines the structuring of the text with regard

to content (subject matter, choice of informative details) and form
(e.g. composition, stylistic-rhetorical characteristics, quotations, use of
non-verbal elements etc.). At the same time, the specific organization
of a text marks the text type and is a pre-signal which tells the receivers in which function they are expected to use the text.

Example 3.1.2./1
A set of operating instructions is meant to inform the user about a certain
piece of equipment, e.g. a hairdryer, and to explain its correct use. Therefore,
the text producer chooses the conventional forms of text organization (composition, sentence structures, lexical clichés, etc.). Taking the text out of the box
with the hairdryer, the receiver recognizes the particular forms of text organization and immediately knows that the sender wants to inform about the hairdryer and the way it has to be used. Therefore receivers will normally utilize
the text in this particular function. In this case, the text type is linked with a
particular intention on the part of the sender, which leads to the corresponding
text function on the part of the receiver. The effect will be that of "conven-
tionality" (cf. ch. 3.3.d).

The sender's intention is also important in connection with the principle of loyalty (ch. 2.1.4.). Even if the text function is changed in translation, the translator must not act contrary to the sender's intention (if
it can be elicited).

The information on the dimension of intention can throw some
light on other external factors (e.g., what effect on the receiver might
be intended, which medium may be most appropriate or conventionally used to realize the intention in question, or whether there is a link
between intention and genre), and, to a large extent, on the intratextual
features (e.g. composition, use of rhetorical devices or non-verbal elements, tone, etc.).

b. What to find out about the sender's intention
What different types of intention can be associated with a text? There
may be forms of "communication", where the sender is his or her own
addressee: somebody may write something down either to ease the
burden of their memory or to sort out their ideas and thoughts, or they
may just scribble something on a piece of paper while making a phone
call ("zero-intention"). These forms would not appear to be relevant to
translation. In normal communication with two or more participants,
the possible intentions correspond with the four basic functions of
communication described above in connection with the systematic
framework. We may ask, for example, whether the sender wants to inform the receiver about a certain issue (referential intention) or intends

to express her/his feelings or attitude towards things (expressive intention), whether s/he plans to persuade the receiver to adopt a particular opinion or perform a certain activity (appellative intention), or whether s/he just wants to establish or maintain contact with the receiver (phatic intention).

Of course, a sender may well have more than just the one intention. Several intentions can be combined in a kind of hierarchy of relevance. For pragmatic reasons, this hierarchy may have to be changed in translation.

c. How to obtain information about the sender's intention

Normally, the receiver is not informed explicitly about the sender's intention, but receives the text as the result of the sender's communicative purposes. One means of obtaining explicit or implicit information about the intention(s) of the sender or text producer, therefore, is the analysis of intratextual features (see ch. 3.2.).

However, if we stay with the extratextual factors (sender, receiver, medium, place, time, motive, and function), these can throw some light on the intention the sender may have had in transmitting the text. Paralinguistic phenomena, such as manifestations of the sender's excitement or indignation, may have to be taken into account as well.

In determining the sender's intention we have to consider the role the sender adopts towards the receiver in or through the text, a role which is quite separate from the "real", status-based relationship between the two. A sender who is superior to the receiver because of greater knowledge about the subject in question may nevertheless try to play down this knowledge in order to gain the receiver's confidence. If the analyst knows the sender's role (in relation to status), s/he may be able to draw some conclusions as to the sender's intention.

The sender's intention is of particular importance when analysing literary texts or texts marked as a personal opinion (e.g. political commentaries, editorials) because there is no conventional link between genre and intention. In these cases, the translator may have to take account of the author's life and background, events that have influenced his or her writings or any literary classification (such as "romantic" or "politically/socially committed literature"). There is no doubt that for a translation-relevant text analysis translators must exploit all sources at their disposal. But they must keep in mind that the details they have found out should have a bearing on the particular source text they are analysing. The translator should at least strive to achieve the information level which is presupposed in the receiver addressed by the author. For a literary text this will not be the level of a literary scholar, but certainly that of a "critical receiver".

> **Example 3.1.2./2**
> a) Bertolt Brecht is a representative of German politically committed literature. If the receivers know that his story "Measures against Violence" was first published in 1930, they may take this as a clue that the author intended to warn his readers about Nazi tendencies. b) If a text is published in a newspaper on the pages specially devoted to political commentaries (which in quality papers is often separate from news and reports), this medium of publication can be taken as a clear hint that the sender's intention was that of "commenting" on recent political events or tendencies. c) In a text marked as a "recipe" the reader can be quite sure that the sender's intention was to give directions for the preparation of a particular dish and to give a list of the necessary ingredients. However, if the same recipe is embedded into a larger unit, e.g. a novel, the sender's intention may have been quite different.

Sometimes senders themselves give a metacommunicative explanation as to their intentions, as is shown in the following example.

> **Example 3.1.2./3**
> In the preface of his story *Los cachorros* (Barcelona 1980), the Peruvian author Mario Vargas Llosa writes: "I wanted *Los cachorros* to sound like a story that is sung rather than told, and therefore the criterion for the choice of each syllable was not only a narrative but also a musical one. I somehow had the impression that the authenticity of the story depended on whether the reader really felt that he was listening to the story and not reading it. I wanted him to perceive the story with his ears." (My translation)

Vermeer ([1979]1983: 69) aptly points out, however, that such a statement by the author is no guarantee that the source text (actually, or even in the author's opinion) conforms to this intention.

d. Checklist

The following questions may help to find out the relevant information about the sender's intention:

1. Are there any extratextual or intratextual statements by the sender as to his or her intention(s) concerning the text?

2. What intention(s) are by convention associated with the genre to which the analysed text can be assigned?

3. What clues as to the sender's intention can be inferred from other situational factors (sender – especially his or her communicative role –, receiver, medium, place, time, and motive)?

4. What conclusions can be drawn from the data and clues obtained about the sender's intention with regard to
(a) other extratextual dimensions (receiver, medium, and function) and
(b) the intratextual features?

3.1.3. Audience
a. The importance of audience orientation
In almost all approaches to translation-relevant text analysis, the addressee (who is mostly referred to as the "receiver") is considered to be a very important, if not the most important, factor. A good deal of attention is paid to the addressee's communicative role (Wilss 1977) and expectations towards the sender (Thiel 1974a, 1980), communicative background ("knowledge presuppositions", Thiel 1978a) and sociological environment (Cartellieri 1979), position with regard to the subject matter presented in the text (Cartellieri 1979) and the linguistic features (Reiss 1980a). For Koller (1979) the addressee's situation is the pragmatic dimension par excellence. Drawing on Neubert (1968), he classifies source texts as being "specifically SL-oriented", "SL-oriented but not only SL-oriented", "not specifically SL-oriented", or "TL-oriented".

The specification of the addressed audience may be linked to the text type or may not be linked at all. Wittich (1979: 769), for example, points out that the genre "popularizing scientific text" can be addressed to various types of audience: children, adolescents, adults, the latter group comprising scientists as well as non-scientists.

Although the importance of the addressee is commonly acknowledged in translation theory, there is no other factor which is neglected so frequently in translation practice.

Example 3.1.3./1
In his article "Translation as a Decision Process" (1967: 1174, note 2) Jiří Levý refers to his book *Umění překladu*. In the German version of this article, the book is cited under the same title, although there is a German translation available (Levý 1969), which would probably be of greater interest to the average German reader than the Czech original.

b. Source-text audience vs. target-text audience
During the process of text analysis the translator elicits those textual elements or features which can be considered to be determined by the particular audience-orientation of the source text. Since each target

text is always addressed to receivers-in-situation different from those
to whom the source text is or was addressed, the adaptation of precisely these elements is of particular importance.

Example 3.1.3./2
If the source text is a report on a recent event published in an American newspaper, it is addressed to a large, non-specific audience in the United States. In
order to capture the attention of the readers the author chooses a sensational-
istic title plus an additional, informative subtitle and uses small text segments
and quotations as sub-headings for the paragraphs. The text is accompanied by
two photos. All these features are intended as "reading-incentives" for the receiver. If this text is translated for a journalist who has herself initiated the
translation because she is interested in the information provided by the text,
the reading-incentives are superfluous, and the paragraph headings may even
have a confusing effect.

Every TT receiver will be different from the ST receiver in at least
one respect: they are members of another cultural and linguistic community. Therefore, a translation can never be addressed to "the same"
receiver as the original.

c. Addressee vs. chance receiver
First of all, we have to distinguish between the addressee of a certain
text (i.e. the person or persons addressed by the sender) and any
chance receivers who happen to read or hear the text, even though
they are not addressed directly, such as people listening to a panel discussion or watching a televised parliamentary debate. In some cases,
the "chance receiver" is actually a secondary addressee; for example,
when a politician pretends to be answering a question asked by an interviewer but is, in reality, addressing his/her words to potential vo-
ters.

This aspect is relevant not only in cases where the chance receiver's comprehension of the message differs from that of the real addressee (which may have consequences for the participants), but particularly where translation or interpreting is concerned. The transfer decisions of the translator will have to depend on which of the two audiences is supposed to be addressed by the target text.

The case may even arise where the translator has a "chance receiver". If the SL participant in an interpreting session has a passive
command of the target language or if a translation is published page-
to-page with the original in a parallel text edition, the afore-mentioned
SL participant or the reader with some SL knowledge, who compares
the translation with the original, might be regarded as being a kind of

"secondary receiver" as well. They are interested not only in the message of the text but also in the way this message is transmitted to the TL reader. In view of such secondary receivers it may be advisable for the translator to comment on certain translation strategies in a preface or post-script.

d. What to find out about the audience

After all the available information about the intended TT receiver has been extracted according to the normal circular course of the translation process, then the translator can check this against the characteristics of the ST receiver: age, sex, education, social background, geographic origin, social status, role with respect to the sender, etc.

> **Example 3.1.3./3**
> A report on drugs published in a magazine for young people is written with teenage readers in mind. In order to appeal to the receivers and warn them of the risks of drug addiction, the author uses words and phrases from juvenile slang and drug jargon. A translation of the text which is also addressed to young people may use the corresponding TL slang, whereas if the same translation text (using slang words and jargon) were to appear in a section of a news magazine, whose readership is a mainly adult one, it would either not be understood or would not be taken seriously.

The communicative background of the addressees, i.e. all their general background knowledge and their knowledge of special areas and subject matters, is of particular importance for translation-oriented text analysis. According to the assessment of the audience's communicative background[22], a text producer not only selects the particular elements of the code that will be used in the text but also cuts or omits altogether any details which can be "presupposed" to be known to the receiver, whilst stressing others (or even presenting them with extra information) in order not to expect too much (nor too little) of the addressed readership.

How much knowledge can be presupposed in a reader depends not only on their education or familiarity with the subject but also on factors relating to the subject matter itself, e.g. its topicality. In this respect, the situation often varies widely for ST and TT receivers, as

---

[22]It may even be wise to take account of the fact that the TT receiver may be familiar with earlier translations of the same text. The historical reception of one translation (such as that of Luther's Bible translation or the King James Version, just to mention two famous examples) has a considerable influence on the reception of a new translation, which should not be neglected by a modern translator.

there is usually (at least in written communication) a considerable time lag between ST and TT reception.

Example 3.1.3./4
For a Spanish receiver, the heading "Nuestra integración en Europa" above a commentary published in the Spanish paper *El País* in February 1984 is not a thematic title which informs about the content of the text, but refers to the then current discussion on special agricultural problems connected with the negotiations on the Spanish entry into the European Community. For German or French newspaper readers the issue was not of topical interest at that time; under the heading "Spain's entry into the EC" (or "Our integration into Europe", for that matter) they would have expected an article on the issue of Spanish (or German/French!?) integration into the European Community.

Like the author, who has a specific intention in transmitting the text, the receiver, too, has a specific intention when reading the text. The receivers' intention must not be confused either with their expectations towards the text, which is part of their communicative background, or with their reaction or response to the text, which takes place after text reception and is thus part of the text effect.

The information obtained about the addressee may throw some light on the sender's intention, on the time and place of communication (in relation to the receiver's age and geographic origin), on text function (in relation to the receiver's intention), and on the intratextual features (e.g. the presuppositions).

As was pointed out in connection with the sender, a fictitious receiver is part of the "internal" communicative situation and not of the external communicative situation. But even externally a text can be directed at different possible receivers.

Example 3.1.3./5
Whilst imprisoned for being a member of the Resistance movement against the Nazi regime, the German writer G. Weisenborn (1902-1962) wrote some letters to his wife, Joy Weisenborn, which were published after the war. In the original situation, these letters had one precisely defined and addressed receiver. Published later in a book together with some answering letters from his wife and some songs and poems, they address a group of receivers that is much larger and not so clearly defined, i.e. anyone interested in the documents and personal testimonies of Resistance in the Third Reich. If a young man gives this book, which contains many tender love-letters, to his girlfriend many years later, the conditions of reception will be different again, not to mention those of a translation of the book into English, Dutch, or Spanish.

Therefore, the translator must analyse not only the characteristics of the ST addressees (or receivers) and their relationship to the source text, but also those of the TT receiver, whose expectations, knowledge and communicative role will influence the stylistic organization of the target text.

The stronger the orientation of the ST towards a particular SL addressee or audience, the higher the probability that the ST has to be translated in a documentary way (see ch. 3.1.8.c), which means that the target text can only give information about the source text in its situation but not fulfil an analogous function. It would therefore seem unrealistic or even absurd to postulate an equivalent effect or the "same function" for a translation of Pompidou's address "to the French", as discussed by Paepcke (1974).

e. How to obtain information about the addressed audience

As in case of the sender, information about the addressees can first of all be inferred from the text environment (e.g. dedications, notes), including the title (e.g. *Bad Child s Pop-Up Book of Beasts*). It can also be elicited from the information obtained about the sender and his/her intention or from the situational factors, such as medium (cf. example 3.1.3./2), place, time, and motive (cf. example 3.1.3./3). Standardized genres often raise equally standardized expectations in the receivers.

Example 3.1.3./6
A housewife normally expects a recipe to contain instructions for the preparation of a certain dish, and, indeed, that is why she reads it. Her attention is directed at the content of the text (e.g. what ingredients will she need, what has she got to do?). Recipes usually have a rather conventionalized form, not only with regard to their composition (first a list of ingredients, then the instructions in chronological order) but also with regard to syntactical structures (e.g. imperatives, parataxis) and lexical features (e.g. terminology and formulaic expressions, such as "bring to the boil", "stirring constantly", etc.). The reader will only become aware of the text form if it is not as expected: if, for example, the recipe is written as a poem or if the list of ingredients is missing.

The expectation of the receiver can sometimes lead to a certain tolerance. For example, when reading a menu, whose text function can clearly be inferred from the situation, but which is translated badly into their own language, tourists in a foreign country may not feel annoyed, as they normally would, but rather amused by the orthographic mistakes or unidiomatic collocations as long as they get some information about what to eat or drink.[23]

---

[23]We could take advantage of this consideration in translator training, admitting a certain degree of "interlanguage" (Selinker 1972) or "translationese" (Toury [1978] 1980: 75) for a translation into the foreign language at an early stage of translation

Normally, of course, the text producer will try as far as possible to
meet the expectations of the addressed audience. There are cases,
however, where an author disregards or even deliberately ignores the
addressees' expectations in order to make them sit up and take notice
or to make them aware of certain patterns of thinking, etc.

f. Checklist
The following questions may help to find out the relevant information
about the addressed audience and their expectations:

> 1. What information about the addressed audience can be in-
> ferred from the text environment?
> 2. What can be learned about the addressees from the available
> information about the sender and his/her intention?
> 3. What clues to the ST addressee's expectations, background
> knowledge etc. can be inferred from other situational factors
> (medium, place, time, motive, and function)?
> 4. Is there any information about the reactions of the ST recei-
> ver(s) which may influence translation strategies?
> 5. What conclusions can be drawn from the data and clues ob-
> tained about the addressee regarding
> (a) other extratextual dimensions (intention, place, time, and
> function), and
> (b) the intratextual features?

3.1.4. Medium
a. Speech vs. writing
The concept of medium (cf. Thiel 1974b) or channel (cf. Reiss 1984)
has to be interpreted rather broadly. We refer to "medium" as the
means or vehicle which conveys the text to the reader (in communication theory, "channel" stands for sound waves or print on paper). The
translator is, however, interested less in the technical distinctions and
more in the aspects of perceptibility, storage of information and the
presuppositions of communicative interaction.

First of all we have to ask whether the text is being transmitted
in a face-to-face communication or in writing. The means of transmis-
sion affects not only the conditions of reception, but more particularly
also those of production. It determines how the information should be

---

teaching. This should be stated in the translating instructions and taken into account
in the evaluation of the results.

presented in respect of level of explicitness, arrangement of arguments, choice of sentence types, features of cohesion, use of non-verbal elements such as facial expressions and gestures, etc. The effect of the chosen medium on the intratextual factors can be illustrated by looking at the deictic aspect: situational references (Halliday & Hasan, 1976: 33, talk about "exophoric reference"), which in face-to-face communication do not have to be verbalized explicitly because the participants are a part of the situation, must be expressed much more clearly in written communication.[24]

Example 3.1.4./1

In face-to-face communication, deictic expressions, such as *here, by my side*, or *today*, or expressions referring to the participants of communication, such as *I, all of us*, or *as the speaker before me correctly remarked*, are unambiguous. However, in a written text they can only be decoded correctly in connection with the information on time, place, sender, receivers, etc. given in the text itself or in the text environment, such as title page, imprint, introduction lead, etc.

The categories of speech and writing cannot, however, always be separated completely, as there are spoken texts which are reproduced in a written form (e.g. a statement made by a witness) and written texts which are spoken (e.g. lectures). Crystal & Davy (1969: 68ff.) therefore introduce the concept of complex medium, comprising "language which is spoken to be written, as in dictation, or language written to be spoken, as in news-broadcasting", and even subclassifications such as "language written to be read aloud as if written".[25]

This shows that for our purposes it would not be wise to aim at a mere "labelling" of texts as regards medium. What we have to do is elicit specific features of the medium such as coincidence or discontinuity of text production and reception, indirect or direct form of communication, spontaneity of text production, opportunities for feedback operations, one-way communication, etc.

---

[24]Beck (1973: 84, my translation) gives three important reductions which justify the classification of written language as a special category: "1. General unidirectionality (i.e. reduction of interactivity: the greater the number of people participating in the communication act, the fewer communicative partners there will be), 2. reduction of the opportunities for extra-verbal communication (especially as regards the level of interhuman relations), and 3. reduction of pragmatic contextuality."

[25]House (1981a: 43) refines the category of complex medium, at least as far as written texts are concerned, by using some of the distinctions suggested by Gregory (1968). The category of "writing" is subdivided into "to be spoken as if not written", "to be spoken", and "not necessarily to be spoken"/"to be read as if heard".

b. What to find out about the medium

In spoken communication, the dimension of medium includes the technical devices for information transfer (such as telephones or microphones), and these, of course, affect the production, reception and comprehension of the text. In written communication, on the other hand, it is the means of publication that is referred to as the "medium", i.e. newspaper, magazine, book, multi-volume encyclopedia, leaflet, brochure, etc., as well as subclassifications such as business news, literary supplement, etc.

The dimension of medium is relevant because it provides some clues as to the size and identity of the addressed audience. The readership of a national daily newspaper is not only much larger, but usually represents a different level of education and information with different expectations and different standards of stylistic quality from that of a medical, not to mention a neurosurgical, journal. The cheap paperback edition of a novel would be expected to reach a wider public than an expensive, multi-volume collection of Cantonese love poems. A personal letter is directed at one individual receiver whereas a standard business letter can be addressed to any number of companies on a mailing list, and a poster on an advertising board is targeted at anyone passing by, etc., etc.

In addition, the specification of the medium may give some clue as to the sender's intention (e.g. in the case of a poster or a picture postcard) and to the motive for the communication (e.g. in the case of a death announcement in a newspaper). Since the range and conventions of medium use may vary from culture to culture and from one generation to another, the specification of medium may even give some idea of the time and place of text production.

Although the choice of a particular medium obviously provides pre-signals for the receiver's expectations regarding the intended text function, function and medium must not be automatically associated or even equated. The receivers' expectations are certainly based on their experience with the medium in question, but, again, a particular sender may intend to surprise or disappoint the receiver by using a medium for a purpose quite different from that usually associated with it. For the translator it is important, too, to take into account the fact that the "same" media may have quite different functions in another culture.

As a general rule, however, the medium determines the receiver's expectations as to text function. A leaflet distributed at the entrance of a famous church is expected to contain basic information on the objects of interest in the form of a guided tour. The text in a guidebook usually has the functions of information plus advertising, and an article in an encyclopedia is expected to provide detailed information not only on the positive but also on the negative aspects of a place (for more examples see Sample Text 3, ch. 5.3.).

To illustrate this, I have taken the paragraphs on York Minster from four different written media:

Example 3.1.4./2
a) This plan draws your attention to some of the main features of the building. More details may be obtained from guide books on sale in the shop. The Nave, begun in 1291 and finished in the 1350's in the Decorated Gothic style, is one of the widest Gothic naves in Europe. It is used for services throughout the year. The pulpit on the left commemorates Archbishops Temple and Lang, and the brass lectern has been used since 1686. The Great West Window is being repaired and cannot at present be seen. (First paragraphs of the information leaflet *Welcome to York Minster*. There is a plan with numbers on the opposite page.)

b) THE MINSTER (by the late Chancellor F. Harrison)
Beloved to Yorkshiremen, renowned the world over. This is true. Of great and noble churches in this country, probably three attract the greatest number of visitors. These three are Westminster Abbey, St. Paul's Cathedral and York Minster). (...) The east window deserves a note of its own. Seventy-six feet high and thirty-two feet broad, containing therefore more than two-thousand square feet of medieval glass – the great window at Gloucester Cathedral measuring seventy-two feet by thirty-eight feet, and containing more than two-thousand-three-hundred square feet of glass, but not wholly coloured – this great and grand window never ceases to excite admiration and wonder. The master-glazier, John Thornton, of Coventry, received for his work, in all, the sum of £ 55 in three years, worth in modern currency – £ 2,000? Who knows, even approximately? This was the pay of only one man. (From the brochure *City and County of the City of York*, Official Guide, 112 pages. I have left out the 12 pages on the history of the Minster.).

c) There are many small old churches, quaint and often glorious towers and the breathtaking spectacle of the Minster. It took two-and-a-half centuries, from 1220 to 1470, to complete this poem in stone. Inside, a kaleidoscope of light explodes from windows of medieval stained glass that are among the art treasures of the world. (Last of the three paragraphs on York, from the book *AA Illustrated Guide to Britain*, 544 pages)

d) York Minster is the largest of England's medieval cathedrals. The result of 250 years of building, it shows a variety of styles. The transepts are the earliest part of the present building, dating from 1220-1260; the nave, chapter house, and vestibule were built in 1291-1345 in Decorated style; the choir in 1361, the central tower in 1400-1423, and the western towers in 1433-1474 in early and late Perpendicular. The Minster contains some of the earliest glass and the biggest acreage of stained glass in Britain. The lancet lights of the "Five Sisters" in the north transept are a particularly fine example of 13th-century grisaille glass. (Paragraph on York Minster – under the heading "York" – from *The New Caxton Encyclopedia*, 18 vols.)

For translation-oriented text analysis, it is most important to elicit features typical of the medium, i.e. features of content and/or form, and to classify them as culture-specific or transcultural or even universal. This is particularly relevant in those cases where the target text is to be transmitted through a medium or channel different from that of the source text.[26]

c. How to obtain information about the medium

If the source text is not available in its original medium, but only in a copy or typescript (which actually occurs fairly frequently in translation practice), the translator must insist on having detailed information about the medium, as it is rather difficult to identify the medium from intratextual analysis alone. There may be some clues in the dimensions of the sender and his/her intention or motive; time and place, too, sometimes narrow the field of possible media. In some cases, the choice of medium is determined by convention since there are favourite media for particular communicative purposes in every culture (e.g. posters or newspaper advertisements for product promotion, leaflets for tourist information, etc.).

d. Checklist

The following questions may help to find out the relevant information about the dimension of medium or channel:

1. Has the text been taken from a spoken or a written communication? By which medium was it transmitted?

2. Which medium is used to present the text to the target audience? Is there any extratextual information on the medium?

---

[26] Nida (1976: 62) quotes an example: "A group of students in one country of Latin America wished to reproduce in a printed flyer a selection from one of the Old Testament prophets dealing with the issues of social justice. In place of a well-constructed translation in traditional biblical language, they chose to produce an extemporaneous type of translation, poorly mimeographed on cheap paper. The production had considerable success, because it closely parallelled in form and content the types of revolutional documents students were eager to read."

3. What clues as to medium or channel can be inferred from other situational factors (sender, intention, motive, function)?

4. What conclusions can be drawn from the data and clues obtained about the medium as regards

(a) other extratextual dimensions, such as the addressees and their expectations, motive, and function, and

(b) the intratextual features?

3.1.5. Place of communication

a. Place of text production vs. place of text reception

The dimension of space is dealt with explicitly only in the publications based on the New Rhetoric formula (Bühler 1984 and Reiss 1984). Of course, in translation the question of culture and its influence on the source text forms the centre of interest anyway, and so it may seem superfluous to stress this aspect once again. This is probably why Reiss (1974a) and Thiel (1978a) combine the dimensions of time, space, and motive in one global dimension called "geographical, historical, and socio-cultural background" (Reiss) or "implied (situational) presuppositions" (Thiel).

However, as these factors can be of varying relevance to different texts or genres, they are, in my opinion, worth dealing with separately in ST analysis. Moreover, as has been pointed out before in connection with our systematic framework, time and space are basic categories of the historical situation of a text.

The dimension of space refers not only to the place of text production, i.e. the actual situation of the sender and the text producer, but also, at least in connection with certain media, to the place of text reception (cf. examples 3.1.1./4 and 3.1.3./4). It cannot be equated with the dimension of medium, as Hönig & Kußmaul (1982: 71) seem to use the term. The dimension of space is of particular importance where languages exist in various geographical varieties (such as the Spanish spoken in Spain as opposed to Latin America or even Peru, Mexico, Argentina etc., and the English spoken in Great Britain as opposed to the United States, Australia, India etc., cf. example 3.1.1/3a). If one of these languages is the source language, the place of text production may provide a pre-signal for the variety used in the ST, and if one of these languages is the target language, the place of text reception determines the variety the translator has to use in the translation.

Example 3.1.5./1
The Portuguese version of the information brochure published by the Tourist
Office of Munich was accepted unhesitatingly as being correct and appropriate by a group of Brazilian teachers in a seminar on translation, whereas
their colleagues from Portugal classified the text as "more or less understand-
able, but unidiomatic and not conforming to normal usage". In this case, an
analysis of the dimension of place could not throw any light on this problem
because the text had been produced in Munich for "Portuguese"-speaking receivers. As the name of the translator was not specified in the text imprint, the
participants in the seminar could only assume that the translator – whether he
or she was a native speaker or not – had used the Brazilian variety of Portuguese. The sender/initiator (the Tourist Office) had probably not been aware
of the problem. For the German version of this brochure, however, the dimension of place (of reception) would suggest that the text is written in the variety
used in Germany (as opposed to Austria or Switzerland).

In addition to the linguistic aspects, the dimension of space can be important for the comprehension and interpretation of a text in that the
place of text production may be regarded as the centre of a "relative
geography". The distance or significance of other places must often be
judged in relation to this centre. The translator has to take into account
that the "relative geography" from the standpoint of TT production
may be quite different from that of ST production.

Example 3.1.5./2
a) The difference in cultural or social level could be called "downgrade" or
"upgrade", depending on whether it is seen from the lower or the higher level.
b) The distance between London and Liverpool is much "shorter" as perceived by a Texan than by an Englishman. c) The names of places, areas and
tribes listed in Act 2, 9-11, do not make sense as a description of the "horizon
of the Jewish world" unless Syria is assumed to be the place of text production, and not Jerusalem, where the Pentecostal event is set (cf. Roloff 1981:
44f.).

b. What to find out about the dimension of space

In the dimension of space we have to consider not only linguistic aspects but also cultural and political conditions. A text published in a
country where literature is censored must be read "in another light"
than a text whose author has not been subject to any restrictions, since
authors under censorship often write "between the lines".

In addition to the name of the state or country the text comes
from, it may even be necessary to know the exact area or town of text
production in order to be able to interpret the deictic elements correctly (cf. example 3.1.4./1). This applies to the ST as well as to the TT,
which would normally be read in the target cultural environment.

Example 3.1.5./3
In the case of newspaper articles, the place where the paper is published is normally taken to be the place of text production as well. Therefore, readers of the Sunday Times can assume that the information "Mortgage cut in sight" refers to Great Britain, while all articles on the first page of the international edition of the Herald Tribune have to indicate the place the article refers to: "U.S. Banks Lower Prime Interest Rate", "In Leipzig, Protesters Fear Resurgence of Communist Power", "Tamil Guerrilla Army Nears Goal in Sri Lanka", etc. If correspondents send their reports from somewhere else, the place of text production is usually specified together with the author's name ("By David Binder, New York Times Service, Bucharest") or at the beginning of the text ("LEIPZIG, East Germany"), so that the reader can interpret a sentence as "Now everything is quiet around here again" correctly. In a translation, too, the dimension of place has to be specified either externally (e.g. in an introduction) or internally (e.g. "Now everything is quiet around Leipzig again").

Information about the place of text production also gives an indication of the cultural affiliation of the sender and/or the addressees, the medium (in the case of culture-bound or culture-specific media), the motive (at least where combined with the dimension of time) and the intratextual features (such as regional dialect or deictic expressions).

c. How to obtain information about the dimension of space
As a rule, information about the dimension of space can be found in the text environment in the form of the place of publication, the name of the publishing company, the first edition details, or newspaper headlines, or in the secondary literature. Sometimes, it is presupposed to be part of the receiver's general background knowledge (e.g. in the case of publications by international organizations or institutions or by world-famous writers). From the intratextual point of view, certain linguistic features may provide a clue as to where the text was written or intended to be read.

Other clues may be obtained from the information about the sender (e.g.: Where did s/he live, work, etc.?), the addressed audience (e.g.: What culture-specific information may be presupposed to be known by the receiver?), medium (e.g.: Is it bound to a certain culture?), or motive (e.g.: Is it a culture-specific motive?).

d. Checklist
The following questions may help to find out the relevant information about the place of communication:

1. Where was the text produced or transmitted? Is any information on the dimension of space to be found in the text environment? Is any information on space presupposed to be part of the receiver's general background knowledge?
2. What clues as to the dimension of space can be inferred from other situational factors (sender, receiver, medium, motive)?
3. What conclusions can be drawn from the data and clues obtained about the dimension of space as regards
(a) other extratextual factors (sender, receiver, medium, motive) and
(b) the intratextual features?

3.1.6. Time of communication

a. The relevance of the dimension of time

The dimension of time has been dealt with explicitly not only by Bühler (1984) and Reiss (1984) but also by Thiel (1980) and Cartellieri (1979). However, with the analytical question "In what time is the plot set?" Cartellieri alludes to the internal situation (see above, ch. 3.1.0.b). Other authors include the dimension of time in the "situational presuppositions". In my opinion, the dimension of time, like the dimension of space, has to be dealt with separately and in detail.

Every language is subject to constant change in its use and its norms. So the time of text production is, first and foremost, an important pre-signal for the historical state of linguistic development the text represents. This applies not only to language use as such (from the sender's point of view) but also to the historical comprehension of linguistic units (from the receiver's point of view), which is itself bound to a certain period or epoch, since linguistic changes are usually determined by socio-cultural changes.

Moreover, this process of change affects the area of text types. Certain genres are linked to a particular period (e.g. oracles and epic poems as opposed to weather reports and television plays), and, of course, genre conventions also undergo change. Depending on the age of the text, the receiver/translator may have totally different expectations as to the typical features of the text type in question. S/he may even expect obsolete forms that are not used any more.

Example 3.1.6./1
Being asked what they thought to be the typical syntactic feature of a German recipe, the majority of competent native speakers of German mention the subjunctive of the present tense: "Man nehme...", whereas modern German reci-

pes are written exclusively in infinitive constructions. Today, the subjunctive is used only to give a recipe an old-fashioned touch, as if it was from *Grand- mother s Recipe Book.*

In addition to the linguistic aspects, the dimension of time can throw some light on the communicative background of the sender and the addressed audience, and thus provide a clue to understanding the sender's intention. In the case of text types of topical interest, such as news items and news reports, political commentaries, election speeches, weather reports, etc., the dimension of time can be the decisive criterion as to whether there is any point in a text being translated at all, or, if there is, under which circumstances and with which skopos it may be worthwhile.

Example 3.1.6./2
In translator training, teachers seem to prefer newspaper reports as translation texts because they assume that the students are familiar with both the topical subjects and the corresponding vocabulary. In the practice of translation, however, these texts are rarely translated, because they are produced "for the day" and will be obsolete tomorrow. A translation of such a text only makes sense if it is in document function.

As I have pointed out in connection with the dimension of space, deictic elements refer directly to the situation. Like spatial deixis, temporal deixis can only be interpreted correctly if the receiver knows the time of text production.

Example 3.1.6./3
In the *International Herald Tribune* of January 9, 1990, we find the following notice: "NEW YORK – The hopes entertained that the grippe was relaxing have been destroyed by the mortality returns of yesterday (Jan. 7), which show an increase of nearly 100 over the toll given three days ago, with 134 deaths traceable to the epidemic." No need to be alarmed: the notice is to be found under the heading "100, 75 and 50 years ago", and dates from 1890.

However, it may also be necessary to know the genre conventions in this respect, as the following example shows.

Example 3.1.6./4
In Madras, I was surprised to read in the morning paper lying on my breakfast table that "there was a train crash this afternoon". Of course, the text had probably been written late at night, and the author was quite right to say "this afternoon" – but in a German newspaper (and normally in British and American papers as well) the author would have written *yesterday afternoon* because it seems to be a convention here for newspaper writers to imagine themselves in the situation of the reader who receives the text the next morning, whereas obviously the Indian readers are expected to put themselves in the writer's shoes.

Sometimes it may be wise for the translator to check on the validity of the information given in the source text (if possible) or at least to point out to the initiator that some information in the text may not be up to date.

Example 3.1.6./5
In some tourist information leaflets, the information on opening hours, prices etc. or warnings such as "is being repaired" (cf. example 3.1.4./2a) are not up to date. For example, the latest (translated) published information on the famous Altamira caves in Northern Spain specifies that the caves can be visited by anybody "on request". When I went there to have a look at the prehistoric paintings, I found out that there was a pavilion with beautiful reproductions of the paintings – but the caves had not been open to the public for the past few years. Only persons presenting proof of a particular research project were allowed to enter.

The dimension of time influences directly or indirectly the dimensions of sender (e.g.: Is s/he a contemporary of the receiver/translator or not? What situational presuppositions can be made?), intention, audience (expectations, temporal distance between ST and TT addressees), medium (historical or modern forms of medium), motive (e.g. topicality), and, above all, intratextual features (e.g. presuppositions, historical language variety, deictic elements).

b. The traditions and conventions of translation
The dimension of time encompasses not only the time of ST production and reception but also that of TT production (= translation) and reception. The original communicative situation as well as the intercultural communicative situation are determined by their respective temporal contexts.

In connection with the dimension of time, we must therefore look at the traditional translations of classical texts and consider the problems involved in translating or re-translating old texts. Whether and how the dimension of time has to be taken into account for the translation of, say, Homer's *Iliad*, Shakespeare's *King Lear*, or Cervantes' *Don Quixote* depends on the translation skopos. Popovič ([1977]1981: 103f.) distinguishes between the "synchronous translation" of a contemporary author and modern translations of older texts, which in his opinion can be either "re-creative" (i.e. actualizing) or "conservative" (i.e. historicising).

Which approach is regarded as the "correct" one depends on the prevailing translation tradition or concept, which may be regarded as a kind of culture-specific convention. Analysing the modern reception of Homer's works in Germany, which has been strongly influenced by the hexameter translations by Johann Heinrich Voss (1751-1826), Vermeer points out:

> Translations and imitations of classical Greek poetry have meant that hexameter verse has become absorbed into German culture and can no longer be regarded as an innovation. However, it does have connotations not found in classical Greek in that it creates a distance regarding the text and signals the feature "classical", possibly even "archaic", but certainly "alien" and hence "unusual" ([1981]1983: 100, my translation).

Tradition has created here a particular "translation language", which is, as a general rule, accepted without criticism and regarded as being characteristic of a specific text type. The same applies to the language of Bible translation. From our own reactions to modern Bible translations (e.g. *Good News Bible*), which we intuitively judge to be "inadequate", we can easily see how strongly we are bound to translation traditions.

The short-lived nature of a comic effect based on the jargon of the day is illustrated by Kloepfer (1967) in his translation of a few verses from Plautus' comedy *Epidicus*. To achieve the same effect as the original, Kloepfer uses some "technical terms" describing the latest fashion of the mid-sixties which now seem hopelessly out of date – if not totally incomprehensible to any receiver under fifty.

On the other hand, it appears to be equally problematical to translate an old text in a "historicising" manner, i.e. into the variety of the target language common at the time of origin, "as if" the text had been translated synchronously, such as Borchardt's translation of Dante's *Divina Commedia* into (what he considers) 14th century German. This translation, though an interesting experiment, cannot possibly have the same effect on the modern receiver as the original, mainly because German has changed much more profoundly in the past five hundred years than the Italian language (cf. Stackelberg 1978: 16f.).

c. How to obtain information on the dimension of time

Information on the dimension of time can sometimes be inferred from the date of publication of the text or other clues from the text environment, although this is not always reliable, as texts are often published years after they have been written. However, they cannot be published

before they are written – thus, the date of publication always offers a
"terminus ante quem".

   If the time of text production is not hinted at in the text itself, or
presupposed to be part of the receiver's general background knowledge, it may be necessary to refer to secondary literature in order to
come to an approximate age or at least to identify the period of time in
which the text might have been written (e.g. the author's lifetime or a
certain period in his or her life; some time before the date of reception,
if this is known; during the time when a certain medium was used, if
the text is transmitted by a historical medium; some time after the
occasion that motivated the text, if this is known, etc.). Last but not
least the time of text production can be inferred from any features
representing a historical variety of the source language.

d. Checklist
The following questions may help to find out the relevant information
about the time of communication:
   1. When was the text written/published/transmitted? Does the
   text environment yield any information on the dimension of
   time? Is any information on the dimension of time presupposed
   to be part of the addresse's general background knowledge?
   2. What clues to the dimension of time can be inferred from
   other situational factors (sender, medium, receiver, motive, and
   text function)?
   3. What conclusions can be drawn from the data and clues obtained about the dimension of time as regards
   (a) other extratextual factors (sender and intention, communicative background of the receiver, possible media, the motive for
   text production, function), and
   (b) the intratextual features?
   4. What fundamental problems arise from a possible time lag
   between ST and TT situation?

3.1.7. Motive for communication
a. The importance of motive in text production and reception
None of the authors consulted deal explicitly with the motive which
leads to the production or reception of a certain text, although we can
certainly assume that it is implied in what Reiss (1974a) calls the "historical situation" or in what Thiel (1978a) refers to as "situational presuppositions". The question "For what reason (was the text written)?"

(Thiel 1974a) seems to point to the motive for text production as I understand it, but Thiel does not discuss the problem in any detail. Communication-oriented approaches to text analysis, however, usually include the interrogative "why?" in their catalogues of text-analytical questions, which in my opinion asks for information about the reason or motive for communication.

For some text types, this question is relatively easy to answer. A wedding announcement is made because someone is getting married; a news report is written because something of importance has happened; a play review is published because there was a première, etc.

However, the dimension of motive applies not only to the reason why a text has been produced but also to the occasion for which a text has been produced. Somebody may write a poem because he or she has fallen in love, or because it is Grandfather's 70th birthday. In the first case, the text producer's motive for text production is in the focus of interest, whereas in the second case we look at the receiver's motive for text reception.

There are motives or classes of motives which are conventionally linked with certain text types or media. This means that on certain occasions (e.g. death of a relative, immigration into a foreign country, arrival of an invitation for dinner), it is necessary or conventional to produce a text of a certain type (e.g. announcement, registration, acceptance) and/or use a particular medium to transmit it (e.g. newspaper, registration form, formal headed notepaper). After the death of a personality in political or cultural life, for example, there will be an obituary in the paper. Such singular, recurring, or "standard", occasions can be classified as "motive types".

The dimension of motive can provide certain clues as to other situational factors, especially if these are conventionally linked with the motive or motive type. For example, it is normally the sports reporter who reports a world cup final (= sender); a death announcement in the paper is meant to inform readers and perhaps invite them to be present at the funeral service and/or to send flowers (= intention) and is usually addressed to the friends and colleagues of the deceased and not to every reader of the paper in question (= audience); if the time and place of the event that serves as the motive are known, they sometimes give an indication of the time and place of text production.

The motive may also be a pre-signal announcing certain conventional features of the text itself, such as formulas or non-verbal symbols, and thus guide the receiver's expectations. Depending on the text type, it will be mainly the following intratextual features that are determined by the motive of communication: content (insofar as the motive is explicitly mentioned in the text), vocabulary and sentence structure (e.g. in a memorial address), suprasegmental features (memorial address vs. election speech), and non-verbal elements (e.g. black edging round a death announcement).

b. How to obtain information about the motive for communication
Although the motive for communication is closely linked with the dimension of time, the two factors must not be confused. While the dimension of time is part of the communicative situation (in the narrower sense), the dimension of motive relates the communicative situation and the participants to an event that is outside, or rather prior to, the situation.

It is not always easy therefore (and not always relevant to translation!) to find out which event has motivated a certain text. Sometimes the motive is referred to in the text or mentioned in the text environment (e.g. in the title: *To Honor Roman Jakobson on the Occasion of his 70th Birthday*, cf. Levý 1967); but there are communicative situations in which the motive is only an indirect reason for the author to deal with a loosely connected subject.

> **Example 3.1.7./1**
> On March 12th, 1984, the Spanish daily paper *El País* published a commentary under the title "El Día de la Mujer" (International Women's Day). It is the motive for text production this title alludes to and not the subject matter, because the text deals with the situation of working women in Spain in 1984. The newspaper reader was expected to be familiar with the occasion, International Women's Day, since it had been commented on quite frequently at the time. If the text is to be translated, it is the motive for translation (as well as the dimensions of time and place) that has to be taken into account. Only a few days later the date will have been pushed into the background by other events, and a title like "International Women's Day" will arouse specific expectations about the subject matter, which the text cannot meet.

As is illustrated by the example, the dimension of motive is of as much interest to the translator as that of time, because s/he has to contrast the motive for ST production with the motive for TT production and find out the impact this contrast has on the transfer decisions. While the motive for ST production is often to be found in the "environment" of the sender or text producer, the motive for TT production can be inferred from what is known about the transfer situation, i.e. the initiator and the translation brief. The effect of the motive on intratextual features – as opposed to that of the dimension of time – is often merely an indirect one.

We can restate that the clues as to the motive or motive type are to be inferred from certain situational factors, such as medium (e.g. political section of a newspaper), place and time (in connection with the receiver's general background knowledge, cf. example 3.1.7./1), and, of course, text function, if this is specified by unambiguous pre-signals, such as genre designations (e.g. "protocol") or text-type features (e.g. black edging). The information obtained on the sender and the intention usually permits only indirect conclusions as to the motive for communication.

c. Checklist

The following questions may help to find out the relevant information about the motive for communication:

1. Why was the text written or transmitted? Is there any information on the motive of communication to be found in the text environment? Is the ST receiver expected to be familiar with the motive?

2. Was the text written for a special occasion? Is the text intended to be read or heard more than once or regularly?

3. What clues as to the motive for communication can be inferred from other extratextual dimensions (sender, intention, receiver, medium, place, time, function)?

4. What conclusions can be drawn from the data and clues obtained about the motive for communication as regards

(a) other extratextual factors (expectations of the receiver, sender and intention), and

(b) the intratextual features?

5. What problems can arise from the difference between the motive for ST production and the motive for translation?

3.1.8. Text function

a. The relationship between text function and genre

Let me briefly restate that the notion of text function means the communicative function, or the combination of communicative functions, which a text fulfils in its concrete situation of production/reception. It is derived from the specific configuration of extratextual factors (sender/sender's role, intention, receiver/receiver's expectation, medium, place, time, and motive). Certain configurations (= text functions) oc-

cur so frequently that the texts acquire conventional forms and constitute genres (cf. ch. 1.2.3.). In other words, a genre is the textual result
of a certain type of communicative action. Text function and genre
must not be confused (although designations like "instruction" seem
to suggest that they refer to the same thing). As I understand it, the notion of text function is related to the situational aspect of communication, whereas the notion of genre is related to the structural aspect of
the text-in-function. It is like looking at the two sides of a coin: they
cannot be separated, but they are not the identical.

As was pointed out above, text can be classified on various levels of generalization. It is therefore not surprising that some authors
specify text types as "newspaper reports", "sermons", or "resolu-
tions", while others prefer a more general categorisation into "informative", "expressive", or "operative" texts (cf. Reiss 1971).

Text function is a crucial factor in most approaches to translation-oriented text analysis. Thiel (1974a) gives "plea", "question",
"promise", "reproach", "request", etc. as communicative functions of
sentences, but does not discuss the problem in relation to texts. Although of course an exhaustive listing of functions will not be possible, I think it can be taken for granted that texts can be intended to
serve these sub-functions, which have to be subsumed under the four
super-functions described above (ch. 3.1.0.).

b. Literariness as a text function
The notion of text function as a particular configuration of situational
factors can be illustrated by the special function of literary texts. The
senders of a literary text are usually individual authors who are also
text producers and who in the literary context are known as "writers".[27] Their intention is not to describe "reality", but to motivate personal insights about reality by describing an (alternative) fictitious
world.[28] Literary texts are primarily addressed to receivers who have a
specific expectation determined by their literary experience, and a

---

[27]Kayser involuntarily gives an illustrative example which proves that literary texts
are often "recognized" by the fact that they are written by a person known as a writer or poet. He criticizes Croce, complaining that in his *Critica e Storia della Poesia*
he does not regard Horatio, Byron, Camões, and Molière as "poetry" (cf. Kayser
1962: 15). In the case of translated literature written by authors who are not known
in the target culture, this fact often causes reception problems.

[28]Cf. de Beaugrande & Dressler 1981: 185. The mimetic reproduction of the world is
supplemented by the element of expressivity; the expressive function of language
(according to Jakobson 1960) is stronger than the referential function.

certain command of the literary code.[29] As a rule, literary texts are transmitted in writing (= medium), although sometimes orally transmitted texts (such as fairy tales) are included in literature as well. The situational factors (place, time, motive) may not be of great significance in intracultural literary communication but they do play an important part in literary translation because they convey the culture-specific characteristics of both the source and the target situation (cf. Nord 1988b).

If we recognize the fundamental influence that the special literary intention of the sender and the "literary" expectations of the receiver have on the function and effect of literary texts, we can say that literariness clearly is a pragmatic quality which is assigned to certain texts by the sender and the receiver in a particular communicative situation. The intratextual features of these texts are not marked "literary" as such, but are interpreted as "literary" by the receivers in connection with their own culture-specific expectations which are activated by certain extratextual pre-signals (such as the name of the author, designations such as "novel" or "short story", etc.).[30]

Because of its culture orientation, this dynamic concept of literariness appears to be more satisfactory as far as the translation and translatability of literature are concerned than a static concept based more or less exclusively on linguistic features (for more details cf. Nord 1997a: 80ff.).

c. The importance of ST function for translation

The basic principle of functionalism in translation is the orientation towards the (prospective) function of the target text. Since I have argued that a change of function is the normal case, and the preservation of function the special case in the process of intercultural text transfer

---

[29]Schmidt (1970: 65) points to the fact that certain literary texts (such as visual poetry) can only be fully understood by those readers who have at their disposal systems of interpretation by which they can make the text "significant" for themselves.

[30]If literature must of necessity use "normal" language to create its own literary system, a text belonging to this system has to be marked in such a way that the reader's attention is drawn to the non-normal, secondary and, to be more precise, literary character of the text. If the text is not marked as literary, it may happen that the reader does not recognize its literary function. Literary markers can be set in the extratextual environment, announcing a book, for example, in a bookshop catalogue under the heading of "fiction", or publishing a text in a "literary" magazine (cf. Titzmann 1977: 72f.). The same considerations apply, in many cases, to the fictionality of content.

(cf. ch. 2.1.1.), it might appear superfluous to analyse the function of the source text. But if, in our culture, translation requires not only functionality of the target text but also loyalty towards the ST sender and his/her intention (which is a constitutive factor of ST function), it is only by analysing the ST function that the translator can decide which TT function(s) will be compatible with the given ST.

If a translation is an offer of information about the (offer of information of the) source text, there can be two fundamental kinds of relationship between source and target text. Here again we find the two translation theories which have split translation scholars into two camps since the days of Cicero: the supporters of liberty and the adherents to fidelity. The target text can be (a) a document of a past communicative action in which an SC sender made an offer of information to an SC receiver by means of the source text, and (b) an instrument in a new TC communicative action, in which a TC receiver receives an offer of information for which the ST provides the material. Accordingly, I distinguish between two translation "types": documentary and instrumental translation.[31]

Documentary translations (such as word-for-word translation, literary translation, philological translation and exoticizing translation) serve as a document of an SC communication between the author and the ST receiver, whereas the instrumental translation is a communicative instrument in its own right, conveying a message directly from the ST author to the TT receiver. An instrumental translation can have the same or a similar or analogous function as the ST.

In a documentary translation, certain aspects of the ST or the whole ST-in-situation are reproduced for the TT receivers, who is conscious of "observing" a communicative situation of which they are not a part. A documentary translation can focus on any of the features on each rank of the source text, pushing others into the background. In a word-for-word translation, for example, which aims to reproduce the features of the source language system, the focus is on the morphological, lexical, and syntactic structures presented in the source text,

---

[31]The distinction of documentary vs. instrumental translation bears some resemblance to House's differentiation between "overt" and "covert" translation (1981a: 188f.). House suggests, however, that the TT function depends on the type the ST is assigned to. In my view, the TT function(s) are determined by the TT skopos (as long as it is compatible with the principle of loyalty). Even in instrumental translation, the TT function does not have to be identical (House says "equivalent"), but only compatible with the ST function.

whereas textuality is bound to be neglected. Other forms of documentary translation are literal translation, philological translation, and what I call "exoticizing translation" (because it tries to preserve the local colour of the source text).

An instrumental translation, on the other hand, serves as an independent message-transmitting instrument in a new communicative action in TC, and is intended to fulfil its communicative purpose without the receiver being aware of reading or hearing a text which, in a different form, was used before in a different communicative action. This translation type comprises three forms. First, if the target text can fulfil the same function(s) as the source text, we speak of an "equifunctional" translation (used, for example, in the case of operating instructions or business correspondence). Second, if the ST functions cannot be realized as such by the TT receiver, they may be adapted by the translator, provided that the TT functions are compatible with the ST functions and do not offend against the sender's intention (e.g. the translation of Swift's *Gulliver s Travels* for children). This form is referred to as "heterofunctional translation". The third form, which I call "homologous translation", is intended to achieve a similar effect by reproducing in the TC literary context the function the ST has in its own SC literary context. This form is often found in the translation of poetry.

Within the framework of our culture-specific concept of "compatibility", an instrumental translation is legitimate only if the intention of the sender or author is not directed exclusively at an SC audience but can also be transferred to TC receivers, so that the information offer of the TT is included in the information offer of the ST. If this is not the case, the translation must be realized in document function, "documenting" the ST situation in the text environment (e.g. in a few introductory lines) and thus giving the TT receivers an indication that they are reading a (documentary) translation (for more details see Nord 1997c and 1997a: 47ff.).

d. How to obtain information about text function
The most important source of information is, again, the text environment, since designations like "operating instructions" or "anecdote" call on the receivers' reading experience of the text type in question (i.e. their experience of "intertextuality", cf. de Beaugrande & Dressler 1981: 183ff.) and build up a specific expectation as to text function(s). It is obvious that these "labels" can be misleading if they are

used inadequately by the author or sender (whether intentionally or unintentionally). On the other hand, it may be assumed that in normal communication such designations are in fact intended as a guideline for the receiver.

If there is no genre designation, the text function or functions have to be inferred from the configuration of the external factors. This is why text function should be analysed last when as much information as possible is available. As was illustrated by the example of literary texts, the intention of the sender and the expectations of the receiver are the crucial dimensions in this respect. However, other factors may also narrow the range of possible functions, such as sender (e.g. a candidate for presidency), medium and place (e.g. a public speech in the market place of a mountain village), time (e.g. shortly before the general elections), and motive (e.g. an election campaign).

The pragmatic relationships between sender, receiver, medium, and motive, provide the translator with a number of pre-signals announcing a particular function, which will be either confirmed or rejected by the subsequent analysis of the intratextual features. If the translator finds his or her expectations confirmed, s/he has reason to believe that s/he has elicited the correct function – if not, there are two possible explanations: either the author has intentionally violated the norms and conventions of the text type, or the translator has interpreted the pre-signals wrongly and therefore has to go through the process of eliciting the text function on the basis of pragmatic pre-signals again.

e. Checklist
The following questions may help to find out the relevant information about text function:

1. What is the text function intended by the sender? Are there any hints as to the intended function in the text environment, such as text-type designations?

2. What clues as to the function of the text can be inferred from other extratextual dimensions (motive, medium, receiver, intention)?

3. Are there any indications that the receiver may use the text in a function other than that intended by the sender?

4. What conclusions can be drawn from the data and clues obtained about text function as regards

(a) other extratextual dimensions (sender, intention, receiver, medium, time, place, and motive), and
(b) the intratextual features?

3.1.9. The interdependence of extratextual factors

The checklist questions suggested in connection with the extratextual factors illustrate the interdependence of the extratextual factors on the one hand, and of the extratextual and intratextual factors (which have so far not been specified), on the other. Data and clues about a single factor can be derived from the data and clues obtained about the other factors. This is why the order in which the analytical steps are carried out should not be regarded as being entirely arbitrary at least in the classroom situation.

The most important principle, however, is that of recursiveness. This type of analysis is no one-way process, but contains any number of loops, in which expectations are built up, confirmed, or rejected, and where knowledge is gained and extended and understanding constantly modified. This applies not only to the analysis of the text as a whole and to the individual text factors but also, if the analysis and translation of microstructures leads incidentally to new discoveries requiring previous transfer decisions to be corrected, to the processing of smaller text units such as chapters or even paragraphs.

The extratextual analysis developed in chapter 3.1. will be demonstrated by means of a short text, but here we shall only give the environmental data and clues. The interdependence of the extratextual factors is illustrated by a diagram (Figure 5), in which arrows are used to show the course of the analytical procedure. Those steps which yield reliable data are depicted by a continuous line, while the steps which merely lead to clues are represented by a dotted line. Since we have not yet analysed the intratextual factors, there are no arrows so far which depart from this area (see below, Fig. 7).

Example 3.1.9./1
Bertolt Brecht: "Maßnahmen gegen die Gewalt" (Measures Against Violence) The story is taken from an anthology of modern German short stories, *Deutschland erzählt* (p. 128f.), edited by Benno v. Wiese and published in the series Fischer Bücherei by S. Fischer Verlag in Frankfurt and Hamburg in 1965. The volume contains a bibliography in which we find the following reference to the story in question (p. 329): Bertolt Brecht (Augsburg 10-2-1898 – Berlin 14-8-1956) "Maßnahmen gegen die Gewalt", from: *Versuche* vol. I, Suhrkamp Verlag Berlin/Frankfurt 1959, p. 25-26. First edition: *Versuche* vol. I, Gustav Kiepenheuer Verlag, Berlin 1930.

Figure 5: The interdependence of extratextual factors

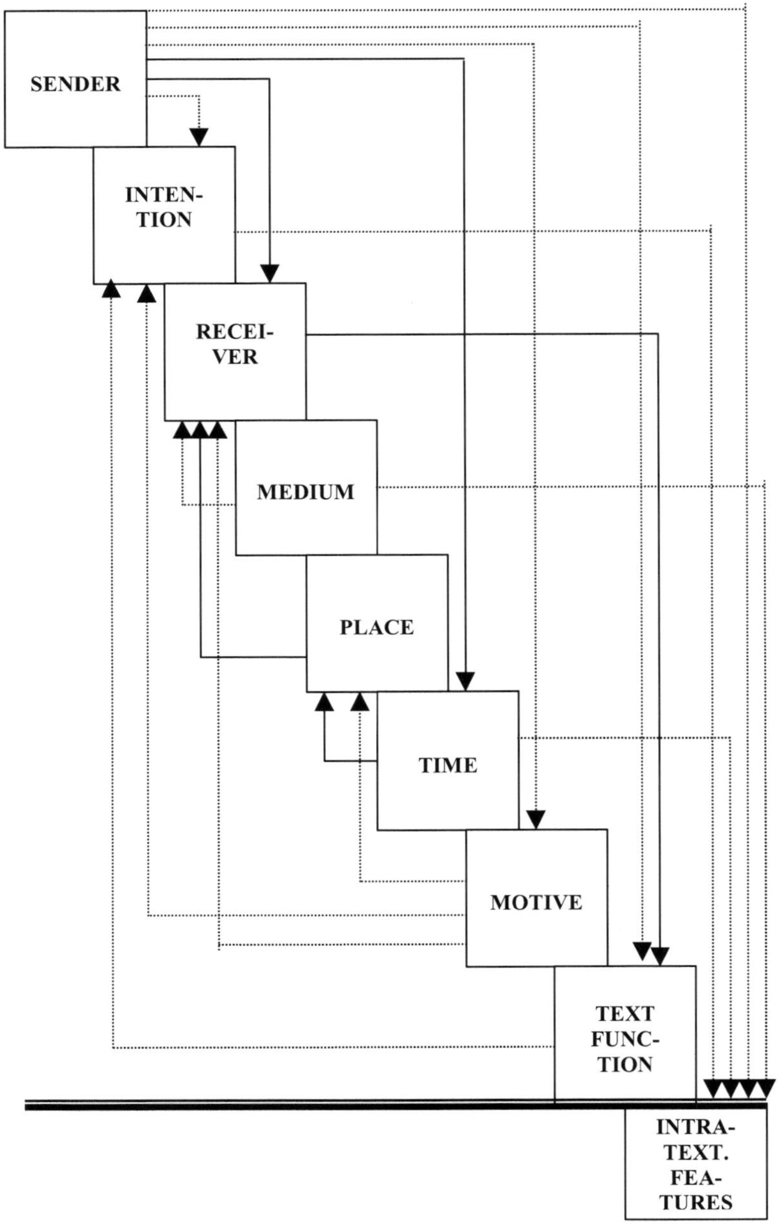

The text environment gives the name of the sender, who is at the same time text producer (Bertolt Brecht), and the dates of his birth and death (1898-1956). From this information the reader can infer that the text must have been written between 1898 and 1956 ($\rightarrow$ time$_1$), or rather, looking at the date of the first impression, before 1930 ($\rightarrow$ time$_2$). It is therefore addressed to receivers separated from today's receivers (let us say: a 25-year-old translator in 2005) by more than two generations ($\rightarrow$ background knowledge and $\rightarrow$ expectations of the receiver ST-R$_1$/ST-R$_2$).

The readers can assume that the text is written in German. They can expect that it is written in modern German (but not according to the latest "fashion") (= intratextual feature) and that it is a literary text ($\rightarrow$ text function).

Even if they have only a minimum of encyclopedic knowledge about the author, whose works are set texts in almost every German school, they expect a politically committed literary text ($\rightarrow$ intention) and perhaps even know that Brecht's first works were published in 1918/19. The time of text production therefore can be fixed between 1918 and 1930. Together with the information about the dimension of time, the title of the story gives a clue as to the motive for text production, namely the imminence of Nazi violence. This leads to a conclusion as to the place of text production and, possibly, the first reception ($\rightarrow$ place), which is confirmed by the fact ($\rightarrow$ encyclopedic knowledge) that Brecht did not emigrate from Germany until 1933.

The intention Brecht may have wanted to realize with this particular story cannot be inferred neither from the text environment nor from external enquiries. The title suggests that the author wants to suggest "measures against violence" to the reader, and this leads to the expectation that the text may be intended as a kind of instruction, although in view of the expected literary function it is unlikely that the text is written in the conventional form of instructing texts.

As for the original addressee, there is little to be inferred from the text environment. The text seems to have been intended in the first place for a contemporary of Brecht's who was interested in literary experiments (*Versuche*, $\rightarrow$ medium$_1$), with roughly the same communicative background as the author (at least as far as the political situation in Germany was concerned), and who expected the author to take up a critical, though indirect, attitude towards the situation ($\rightarrow$ motive$_1$). The modern paperback edition in the Fischer Bücherei series

($\rightarrow$ medium$_2$), however, addresses receivers whose age, communicative background, political and literary interests, and socio-cultural environment are quite different and whose comprehension and interpretation will consequently also be quite different ($\rightarrow$ motive$_2$). This second medium might even include German-speaking foreigners as possible addressees ($\rightarrow$ AT-R$_3$).

The translation brief would have to specify from whose point of view the translator is expected to analyse the text or which of the two types of ST audience is supposed to serve as a "model" for translation. This decision can serve as a basis for the next step: the definition of the TT skopos, i.e. of the function which the target text can fulfil in the target culture (e.g. to inform foreign readers about a "historical" German writer, to appeal to receivers in an analogous situation, to inform receivers in an analogous situation on how Brecht in Germany in 1930 appealed to his German readers..., etc.).

The definition of the possible TT functions also depends on what medium is planned for the target text. The source text is transmitted by two different media, which identifies the two groups of receivers. What they have in common, however, is that the text is transmitted in writing. This fact would have to be taken into account if the TT was intended for oral presentation (e.g. for broadcasting).

The exact place of text production is not mentioned in the reference; however, from the information obtained about the dimensions of sender and time we can infer that the text was written in Germany. Since the text function "literary text" is often associated with fictionality of content, we can expect that the place of text production is not relevant for intratextual deixis. The places of publication can therefore only be used for identification of possible addressees, namely readers in the area of the German Reich in the case of place$_1$, and in the area of the Federal Republic of Germany in the case of place$_2$.

The time of text production has been narrowed down to the period between 1918 and 1930. The time of reception must have been after 1930, which taken with the dimension of motive gives an indication as to the text function (i.e. an additional specification of the general function of "literary text").

The definition of the motive as "imminence of Nazi violence" places even further restrictions on both the dimensions of intention (to make the reader think and to appeal to him to "take measures" against violence) and audience (those readers for whom Brecht's story may signify a kind of instruction, and who will certainly not be sympathis-

ers of the Nazi ideology). At the same time, other (intended) functions
are rendered improbable (e.g. to teach the receiver the German language), although no receiver can be prevented from using the text in a
function other than that intended. A translation for the function of language teaching would, however, make very little sense.

At this point we have defined, as far as is possible, the text
function from the extratextual point of view, without taking into account the genre (parable) which this story can be assigned to. Such an
analysis does not yield any information on the intratextual features,
and there is only a vague expectation as to content (allusion to
violence and claims to power, the possible reactions of people towards
these).

This analysis is by no means complete – indeed, one of the constitutive features of a recursive model seems to be that the process of
interpretation never really comes to an end. However, what it does
show is that a purely external analysis of the communicative situation
of a text, which in the beginning appeared to be totally obscure, can
provide a foundation for the analysis of intratextual features.

3.2. Intratextual factors

3.2.0. Basic notions
a. Specification of the intratextual factors
The New Rhetorics formula, together with its amplifications, which
was chosen as a starting point for our set of analytical WH-questions
(cf. note 13) contained only two questions referring to the text itself
(i.e. What does the sender say? and How does s/he say it?) which encompass the traditional aspects of content and form. The discussion as
to whether or not it is possible or wise to separate the content and
form of a linguistic sign is by no means at an end[32], and in the case of

---

[32]It can be shown quite easily that in every text semantic phenomena, such as coherence, have formal correspondences, such as the linking devices of cohesion, and
every formal feature carries a semantic element whenever it informs the reader about
the speaker's attitude, his/her assessment of the information given, or about the intention with regard to the receiver. In some areas of communication (e.g. in LSP
communication), the semantic element of formal features is severely reduced (cf.
Wilss 1977: 673), and sometimes the translation skopos requires content and form to
be differentiated. We cannot, therefore, abandon the idea of distinguishing (not separating) semantic and formal factors in translation-relevant text analysis. For instance,
when the initiator asks for a "rough translation" or for a quick TL summary of the

a translation-oriented text analysis it did indeed prove extremely difficult to take these two categories as a basis for intratextual analysis.

Working on the hypothesis that the reversal of a model of text synthesis must lead to a model of text analysis, I have taken the perspective of a sender, who produces a text for a communicative purpose, in order to ascertain what intratextual factors should be taken into account in text production.

The sender usually initiates the process of communication because s/he wants to convey a message to a receiver. I use the concept of message in the broad sense to include requests and orders, questions or attempts to get into contact, etc., in other words, all utterances that fulfil the basic functions of human communication described above. Through the message the sender refers to a part of extralinguistic reality, which will constitute the subject matter of the utterance. Having decided on the subject matter, the sender selects those items of information which may be of interest or new to the receiver, and these items will form the content of the text that is being produced.

When formulating the message, the sender has to take into account the assumed general background knowledge of the receiver. The sender wants the text to be "communicative" and will therefore try to avoid including too much of the kind of information that might be "pre-supposed" to be known by the receiver. Although not verbalized, this information is, of course, present in the text in the form of presuppositions.

As soon as subject, content and presuppositions have been fixed, the sender goes on to decide in which order the content should be presented and how the various pieces of information can be interconnected. This aspect is covered by the category of composition, which comprises both the macro-structure of the text as a whole (chapters, paragraphs, etc.) and the micro-structure of sentences and sentence-parts.

The composition of a text is often signalled by its outward appearance. Indentations, chapter headings and numbers, asterisks, but also layout, illustrations, tables, initials, boldface types or italics, or, in face-to-face communication, gestures and facial expressions, which can, of course, serve other purposes as well, will be referred to as non-verbal elements.

---

content, all ST elements belonging to the formal component, such as stylistic markers, rhetorical devices, original choice of lexis, etc., are of secondary importance.

However, it is the verbal elements (lexis, sentence structure and the suprasegmental features, i.e. the "tone" of the text) which are most important for conveying the message. In both written and spoken texts suprasegmental features serve to highlight or focus certain parts of the text and to push others into the background. All these elements have not only an informative (i.e. denotative), but also a stylistic (i.e. connotative) function.

As has already been pointed out, the intratextual features are influenced to a large extent by situational factors (e.g. the geographical origin of the sender, the special requirements of the chosen medium, the conditions of the time and place of text production, etc.), but they can also be determined by genre conventions or by the sender's specific communicative intention, which affects the choice of the intratextual means of communication. We also have to account for the fact that stylistic decisions are frequently interdependent. If, for example, the sender decides on a nominal style in the area of lexis, this will naturally affect the choice of sentence structure.

In our sender-oriented approach we distinguish eight intratextual factors: subject matter, content, presuppositions, composition, non-verbal elements, lexis, sentence structure, and suprasegmental features. In practical analysis it has proved effective to deal with the factors in the order in which they appear here. However, there is no real reason why this cannot be changed, since the principle of recursiveness again allows any feedback loops which may be deemed necessary.

The separation of the factors is a mere methodological device. In practice, they form an intricate system of interdependence, which is illustrated in Figure 6. For instance, the subject matter may have determined the composition of the text (e.g. chronological order of events in a report) or the choice of lexical items (e.g. legal terminology in a contract), and the insertion of non-verbal text elements may have influenced the composition of the text, which in turn may affect the choice of sentence structure, etc.

In the practical application of the model it may not always be necessary to go through the whole process of intratextual analysis step by step. Some translation briefs will be such that merely a cursory glance at the intratextual features is sufficient (just to find out, for example, whether or not the framing of the text corresponds to genre conventions), whereas others may require a detailed analysis right down to the level of morphemes or phonemes.

Example 3.2.0./1
If a strongly conventionalized text, such as a weather report, has to be translated in such a form that the target text conforms to the target-culture conventions of the text type, there is no need to analyse all the intratextual details of the source text, once it has been stated that they are "conventional". Since the intratextual framing of the TT has to be adapted to TC conventions anyway, the intratextual framing of the ST may be regarded as irrelevant for translation.

In some text types, the analysis will have to focus on certain specific intratextual aspects, whereas in others these aspects will be conventional and, therefore, predictable. This consideration opens up the possibility of schematization in the didactic application of the model, which would permit text analysis to become established in translation classes without it being given too much time at the expense of translation practice (cf. Nord 1987b).

b. State of the art
Let me briefly review how, and to what extent, existing approaches to translation-oriented text analysis take account of the intratextual aspects described above.

They all stress the importance of the reference to extralinguistic reality. Subject matter and content are not usually dealt with as two separate factors (e.g. Wilss 1977, Reiss 1984); sometimes only one of them is mentioned (e.g. content in Thiel 1974a, 1978b; subject matter in Cartellieri 1979, Thiel 1980, Wilss 1980a, Bühler 1984).

The importance of the presuppositions is mentioned explicitly only by Reiss (1984a). Koller makes no specific mention, but seems to hint at the aspect of presuppositions when he bases his text typology on the criterion as to whether or not the ST content is bound to SL surroundings and whether or not the SL context is verbalized in the source text (cf. 1979: 213). Thiel (1974a) maintains that the translator should elicit the "expert knowledge required for text comprehension", which also seems to point to the question of presuppositions.

As for text composition, it is Thiel who never ceases to emphasize this aspect in her contributions. Wilss (1977), too, deals with this factor in connection with the practical analysis of his sample text (1977: 641), when he talks about the "thematic composition" of the text. He refers to opening paragraphs, quotations, thematical sequences, etc. as separable text segments.

As far as non-verbal elements are concerned, they are not usually mentioned in those approaches that are based on a narrower concept of text which does not include elements other than linguistic ones. Only Thiel (1978a) underlines the importance of "formal text structure" and "optical markings".

Lexis and sentence structure are generally dealt with in connection with the linguistic or stylistic aspects of text analysis. These aspects comprise rhetorical figures of speech such as metaphors, similes, word formation, ellipses, etc. (cf. Wilss 1977) as well as levels of style (Thiel 1974a), text-type conventions (Reiss 1974a, Cartellieri 1979), and the "artistic organization" of literary texts (Reiss 1980a). To my mind, however, onomatopoeic elements, rhyme, rhythm, and other features that Koller subsumes under the category of "formal-aesthetic characteristics" must be classified as suprasegmental features.

The specification of the "dominant language function"[33], which Koller (1979) considers to be one of the most important steps in translation-relevant text analysis, seems to go beyond the limits of intratextual analysis, since it cannot be determined without taking into consideration the external characteristics of the communicative situation.

When we analyse the linguistic features of a particular text, we soon realize that they all have to be evaluated in a different way, depending on the function they have in the text. There are features that depend on situational conditions which cannot be controlled or modified by the sender (e.g. pragmatics of time and space, geographical or socio-cultural background of the sender himself) or features that may have been determined by a decision taken prior to text production (e.g. choice of medium or addressee orientation). Then, there are other features which are dictated by social norms (e.g. text-type or genre conventions and so on). During the process of analysis, therefore, the translator constantly has to go back to factors which have already been analysed (= principle of recursiveness). Lastly, there is a type of feature which depends on the sender deciding on one out of several alternative means of expression, a decision determined by the intention to produce a certain effect on the receiver. This interrelation between extratextual and intratextual factors is illustrated in Figure 7, which may serve as a kind of matrix for text analysis in translation teaching.

---

[33]The first step in Koller's translation-relevant text analysis (cf. Koller 1979) is to determine the "dominant language function" (according to Bühler 1934). In my view this feature can only be elicited after a careful analysis of all intratextual factors. A more or less "automatic" alignment of dominant language function and (optimum) translation method, which Reiss (1971) and Koller (1979) seem to have in mind, is only conceivable within the framework of an equivalence-based translation theory.

c. General considerations on the concept of style

The semantic information in the text, which is essentially conveyed by the lexical elements, has to be analysed at text level. This means that by including the global functions of cohesion and coherence ambiguous text elements and structures (verbal as well as non-verbal ones) can be more easily clarified. Semantic information can thus be assigned to the categories of subject matter, content, and presuppositions.

The categories of composition, non-verbal elements, lexis, sentence structure, and suprasegmental features, on the other hand, refer mainly to the stylistic implications of text "gestalt". At this point it might be useful to explain the concept of style, as I understand it.

The style of a text refers to the way the information is presented to the receiver. The term is not used here in the evaluative sense (as it is when we talk of a "clear" or "beautiful" style, cf. Crystal & Davy 1969: 9f., or say that something or someone "has style"). Nor is it understood as a means of defining a "deviation" from a literary or stylistic convention or norm, because this would mean that there could be texts "devoid of style". This concept conflicts with the empirical observation that there are deviations without stylistic value, and that there are stylistic values which are not due to deviation.

This concept of style is a purely descriptive one. It refers to the formal characteristics of a text, whether provided by norms and conventions or determined by the sender's intention. In either case, the style of the text tells something about the sender and his/her attitude and sends certain pre-signals to the receiver as to how (i.e. in what function) the text should be received.

In order to be able to understand a stylistic signal or sign, the receiver has to be equipped, like the sender, with a knowledge or command of stylistic patterns and of the functions that they are normally used for. This knowledge is part of text competence and will enable the receiver to infer the intentions or attitudes of the sender from the style presented in the text. It is based on the fact that most communicative actions are conventionalized and that text producers almost always proceed according to a given pattern. In ordinary communication an intuitive, unconscious, or "passive" knowledge of stylistic patterns will be more than sufficient to ensure the comprehension of the text. However, the receiver/translator cannot manage without an active command of such patterns of expression both in SL and TL, since it enables them to analyse the function of the stylistic elements used in the source text, and to decide which of these elements may be appropriate for achieving the target function and which have to be changed or adapted.

It seems to be of advantage to the translator (at least in our Western civilization) that a large number of the stylistic categories used today have been inherited by various cultures from ancient rhetoric, even though their stylistic value may vary slightly owing to the specific characteristics of the different languages.

3.2.1. Subject matter
a. General considerations

The aspect of subject matter is of fundamental importance in all approaches to translation-oriented text analysis, although it is not always referred to under this heading. Reiss (1984) subsumes subject matter and content under the question "What does the sender talk about?", which seems to embrace the "additional potential" of significance that artistic organization can convey to a literary text. Taking the essay on *Miseria y esplendor de la traducción* by José Ortega y Gasset as an example, Reiss (1980a) shows that the "real" subject of a text can be hidden in stylistic devices such as metaphors or similes.

Wilss (1977) classifies the subject matter of the text as pragmatic but does not justify this classification. In describing the subject matter as the "central theme" which, like a "leitmotiv", can be cognitively reconstructed by analysing the means of coherence, he is, in fact, referring to an intratextual factor. Cartellieri (1979), on the other hand, in trying to establish the "sociological relevance" of the subject matter, definitely touches upon the pragmatic aspect.

Apart from Reiss (1980a), who demonstrates her analysis using a sample text, it is only Thiel who deals explicitly with the problem of how to elicit the subject matter of a text. She points out that for some text types (her sample text is a resolution) there is a convention that the subject matter has to be indicated in the title or in some other part of the text.

For the translator, an analysis of the subject matter is important for several reasons:

1. If one subject consistently dominates the text, this seems to prove that the text is coherent. If a text deals not just with one subject or a hierarchy of compatible topics, but with a number of different subjects, then we talk about a "text combination". Plett (1979: 102)

cites "question time in parliament" as an example of such a text combination with varying subjects. A change of subject matter can be signalled by non-verbal elements. This can present a problem to the
translator if the text to be translated deals with a number of different
subjects since the conditions of the target situation may vary accordingly (e.g. as far as the general background knowledge of the receivers is concerned). In this case, the subject matter has to be elicited
separately for the individual components of the text combination.

2. The question as to whether the subject matter is embedded in
a particular cultural context (cf. Popovič 1977) may give an indication
of possible presuppositions and their relevance for translation. If the
cultural context is not universal, it does not necessarily mean that it
must be bound to the source language culture, as stated by Koller
(1979: 213). It might equally well be bound to the target culture (or
what the sender imagines the target culture to be). Moreover, the cultural context may not even be real but fictitious, in which case it might
be anything from almost realistic, or not very realistic, to utopian,
etc.).

3. Since the elicitation of the subject matter restricts the number
of possible extralinguistic realities described in the text (cf. Thiel
1980), it enables the translator to decide whether s/he possesses the
expert knowledge (including terminology) required for the comprehension and translation of the text and/or what research has to be un-
dertaken in advance.

4. If performed in the first phase of ST analysis, i.e. possibly in
the course of compatibility control, the analysis of the subject matter
can yield important information as to the feasibility of the translation
task.

5. When the subject matter has been analysed, the function of
the title or heading can be dealt with. Where titles or headings indicate
the subject matter of the text, as in our culture is usually, or very often, the case in scientific texts (cf. Graustein & Thiele 1981: 10), they
can often be translated literally in accordance with syntactic conventions (cf. Nord 1990b and 2001d).

6. The elicitation of the subject matter occasionally yields some
information about certain extratextual factors (e.g., sender, time, text
function), where these have not already been ascertained by external
analysis. On the other hand, certain expectations about the subject
matter, which have been built up in the course of external analysis,
may be confirmed or adjusted by internal analysis.

b. How to obtain information about the subject matter

As was mentioned above, the conventions of certain text types seem to dictate that the title or heading or the title context (comprising main title, subtitle(s) and the like) represent a kind of thematic programme. An example of this is the following title of a linguistic article: "Understanding what is meant from what is said: a study in conversationally conveyed requests" (Clark & Lucy 1975).

Where the information is not given by a thematic title like this, the subject matter of a text can be formulated in an introductory lead, as is very often the case, for example, in newspaper articles (cf. Lüger 1977: 49ff.) or in the first sentence or paragraph which can then be regarded as a kind of "topic sentence" paraphrasing the thematic essence of the text.

> **Example 3.2.1./1**
> The Soviet Disunion
> UNITED IT STANDS ...DIVIDED IT FALLS
> While 1989 was the year of eastern Europe, 1990 may be the year of the Soviet Union. Confronted by growing nationalist unrest and economic mayhem, the empire is beginning to come apart at the seams. James Blitz in Moscow reports on the crisis in the Kremlin (...). (*The Sunday Times*, 7 January 1990, p. A 10f.)

> **Example 3.2.1./2**
> Title: Ford Is Rebuffed By Mazda
> Sub-title: No Chance Seen For Larger Stake
> TOKYO – Mazda Motor Corp. said Monday that it saw no opportunity for Ford Motor Co. to enlarge its stake in the Japanese company and that Mazda had no plans to raise funds by issuing new shares, warrant bonds or convertibles. (...) (*International Herald Tribune*, 9 January, 1990, p. 9)

This applies not only to titles which are a shortened paraphrase of the text, but also to descriptive titles, e.g. of literary works.

> **Example 3.2.1./3**
> The original title *El siglo de las luces* ("The Age of Enlightenment", cf. Sample Text 1, ch. 5.1.) indicates the subject matter of the novel, while the titles of the English and the German translation (*Explosion in A Cathedral/Explosion in der Kathedrale*) use the name of a picture that plays a symbolic part in the story. The reader, however, cannot recognize it as such and will probably interpret it as an indication of the subject matter or content. This may lead to a (wrong) classification of the book as a kind of thriller.

If the subject matter is not described in the title or title-context, it can be elicited by reducing the textual macro-structures to certain basic semantic propositions or information units, which constitute a kind of résumé or "condensation" of the text. Occasionally, the translator is even asked to produce a short version of the text (i.e. a summary, abstract, or résumé) in the target language. In translation teaching, the production of summaries can be used for checking text comprehension.

Condensing and summarizing, however, does not in all texts lead to an elicitation of the real subject matter, since in some cases this is obscured by a "false" subject occupying the foreground of the text. In these cases it is the analysis of other intratextual factors, mainly of lexis, which may lead to success.

The crucial concept in the analysis of the subject matter at the level of lexical items is that of isotopy. Isotopic features are semes shared by various lexical items in a text, thus interconnecting the lexical items and forming a kind of chain or line of isotopies throughout the text. The lexical items linked by isotopy are referred to as the "isotopic level", which may indicate the subject matter(s) of the text. There can be various isotopic levels in a text, either complementing each other or hierarchically subordinate to one another.

Similarly, the subject matter of a text can be elicited by isolating thematic concepts and analysing their distribution and density in the text, as Gerzymisch-Arbogast (1987: 111) demonstrates using American economic texts.

Since isotopic structures constitute a "network of semantic relations" (Mudersbach & Gerzymisch-Arbogast 1989: 147), they serve to display the coherence of a text. Mudersbach & Gerzymisch-Arbogast suggest (ib.: 148) that the invariance of isotopy, which they call "isomorphy", should replace the commonly used notion of equivalence in translation.

c. The role of linguistic competence
Eliciting the features of coherence represented in a text is not usually sufficient for a complete understanding of what a text is really all about. Coherence explains the relationships between the elements of a text, but it does not explain the relationship between the text and the extralinguistic reality it refers to. Comprehension, however, is achieved by coordinating the information verbalized in the text with some form or manifestation of either reality in general, or of a particular reality. Readers who want to "understand", have to connect or associate the new information given by the text with the knowledge of the world already stored in their memories.

How does this work? Scherner (1984: 68f.) specifies four fundamental factors which enable the reader to understand a text: (a) the "horizon" of sender and receiver, i.e. any previous knowledge they have stored in their memories; (b) the "linguistic competence", i.e. the language proficiency they have acquired; (c) the communicative "situation", i.e. the situation (time, place, etc.) in which the communicative action takes place and which is perceived by sender and receiver alike; (d) the "con-text", i.e. the linguistic environment of the elements in question.

The situational factors have already been discussed in connection with the external part of the analysis; and context is produced by means of cohesion and coherence. But how do "linguistic competence" and "horizon" contribute to the process of comprehension?

This can be illustrated by the following joke (cf. Scherner 1984: 59f.).

> Meisl comes to Vienna on business for the first time in his life, and in the evening he wants to go to see a play at the famous Burg Theatre. So he asks the lady in the booking office: "What is on tonight?" And she answers: *Twelfth Night or What You Will*. "Oh well," says Meisl, "I would prefer *The Blue Danube*."

Meisl has sufficient linguistic competence to understand the information he receives. But in his "horizon" he has not stored the knowledge that *Twelfth Night or What You Will* is the title of a Shakespeare play. Neither does he know that it is not usually the theatre audience that decides on which play is going to be performed, nor does he realize that the Burg Theatre is not a theatre where operettas are performed.

The reader "understands" the content of an utterance by associating the information gained from the lexical and syntactical text elements, by means of linguistic competence, with the knowledge of the world stored in his or her "horizon" and amalgamating these into a new "whole". They establish analogies between the new information of the text and the information that is part of their empirical knowledge. Similes and metaphors can facilitate this process. Thus, the principle of combining new information with existing knowledge also applies to fictional texts, even to science fiction.

These considerations are of special relevance to translation. Since the difference in "horizons" is not only due to individual idiosyncrasies but also depends on culture-specific influences, the translator can never be a mere "uninterested observer", as Scherner (1984: 60) rightly points out. She must be regarded as an "interested observer", who, after understanding the text intuitively against the background of her own "horizon", tries to find an intellectual justification for her intuitive understanding.

When the translator is translating a text written in the foreign language, another complicating factor in the comprehension of the text may be inadequate linguistic competence.

d. Checklist
The following questions may help to find out the relevant information about the subject matter of the text:

1. Is the source text a thematically coherent single text or a text combination?
2. What is the subject matter of the text (or of each component of the combination)? Is there a hierarchy of compatible subjects?
3. Does the subject matter elicited by internal analysis correspond to the expectation built up by external analysis?
4. Is the subject matter verbalized in the text (e.g. in a topic sentence at the beginning of the text) or in the text environment (title, heading, sub-title, introduction, etc.)?
5. Is the subject matter bound to a particular (SL, TL, or other) cultural context?
6. Do the TC conventions dictate that the subject matter of the text should be verbalized somewhere inside or outside the text?

3.2.2. Content
a. General considerations
The analysis of text content has not so far been dealt with satisfactorily in the various approaches to translation-relevant text analysis. The concepts of "content", "meaning", "sense", etc. remain vague, and there are very few hints on how to actually elicit the content of a text.[34] The analysis of content is restricted more or less to the level of

---

[34]In connection with the analysis of content, Thiel speaks of "semantic information" (1974a, 1978b) which is reflected by a "semantic structure", i.e. the "set of semantic relations between the linguistic elements of the text". Reiss (1974a) suggests that the analysis of content should serve to explicate the facts or objects of reference in the text. By analysing the meanings of words, sentences, and the text (1980a) the translator has to elicit the "sense" of the text. Cartellieri (1979) formulates only two questions concerning content ("Does the content of the text belong to various overlapping areas? Is there a relationship between these areas as regards the object of reference and terminology?") Since by "area" Cartellieri refers to the field of

lexical items (Thiel 1978a, Reiss 1984) and only appears in the form of a summary (Thiel 1978a) or a paraphrase (Bühler 1984) of the text.

Where the translator has a good command of the source language and is fully conversant with the rules and norms governing text production, s/he will usually have little or no difficulty in determining the content of a text. Even so, it would still be useful to have some means of checking this intuitive understanding. It would be even more useful, of course, to have some guidelines available in translator training, where competence in this area is still inadequate. In the following paragraphs I discuss some aspects of content analysis which may be helpful.

b. Paraphrase as a procedure for content analysis
By "content" we usually mean the reference of the text to objects and phenomena in an extralinguistic reality, which could as easily be a fictitious world as the real world. This reference is expressed mainly by the semantic information contained in the lexical and grammatical structures (e.g. words and phrases, sentence patterns, tense, mood, etc.) used in the text. These structures complement each other, reduce each other's ambiguity, and together form a coherent context.

Therefore, the starting point for the analysis of content has to be the information carried by the text elements linked on the surface of the text by the text-linguistic linking devices, such as logical connections, topic-comment relationships, functional sentence perspective, etc.

Since at this stage the external analysis of the communicative situation has been completed, the meaning of the text can be elicited, as it were, "through the filter" of extratextual knowledge.

Analysing the content of syntactically or semantically complicated texts can be made easier by a simplifying paraphrase of the information units, which can be formulated independently of the sentence structure. However, in so far as they are explicitly verbalized in

---

specialization, these questions seem to point to the dimension of subject matter rather than to that of content. In Bühler's model (1984), the "cognitive" analysis of content, i.e. the comprehension of the cognitive structures of the text by means of the determination of its semantic "nucleus", is a third step after the analysis of the communicative situation and the linguistic analysis. In translator training, the semantic nucleus has to be paraphrased in sentences that are free of redundancies. In case of difficulties (e.g. if the linguistic competence in the foreign language is not yet sufficiently developed) she recommends a componential analysis.

the text, the logical relationships between these units should be noted. This procedure permits the translator to identify (and possibly compensate for) presuppositions, and even defects in coherence, which frequently occur in texts.

Example 3.2.2./1
Summary of a novel in a review: "Arando la tierra un labrador encuentra casualmente un tesoro celtibérico que va a conmocionar la vida de un pueblecito. Dada la noticia, una expedición de arqueólogos se dirige al lugar, donde los campesinos, que los miran con sospecha, dan paso a su propia codicia..."[35]
The second sentence can be broken down into the following information units. "The news is made known, a group of archaeologists sets out for the village, the inhabitants look at them suspiciously, they give way to their greed..." The first thing we find out from this paraphrase is that the arrival of the archaeologists at the village is only implied. Secondly, the paraphrase shows that the syntactic structure (relative clauses) is misleading in that all the units contain information of equal importance for the plot, which are not subordinate but coordinate to one another.

These paraphrases have to be treated with great caution, however. The paraphrased information units form a new text which is in no way identical to the original. Paraphrases can only be used in order to simplify text structures, making them more transparent. In example 3.2.2./1 we have used "syntactic paraphrases" or "transpositions" (Wilss 1980b: 72 speaks of "back transformations"). When paraphrasing lexical items we also have to take account of the connotative content, which has to be preserved, or at least marked, in the paraphrased text.

In any case, it must not be the simplified paraphrase which should be taken as a starting point for translation, but the original source text.

c. Linking devices (cohesion)
The linking devices which appear in a text, such as anaphora, cataphora, substitutions, recurrence (i.e. repetition of elements or patterns), paraphrase (i.e. expressing the same content in a different form), proforms, etc. (cf. Halliday & Hasan 1977: 14ff., and similarly de Beaugrande & Dressler 1981: 48ff.), can also be used to analyse the content. The linking devices can vary according to the language. In

---

[35]Literal translation: Ploughing the land, a farm labourer happens to find a celtiberic treasure, which is going to disturb the life of a little village. The news made known, a group of archaeologists sets out for the place, where the inhabitants, who look at them suspiciously, give way to their own greed... (C.N.)

Spanish, as illustrated in the following example 3.2.2./2a, a paraphrase (*pasos fronterizos* for *visitantes*) is used to achieve cohesion, whereas the corresponding lexical element in English is not recognized as a paraphrase in the first translation (2b), so that the reader expects "new" information in the second sentence. But since the second sentence is simply a paraphrase of the first, the sequence lacks coherence. The problem could be solved by inserting a cataphoric element at the end of the first sentence (e.g. a colon) or an anaphoric element at the beginning of the second sentence, e.g. *Thus*, *This means*, or a pronominal substitution as in the second translation (2c).

Example 3.2.2./2
a) España ha tenido durante el mes de julio medio millón menos de visitantes que en las mismas fechas del año pasado. Los pasos fronterizos han descendido un 7,2% sobre los 7.356.809 registrados en julio de 1984 (*El País* 21-8-1985, p. 29).
b) Spain recorded half a million visitors less in July than in the same month last year. The number of border crossings decreased by 7.2 per cent from the 7,365,809 registered in July 1984 (transl. by C. N.).
c) Spain recorded half a million visitors less in July than in the same month last year, when 7,365,809 border crossings were registered. This means a decrease of 7.2 per cent (transl. by C. N.).

Experience shows that paraphrases, particularly in source texts written in a foreign language, may cause considerable difficulties. Hartmann (1970: 40) speaks of intratextual "translation procedures", whereas Kloepfer (1984) calls this phenomenon "auto-translation", which the translator can call upon in the analysis of text content. In some cultures, however, paraphrases (instead of recurrences) are a characteristic feature of certain text types or registers (cf. Nord 1986b).

Example 3.2.2./3
If in a Spanish newspaper article the Spanish entry into the European Community (cf. example 3.1.3./4) is successively referred to as *ingreso en la CEE*, *ingreso en el Mercado Común*, *integración en Europa*, *incorporación*, *adhesión al Tratado de Roma*, and *entrar en la Comunidad*, the use of paraphrases instead of recurrences has no informational relevance whatsoever, but conforms to the convention of stylistic variation which is often observed in Spanish newspaper language irrespective of possible comprehension problems or even overt errors (e.g. *Common Market* does not refer to the same phenomenon as *European Community*).

d. Connotations
The amount of information verbalized in a text includes not only denotative but also connotative (or "secondary") meaning, i.e. the infor-

mation expressed by a language element by virtue of its affiliation to a
certain linguistic code (stylistic levels, registers, functional style, regional and social dialects, etc.). By selecting one specific element in
preference to another from a number of possible elements the author
assigns a secondary meaning to the text. Since the connotative meaning can only be analysed in detail in connection with the stylistic values of lexis, sentence structure and suprasegmental features, I would
recommend at this stage of the analysis provisionally marking those
text elements which can be intuitively classified as "probably connotative". The extratextual category of text function (e.g. the conventional
function of a newspaper column, as in example 3.2.2./4) often provides a certain expectation here.

Example 3.2.2./4
Kate Saunders in *The Sunday Times*, 7 January 1990:
Career woman – or just the little woman?
Chic dinner tables are resounding with funereal orations over the twitching
corpse of the women's movement – they come to bury it, certainly not to
praise it. It was so selfish, so uncaring, so unnatural – surely home-building is
nicer and more fulfilling than hacking through the professional jungle? The
Eighties' ideal was the woman who ran a business, made breakfast appoint-
ments with her own husband, and spent 20 minutes' "quality time" a day with
her children. But women are wondering now whether the effort of juggling
home and career was worthwhile. All you got for your pains was nervous ex-
haustion, and kids who spoke Icelandic because they were brought up by the
au pair. How much simpler to give up the struggle and devote yourself to
stoking the home fires. Part of the problem seems to be that women are disco-
vering the real snag about equality – work is a pain. Any man could have told
them this. (...)

Certain connotations are a part of every speaker's communicative
knowledge whether they speak the standard language or a particular
regional and/or social dialect. They are linked so closely to a lexical
item that they would be specified in the dictionary (e.g. *kid* is marked
"slang" in OALD 1963, and "informal" in OALD 1989, whereas *snag*
is marked "colloquial" in OALD 1963 and not marked at all in OALD
1989). Connotations such as these, even though they may change in
the course of time, must be considered to be part of the "linguistic
competence" of sender and receiver. Other connotations, however, are
merely valid for certain persons, since they can only "work" if the participants know particular social, political, regional or cultural phenomena, e.g. *career woman* vs. *the little woman* or the allusion to Shakespeare's *Julius Caesar* in example 3.2.2./4. Such connotations belong
to the "horizon" of sender and receiver.

In his famous book *How to Be an Alien*, George Mikes gives a humorous example.

Example 3.2.2./5

"You foreigners are so clever," said a lady to me some years ago. First, thinking of the great amount of foreign idiots and half-wits I had had the honour of meeting, I considered this remark exaggerated but complimentary. Since then I learnt that it was far from it. These few words expressed the lady's contempt and slight disgust for foreigners. If you look up the word *clever* in any English Dictionary, you will find that the dictionaries are out of date and mislead you on this point. According to the *Pocket Oxford Dictionary*, for instance, the word means quick and neat in movement, skilful, talented, ingenious. (...) All nice adjectives, expressing valuable and estimable characteristics. A modern Englishman, however, uses the word *clever* in the sense: shrewd, sly, furtive, surreptitious, treacherous, sneaking, crafty, un-English, un-Scottish, un-Welsh (Mikes 1984: 42).

e. The "internal situation"

The information in the text can be "factual", i.e. based on the facts of what is conventionally regarded as "reality" by sender and receiver, or "fictional", i.e. referring to a different, fictitious world imagined or invented by the author, which is quite separate from the "real world" in which the communicative action takes place. However, this distinction is not of immediate importance for content analysis. Fictionality is a pragmatic property which is assigned to a text by the participants in communicative interaction. Its definition depends on the notion of reality and the norms of textuality prevailing in the society in question (cf. Nord 1997a: 80ff.). If the notion of reality changes, then a text which was intended to be factual might be read as fictional, or vice versa. If we look at Aldous Huxley's *Brave New World* or George Orwell's *1984* we might come to the conclusion that a fictional text describing a utopian situation could even become factual if reality were to change accordingly. However, the question of fictionality or factuality really becomes relevant to translation when we consider presuppositions.

Nevertheless, an analysis of content will have to specify whether or not the internal situation of the text is identical with the external situation. If it is not, the internal situation will have to be analysed separately, using the same set of WH-questions applied in the external analysis. This is very often the case in fictional texts, and in factual texts of the complex text type (cf. Reiss & Vermeer 1984) which contain embedded texts of another category.

In an internal situation there might be an internal sender (speaker, narrator), who may adopt various attitudes or perspectives towards the narration (e.g. "author's perspective", or "camera-eye" perspective), or there might be an implicit reader or listener, and implicit conditions of time and place; there may also be hints as to the medium used, the motive for communication and the function assigned to the particular embedded text. The internal situation may even, like the famous Russian doll, contain further embedded situations.

The situational factors of an embedded text are normally mentioned explicitly in the frame text, whereas the internal situation of a fictional text (i.e. its "setting") can often only be inferred from hidden clues or indirect hints, such as proper names of persons and places, references to culture-specific realities, elements of regional dialect in a dialogue, etc.

However, there are cases where an analysis of the external situation yields information on the internal situation, as shown in the following example.

Example 3.2.2./6
In one of his short stories written in his French exile in Paris, the Argentinian author Julio Cortázar describes an urban environment which is not named explicitly, but hinted at by the information that from the window of his multi- storey apartment block the auctorial narrator sees a sign saying *Hôtel de Belgique*. The reference to the setting is not crucial to the interpretation of the story, which deals with the problem of daily routine and the hopelessness of life in modern society. The plot might equally well be set in any big city of the Western industrial world. But still, by describing (or pretending to describe) the view from his own window, the author gives a "personal touch" to the story, which makes it more authentic. This may be important for the translator when she has to decide whether to translate the description of a routine break- fast situation (*tomamos café con leche*) by "we drink our morning coffee" (neutral), "we have our coffee with milk" (non-specific strangeness) or "we have café au lait" (specific strangeness, explicitly referring to France as the setting of the story) or even "we have our ham and eggs" (receiver-oriented adaptation).

f. Checklist

The following questions may help to elicit the relevant information about the content of the text:

    1. How are the extratextual factors verbalized in the text?

    2. Which are the information units in the text?

    3. Is there a difference between the external and the internal situation?

4. Are there any gaps of cohesion and/or coherence in the text? Can they be filled without using additional information or material?

5. What conclusions can be drawn from the analysis of content with reference to other intratextual factors, such as presuppositions, composition, and the stylistic features?

Some other questions which may shed some light on the dimension of content will be found in the following chapters.

3.2.3. *Presuppositions*
a. What is a presupposition?

The notion of presupposition is rather complex because "there is not one concept of presupposition, differing but slightly from one person who employs it to another, but several radically different concepts, all of which have been related to the word presupposition" (Garner 1971). What we mean here is neither the "logical presupposition", which refers to the truth value of utterances and/or to the existence of the objects and phenomena referred to by the utterance, nor Frege's "philosophical presupposition", which is the "necessary condition for having reference" and "for the sentence to be wholly meaningful" (Black 1973: 57), but the "pragmatic presupposition", which Schmidt (1976) refers to as "situational presupposition". These presuppositions are implicitly assumed by the speaker, who takes it for granted that this will also be the case with the listener. Communication can therefore only be successful if speaker and listener both implicitly assume the same presuppositions in sufficient quantity (cf. Schmidt 1976: 105).

In the joke quoted above, for example, the answer *Twelfth Night or What You Will* presupposes the knowledge on the part of the receiver that this is the title of a play, and this presupposition forms the basis on which the joke "works".

In everyday communication it is usually the factors of the communicative situation which are presupposed to be known to the participants and which are therefore not mentioned explicitly. Nevertheless, they have to be taken into consideration when the utterance is made. If, for example, the referent of the information is a person present in the room, the speaker may lower or raise his/her voice or choose simple or complicated or even coded formulations, etc. Of course, it is usually superfluous to mention the things and persons one can point at.

Presuppositions often refer to objects and phenomena ("realia") of the culture the sender belongs to, as is illustrated by the following passage, in which Balcerzan (1970: 8) comments on the immense difficulties that Polish translators were confronted with when rendering Pablo Neruda's *Canto General* into Polish:

Example 3.2.3./1
Quand Neruda écrit: *las mariposas de Muzo*, il faut préciser "les bleus papillons Muzo"; lorsqu'il écrit: *jacarandá*, il faut ajouter "arbre violet de jacarandá". Car pour le poète qui voit tous les jours (donc connaît par l'examen immédiat du monde réel) le bleu éclatant et l'arbre de *jacarandá* couvert de fleurs violettes, cette couleur est renfermée dans le nom même; nous, nous devons l'expliquer à notre lecteur.

It is, of course, right that the information presupposed by the author should be made known to the reader of the translation as well, but the translator must be aware of the fact that the explicitation of implicit information, especially in a poetic text, is bound to cause immense changes in the effect that the text will have on the receiver (cf. below, ch. 3.3.c).

As I understand it, presuppositions comprise all the information that the sender expects (= presupposes) to be part of the receiver's horizon. Since the sender wants the utterance to be understood, it seems logical that s/he will only presuppose information which the receiver can be expected to be able to "reconstruct" (cf. Ehlich & Rehbein 1972: 101f.). This is why I prefer the sender-oriented concept of "presupposition" to the receiver-oriented notion of "pre-information", which is used by the East German authors of functional text linguistics (e.g. Bastian 1979, Penkova 1982). Moreover, the term "presupposition" comprises both the dynamic aspect of "presupposing" and the result-oriented aspect of "something presupposed". With its dynamic aspect, the concept fits into the perspective of text production which we have adopted as a basis for our intratextual analysis (cf. above, 3.2.0.).

Presuppositions may refer not only to the factors and conditions of the situation and to the realities of the source culture, but can also imply facts from the author's biography, aesthetic theories, common text types and their characteristics, metric dispositions, details of subject matter, motives, the topoi and iconography of a certain literary period, ideology, religion, philosophy and mythical concepts, cultural and political conditions of the time, media and forms of representation, the educational situation, or the way a text has been handed down.

Since it is one of the social conventions of communication that an utterance must be neither trivial nor incomprehensible, the sender has to judge the situation, the general background knowledge of the addressee, and the relevance of the information that will be transmitted in the text, in order to decide which presuppositions can be made and which cannot. This convention applies not only to the relationship between the ST sender and the ST receiver, but also to that between the TT producer, i.e. the translator, and the TT receiver. The translator has to take account of the fact that a piece of information that might be "trivial" to the ST receivers because of their source-cultural background knowledge (and therefore is not mentioned in the source text) may be unknown to the TT audience because of their target-cultural background knowledge (and therefore has to be mentioned in the target text) – or vice versa.

b. How to identify presuppositions in the text
Since a presupposition is by definition a piece of information that is not verbalized, it cannot be "spotted" in the text. In their role as ST receivers, translators are familiar with the source culture and – ideally – understand the presupposed information in the same way as a source-culture receiver. This makes it rather difficult to discover the presuppositions which are contained in the text.

In order to identify the presuppositions, the translator has first of all to ascertain which culture or "world" the text refers to (which may have already been established in the content analysis). Here, an important distinction must be made between factual and fictional texts. Factual texts claim to make a proposition about reality (as generally accepted in the culture in question) whereas fictional texts make no such claim – or at least not in the same way as factual texts. The difference lies in the relationship between the text and the (assumed) reality. Fictional texts are, of course, as real as factual texts, and fictitious information can be contained both in fictional and factual texts (cf. Grabes 1977: 64f.).

The categorization of a text as factual or fictional does not primarily depend on the structure of the text itself. It is the author and, above all, the reader who classifies the text according to the concept of reality prevailing in their culture – a concept which is, of course, determined by philosophical and sociological conventions. A text intended to be factual by the ST sender can therefore be "understood" as fictional (and vice versa) by a TT receiver who has a different, culture-specific view of what is "real".

In this context we can return to the criterion of the cultural "environment" of a text stressed by Koller (1979), who even speaks of *Verankerung* (= "anchorage"). If the ST is "anchored" in the world of the source culture, some information on this world will usually be presupposed in the text because of the maxim of relevance, to put it in Gricean terms. If, on the other hand, the ST refers to the world of the TT receiver, which cannot be assumed to be familiar to the ST receiver, it would seem logical for the ST producer to verbalize a certain amount of information for the ST receiver which then would seem irrelevant to the TT receiver. In either case, the translator will normally adjust the level of explicitness to the (assumed) general background knowledge of the intended TT audience using, for example, expansion or reduction procedures.

If the ST refers to a world that is equally "distant" to both the ST and the TT receivers, it is less probable that translation problems will arise from the contrast of ST and TT presuppositions. In these cases the subject matter dealt with in the ST can be regarded as "generally communicable", as Koller (1979: 13) puts it, or, at least, as "transculturally communicable", i.e. between the two cultures involved in the translation process.

The level of explicitness varies according to text type and text function. It is interesting in this context to note that in fictional texts the situation is often made more explicit than in non-fictional texts. While the comprehension of factual texts is based on the fact that sender and receiver share one model of reality, the fictional text has to start building up a model of its own, either referring explicitly to a realistic model or creating a fictitious one in the text, which can then be related in some degree to an existing realistic model. It can even be contrary to the normal truth values of non-fictional utterances (e.g. in fairy tales). A fictional text must, however, also contain some reference or analogy to the receivers' reality because otherwise they would not be able to find access to the world of the text (cf. above, 3.2.1.c).

If the information on the internal situation is hidden in certain elements of a fictional text, such as in proper names, regional or social dialect (e.g. Shaw's *Pygmalion*) etc., it is often extremely difficult to transmit it to the target text, as for instance in the following example, because in a literary text it is often not appropriate to use substitutions, explanatory translations or footnotes.

Example 3.2.3./2
In Ana María Matute's short story *Pecado de omisión* (cf. example 3.1.1./2)
the characters are socially classified by their names. The main character, a
simple village boy who in spite of his talents does not get the chance to train
for a profession, is only called by his Christian name *Lope*, whereas his class-
mate, whose father can afford to let him study law, is introduced by Christian
name and surname: *Manuel Enríquez*. Lope's uncle, the village mayor, has the
rather pompous name *Emeterio Ruiz Heredia*; the school teacher is referred to
by the respectful combination of *don* together with his Christian name (*don
Lorenzo*). The simple shepherd with whom Lope has to stay in the mountains
cannot even boast an individual name: he is called *Roque el Mediano* (i.e.
"Roque the middle one").

These hidden clues cannot be explained to the TT receiver without
running the risk of losing the literary charm of the text. Fortunately,
most authors do not rely exclusively on implicit characterizations, but
include some explicit hints, as does Ana María Matute in the above-
mentioned text.

c. Redundancy
If information is verbalized several times in a text (e.g. in the form of
explanation, repetition, paraphrase, summary, tautology etc.) we speak
of "redundancy" or rather "situational redundancy" (Vermeer [1974a]
1983: 5), as opposed to the "linguistic redundancies" prescribed by a
specific language system. Information theory explains redundancy as
a means of counteracting noise; in a text, its function is to assist
comprehension in the face of the "noise" of obscurity, irrelevance, or
complex thought (cf. Newmark 1981: 77). The level of redundancy
chosen in a text depends on how much background knowledge the
sender expects the receiver to have. But it can also be determined by
culture-specific conventions regarding the readability of a text.

d. Presupposition indicators
The probability of presuppositions being present can be calculated
from the distance of the ST and TT receiver to the cultural environment of the subject matter, as well as from the level of explicitness
and the level of redundancy. Apart from this, there are very few ways
to discover the presuppositions made in a source text. Bastian (1979:
93) maintains that a text contains certain "elements of crystallization"
which may indicate presuppositions. As Helbig (1980) points out,
these elements might be attached to certain syntactic or lexical structures, such as the gerund, infinitive, or passive constructions, modal
auxiliary verbs or valences of lexemes, as in the following example.

Example 3.2.3./3
"John will be picked up at the station. Peter is always in time." Since the verb
to pick up requires two actants, semantically specifiable as agent and patient,
the reader will automatically know that *Peter* has to refer to the person who is
going to pick up John at the station. If the two sentences are to constitute a
text, the existence of the agent is presupposed in the first sentence (cf. Helbig
1980: 262).

Other signals pointing to presuppositions can be provided by the intratextual dimensions of subject matter, content, sentence structure, and
suprasegmental features. The negation left out in an utterance meant
to be ironic can, for example, be signalled by a certain intonation:
"How very, very clever of you!" Non-verbal elements, such as a photo
showing the skyscraper environment of the "immaculate garden flat",
can also illustrate presupposed situational conditions.

The analysis of the extratextual dimensions of sender, receiver,
time, place, and motive of communication can also reveal presupposed information, as has been pointed out above. With their TC competence, translators will be able to check the comprehensibility of the
verbalized information from the TT receiver's point of view. Thus,
any possible information gap or surplus in the background knowledge
of the intended TT receiver, as described by the translation brief, can
be localized and, if necessary, compensated for.

e. Checklist
The following questions may help to discover the presuppositions
made in the source text:
   1. Which model of reality does the information refer to?
   2. Is the reference to reality verbalized explicitly in the text?
   3. Are there any implicit allusions to a certain model of reality?
   4. Does the text contain redundancies which might be superfluous for a TT receiver?
   5. What information presupposed to be known to the ST receiver has to be verbalized for the TT receiver?

3.2.4. Text composition
a. General considerations
The aspect of text composition is dealt with in detail by Thiel. She
suggests that the text has an informational macrostructure (i.e. composition and order of information units) consisting of a number of microstructures. According to Thiel, the text segments forming the macro-

structure are marked or delimited primarily by the continuity or discontinuity of tenses.

There are several reasons why both the macro and microstructure of the text are important aspects of a translation-oriented text analysis.

1. If a text is made up of different text segments with different situational conditions, the segments may require different translation strategies according to their different functions.

2. The special part that the beginning and end of a text play in its comprehension and interpretation means that these may have to be analysed in detail in order to find out how they guide the reception process and influence the effect of the whole text.

3. For certain genres, there are culture-specific conventions as to their macro and/or microstructure. The analysis of text composition can therefore yield valuable information about the text type (and, perhaps, the text function).

4. In very complex or incoherent texts, the analysis of informational microstructures may serve to find out the basic information or subject matter of the text.

b. Text ranks

A source text can be part of a unit of higher rank, which we may call a text combination or hyper-text. Thus, a short story or a scientific article might be included in an anthology or a collection, in which the other texts constitute a frame of reference, and a novel might be intended to form part of a trilogy or tetralogy. The different texts can be related and linked in various ways.[36]

In the practice of professional translating, the parts of a text combination are sometimes translated by different translators, as is shown in the following example.

Example 3.2.4./1
The German version of the textbook on linguistics edited by André Martinet (Martinet 1973) was produced by two translators: Chapters 1 to 25 were translated by I. Rehbein, and Chapters 26 to 51 by S. Stelzer. Each of the chapters is an independent text and, at the same time, part of a larger unit, whose characteristics have to be taken into account by both translators.

---

[36]A good example of a combination of interrelated texts is the Sanskrit Panchatantram, the *Five Books of Wisdom*. The string of its main narration is interlaced by several independent stories which are introduced with the argument that they are intended to illustrate a certain situation, an action, or a conflict by giving an example of a similar event (cf. Beer 1982: 405)

The inclusion of a text in a unit of higher rank is usually signalled by the title and/or the title context, which can be regarded as a sort of "hyper-sentence" or "metacommunicative utterance" (cf. Gülich, Heger & Raible 1979: 82, who using James Thurber's fable *The Lover and his Lass* demonstrate how the information implied in the bibliographic reference can be made explicit).

On the highest rank this hyper-sentence is often replaced by the information about the communicative situation which the receiver infers from extratextual clues. If the extratextual analysis shows, however, that the situation of the TT will differ considerably from that of the ST and that the TT receiver cannot infer sufficient information about the ST situation, the translator may feel obliged to add some kind of hyper-sentence (e.g. in the form of an introductory lead) to the translation.

Example 3.2.4./2
In German newspapers, comments taken from other papers are usually introduced by hyper-sentences, such as "President Reagan's speech before the UN is commented on by *The Times* (London)" (cf. *Süddeutsche Zeitung*, Oct. 26/27, 1985; my translation). The form of these hyper-sentences is culture-specific, and they may even be rather elliptic. In the *International Herald Tribune*, for example, texts quoted from other papers are printed in a special column under the heading "Other Comments" and signed with the name and place of publication of the reference paper, e.g. "Asiaweek (Hong Kong)".

c. Macrostructure

Metacommunicative sentences of the type "A says (to B)" can also be signals for the beginning of an embedded text (cf. example 3.1.0./1), these signals separating the different levels of communication. This is particularly important in translation, because, as was pointed out earlier, each level of communication may require a situational analysis of its own. One of the crucial aspects in the analysis of macrostructure is therefore the question of whether there are any sub-texts or in-texts embedded in the ST.

Other forms of in-texts are quotations, footnotes, and examples (e.g. in scientific texts, such as the present study). The main task of the translator is to find out which function the in-text fulfils in the embedding text. Although other extratextual factors (e.g. audience, place, time, medium) may be the same for the embedding text and the in-text, the function must be analysed separately (cf. my studies on the translation of quotations in Nord 1990a, b).

Example 3.2.4./3
Quotations, like other texts, can have an informative, expressive, appellative, and phatic function. The function of a quotation is basically independent of that of the embedding text, although there seems to be a certain correlation between genre and quotation types. For example: In scientific and technical texts we find more informative quotations, whose form is rather conventional (especially where bibliographical references are concerned) than in popularizing texts or (literary) essays, which more often contain expressive quotations stressing the author's own opinion, or quotations appealing to the reader's own experience or which are intended to impress the reader by citing a famous authority, such as Aristotle or Shakespeare.

Footnotes inserted into a target text in order to provide background information or give additional explanations, can also be regarded as intexts. Since the effect that a text with footnotes has on the reader is different from that of a text without footnotes, the translator has to consider carefully whether other procedures, such as explanatory translations or substitutions, would be more appropriate to the genre and function of the target text than footnotes.

The relationship between the in-text and the embedding text can be compared with that between titles or heading(s) and the text they belong to (= co-text, cf. Nord 1988b and 1993). A title is a metatext which tells us something about the co-text in question and can equally fulfil various other communicative functions.

Example 3.2.4./4
The title of Chapter VII of Charles Dickens' *The Pickwick Papers* not only informs the reader about the contents of the chapter but also recommends the text to the reader: "How Mr. Winkle, instead of shooting at the pigeon and killing the crow, shot at the crow and wounded the pigeon; how the Dingley Dell cricket club played All-Muggleton, and how All-Muggleton dined at the Dingley Dell expense; with other interesting and instructive matters." The metacommunicative function of the title is in this case signalled by the form of an indirect question introduced by *how*. In the title of Chapter I of Jonathan Swift's *A Voyage to Lilliput* it is made even more explicit: "The author gives some account of himself and family (...)".

Inclusions commenting on the text itself (e.g. *so to speak* or *as I pointed out earlier* or *to put it into a nutshell*) can also be regarded as metacommunicative utterances. At the same time they have the (phatic) function of giving a signal to the receiver, thus representing the (extratextual) audience orientation by intratextual means (cf. Nord 2001b).

Within the text itself, macrostructure is defined from a semantic point of view. Hierarchical delimitations of text sections (chapter, chunk, paragraph, complex sentence, non-complex sentence, etc., cf. Graustein & Thiele 1981: 5) can only provide a rather superficial orientation. Since the days of classical rhetoric, the beginning and the end of a text are considered to be of particular importance in the interpretation of the whole text (cf. Berger 1977: 18ff.). This is why they should be analysed separately. As is shown in example 3.2.4./5 and in Sample Text 2 (ch. 5.2.), a detailed analysis of the first paragraph(s) of a long text often provides the guidelines for analysing the whole text, when the significance of the features elicited in the text beginning may be confirmed.

The beginning and end of a text can be marked by certain verbal or non-verbal features, which in some genres will be even conventional, such as the moral at the end of a fable or the expression *once upon a time* at the beginning of a fairy tale. The end tends to be less frequently marked than the beginning (the words *The End* at the end of a film are probably a remnant from the time when the end of a text was conventionally marked by *finis*). The imminent end of a text can also be signalled by the shift to a higher level of communication, e.g. a metacommunicative recapitulation like "in conclusion, let me restate...". Thus, in the fable *The Lover and his Lass*, for example, the moral ("Laugh and the world laughs with you, love and you love alone.") establishes a direct communication between sender and receiver.

The example of the fable shows that certain features of text composition are genre specific. Certain text types are characterized by a particular macrostructure and particular structural markers, as well as particular means of conjunction between the text parts. A good example is the text type "letter" with the conventional text segments date, address, salutation, message, and complimentary closing. In an instrumental translation the translator should observe the target-cultural convention for the text type in question.

d. Microstructure

Both in macro and microstructure we have to distinguish formal and semantic or functional structures. If the highest rank is that of metacommunication and the second rank is constituted by macrostructural units such as chapters and paragraphs (formal structure) or beginning and end (functional structure), the third rank will be that of simple and complex sentences (formal structure). From the semantic or functional point of view we can distinguish information units, utterances, steps of the course of action or plot, or logical relations, such as causality, finality, specification, etc. The fourth rank will then be that of sentence-parts and their relation, such as the theme-rheme structure (TRS).

In written texts, a "sentence" is the unit between two full stops (or question marks, exclamation marks, etc.). In spoken texts it is delimited by intonatory devices, such as pitch or lengthy pauses. In either case, grammatical completeness is not taken into account as a criterion. In spite of all possible reservations regarding this definition, the division into sentences can provide a first approximation to the microstructure of a text. Moreover, it will lead into the analysis of sentence structures. In a second step, the analyst has to prove whether the formal division into sentences corresponds to the semantic division into information units.[37] Complex sentences usually have to be subdivided into clauses.

In narrative texts, the information units can coincide with the steps of the course of action. One of the intratextual features of text composition is, in this connection, the order of tenses used in the text. Stempel (1971: 65) speaks of the "diachrony" of a narrative text and works out a "diachronic profile". The changing of the chronological order of narrative units produces suspense, while a strictly chronological narration is characterized by a rather quiet flow of information.

Example 3.2.4./5
The first paragraph of Juan Goytisolo's short novel *La isla* shows how the author uses the instrument of composition in order to produce suspense in spite of a chronological order of information units. I have indicated in brackets what information the (Spanish) readers get and what they infers. The exclamation marks in the last sentence indicate the answers to the questions raised in the process of text reception.
"When we landed (personal narrator, airport? where?), the landscape (countryside, where?) was inundated by the sun (summer? South?). We had left behind the dirty, grey sky (negative, contrast?) of Madrid (not summer, but South, South of Spain?), and when I (first-person narrator) went down the steps from the aircraft (airport!), I put my dark glasses on (very much sun, no shadow). A man with a white cap (sunny climate, Mediterranean) came to offer me peanuts, almonds, and hazelnuts (Mediterranean!). I remembered my walks (memories of earlier stay?) with Rafael (friend?, lover?, husband? – is the narrator a woman?) around Gibralfaro (South of Spain, Malaga?) and bought a bag. The air hostess led us through a pergola with lots of climbing

---

[37]Since the formal division into sentences is culture-specific and therefore not appropriate for intercultural comparison, Vermeer (1970: 386f.) recommends a division into "text parts", which allows the inclusion of sentences that are incomplete or not well-formed. "Text parts" are functional elements which can embrace sentences as well as other grammatical units. Their length is not formally defined. Vermeer's "text parts" seem to correspond largely to what I call "information units".

plants (small airport, Malaga?). On the terrace I saw a group of foreigners (narrator is not a foreigner!), and I went into the lounge. Gradually I got accustomed to the familiar accent (memories of home? childhood?, narrator is a native!) of the airport staff, and when I heard a porter shouting – his coarse voice, somehow boozy, yet soft and almost sweet (tender feelings) – I felt my heart beat more quickly (joy?, feeling at home?), and with a directness that surprised me I realized – and this knowledge made me happy (!) – that I was back (home!) in Malaga (!)." (Transl. C.N.)

This narrative technique illustrates the experience of the narrator (female, indeed, cf. example 3.2.6./2), who is gradually beginning to feel at home again after a long absence, without explicitly verbalizing it.

A composition which follows the course of action represents a structure with an analogy to objects and situations in the real world ("ordo naturalis"), which is not language-specific and therefore does not raise unsolvable problems for the translator – at least where there is no great distance between SC and TC. This applies also to dialogues, which can be regarded as a (chronological) sequence of various monologues.

Composition structures which do not follow the "ordo naturalis" are determined – both on the macro and microstructural level – by culture-specific norms. They are marked by language-specific linking devices (such as renominalization, adversative conjunctions, etc.) or even by means of metre, rhyme, alliteration, and other sonorous figures, which may help to structure the text.

In languages with temporal and verbal aspects (e.g. Spanish), texts can be structured by means of the so-called "mise en relief", stressing perfective, punctual actions by the use of perfective tenses in contrast to imperfective, durative or iterative actions, processes or conditions, which are described in the imperfect tenses. In other languages (e.g. German) a relief of background and foreground can, for example, be achieved by distributing the information into subordinate or main clauses (cf. Sample Text 2, chapter 5.2.4.c). By this means, certain pieces of information receive more stress than others, which also leads to a certain structuring of the text.

e. Thematic organization of sentences and clauses

The semantic and functional division of sentences or information units into theme and rheme (TRS, also topic and comment), which belongs to the microstructure of a text, is independent of the syntactic structures, although it is frequently combined with certain syntactical features. Linking the information units by the device of thematic progression the writer at the same time produces a certain macrostructure. Thus, TRS is a feature overlapping micro and macrostructural composition.

This is not the place to point out all the problematic aspects of TRS (cf., among others, Brown & Yule 1987: 126ff.). For translation-oriented text analysis, we can confine ourselves to the context-bound aspects of TRS. From this point of view, the theme refers to that part of the information presented in a sentence or clause which can be inferred from the (verbal or non-verbal) context (= given information) whereas the rheme is the non-inferrable part of the information (= new information). Irrespective of its grammatical function as subject or predicate or its position at the beginning or the end of the clause, the theme refers to the information stored in what Brown & Yule (1987) call the "presupposition pool" of the participants. This pool contains the information gained from general knowledge, from the situative context of the discourse, and from the completed part of the discourse itself. Each participant has a presupposition pool and this pool is added to as the discourse proceeds (cf. Brown & Yule 1987: 79f.).

According to the distribution of given and new information in a text, we have to distinguish different forms of thematic progression (cf. Daneš 1978: 188f.), which characterize the argumentative structure of the text. There can be no doubt that the "communicative dynamics" of a text with a linear thematic progression, where the rheme of one sentence constitutes the theme of the next sentence, is totally different from that of a text which has one continuous theme with several rhemes.

TRS has to be regarded as a semantic universal which is realized in different ways by different languages. Focussing structures (such as cleft sentences) or functional sentence perspective, however, are the language-specific correlates of TRS on the phonological or syntactical level. The importance of this composition device is illustrated in connection with Sample Text 2 (chapter 5.2.).

f. Markers of text composition

The macrostructure of a text is first and foremost signalled by formal devices used to mark the boundaries of segments of both written and spoken discourse which form large units, such as chapters or paragraphs in written texts and "paratones" (Brown & Yule 1987: 100) in spoken texts. Chapters are marked by chapter headings or numerals, paragraphs by indentations, and paratones by intonation, pauses of more than a second, etc. These non-verbal markers are often combined with lexical markers, e.g. adverbial clauses in initial (*first – then – finally*) or focussed position (*on the one hand – on the other hand*). In text types with a conventional "ordo naturalis" (e.g. reports) the composition is marked according to subject matter and content.

Microstructures are marked by means of syntax structures (main/subordinate clauses, tenses, inclusions, etc.) or lexical devices (e.g. cataphora) and by suprasegmental features (focus structures, punctuation, etc.).

g. Checklist
The following questions may help to discover the main characteristics of text composition:

1. Is the ST an independent text or is it embedded in a larger unit of higher rank?
2. Is the macrostructure of the text marked by optical or other signals?
3. Is there a conventional composition for this type of text?
4. Which form of thematic progression is realized in the text?

3.2.5. Non-verbal elements
a. General considerations
Signs taken from other, non-linguistic, codes, which are used to supplement, illustrate, disambiguate, or intensify the message of the text, are referred to by the functional concept of "non-verbal elements". I would like to stress the view that these elements play a complementary role in verbal communication. (This excludes sign languages which replace the verbal code.) "Non-verbal elements", as I use the term, comprise the paralinguistic elements of face-to-face communication (e.g. facial expressions, gestures, voice quality, etc.) as well as the non-linguistic elements belonging to a written text (photos, illustrations, logos, special types of print, etc.). However, intonational features, pauses, etc. and the graphical devices that perform analogous functions in written communication (punctuation, capitalisation, italicisation, etc.) are classified as "suprasegmental features".

Example 3.2.5./1
If you're an American living abroad* and you need to keep track of your calls, you really ought to get the *AT&T Card.* First of all, you get a monthly itemized bill. A new option even lets you bill your *AT&T Card* calls to your American Express® Card account.** Or, you can choose to be billed to your VISA® or Master Card.***
In addition to itemized billing, the *AT&T Card* makes it easy to reach family,

friends and business associates in the States. And, you can take advantage of
AT&T USADirect® service , which gets you through to an *AT&T Operator* in seconds.
For an *AT&T Card* application, call us collect at **816-6004 Ext. 60**, or
write to AT&T Card Operations, P.O. Box 419395, Kansas City, MO 64141-0434.
So if you want to know who you called, get the *AT&T Card.*
*Exclusively for U.S. citizens living abroad with valid U.S. passports and Social Security numbers.
**Billing will be in the same currency as your American Express Statement.
***Must be issued by a U.A. bank.

**The *AT&T Card* lets you keep track of
your monthly calls to the States.**

Non-verbal elements are particularly audience-oriented. It is therefore
astonishing that of all the authors of articles on translation-relevant
text analysis only Thiel (1978a, 1978b, 1980) underlines the importance of non-verbal text elements (especially formal markers of text
composition) in text analysis. This may be due in part to a narrower
concept of text, which includes only the verbal elements.

b. Forms and functions of non-verbal elements
We have to distinguish non-verbal elements accompanying the text
(e.g. layout or gestures) from those supplementing the text (e.g. tables
or graphs) or those constituting an independent text part (e.g. pictures
of a comic strip) or replacing certain text elements (e.g. the * that re-
places a taboo word).

In face-to-face communication we tend to use gestures of the
face and the body (such as winking or shrugging). Leonhard (1976:
42) distinguishes between gestures used more or less involuntarily by
speakers to express their feelings and those used intentionally with a
specific meaning. While involuntary gestures constitute a universal
phenomenon, which, apart from differences in temperament and certain culture-specific conventions, are common to all the peoples of the
world, intentional gestures are signs belonging to a culture-specific
code. In an interpreting situation it may therefore be necessary for the
interpreter to verbalize certain gestures made by the speaker, if there is
any risk of misinterpretation. The receivers only see the gestures of
the ST speaker and do not usually notice the interpreter in the booth
"translating" the gestures into a TC code.

The interplay of verbal and non-verbal text elements is particularly important on the stage. Bassnett-McGuire (1978: 165) points out
that plays in which the word is subordinate to the gestures (e.g. Fey-
deau and Goldoni, Noel Coward and the Theatre of the Absurd) are
less problematic in translation than plays in which there is a carefully
balanced tension between words and gestures. This tension should be

regarded as an intentional feature of the text, which the translator may have to reproduce in the TT.

In spoken discourse there are situations where the hearer would not perceive any mimical expressions or gestures of the speaker because of the spatial distance between them (e.g. in an electoral speech on a market square). And there are text types or functions where the use of non-verbal signals is conventionally forbidden. In these cases, non-verbal elements are more and more replaced by suprasegmental linguistic signs, such as stress, intonation, slowing down, etc., which can even develop into genre-specific features (e.g. sermon).

In written communication, mimical expressions or gestures cannot be used; but the reduced pragmatic contextuality of written texts must, of course, be compensated for. This is done partly by the selection of particular verbal elements, especially those representing suprasegmental features in writing (e.g. punctuation, dash, bold type), and partly by additional non-verbal means, such as pictures (a photo of the author, a cartoon illustrating the subject, a drawing showing how to hold the handle of a machine). It may happen that the non-verbal elements convey a piece of information that is even more relevant to the reader than the message transmitted by the text. A number in small print on the label of a wine bottle may in itself be of little interest, but it tells the "connoisseur" more about the quality of the wine than the name.

The range of non-verbal elements used in literature extends from the ancient acrostics to the typographical means which are found in the poems of Klopstock or Stefan George, Apollinaire or E. E. Cummings. But it is not only in literature that they are used. The Gothic type used for the title and headings of the *Frankfurter Allgemeine Zeitung* not only points to a certain traditionalist attitude, but also supplies some information on the philosophical and ideological provenance of the paper.

Non-verbal elements can belong to the conventional form of certain text types, such as the shorter lines of traditional poetic texts or the "small print" in contracts. The unusually wide spaces between the paragraphs in Sample Text 1 (chapter 5.1.), for example, are untypical of a scientific text and suggest a literary text.

Of course, it is not always the author or sender with their specific communicative intention who is responsible for the layout and format of a text. But no matter who makes the final decision on text organization – the effect that these elements produce on the receiver remains the same. If the translation skopos requires "equivalence of effect", the translator must, therefore, take account of all types of non-verbal elements.

Illustrations, diagrams, drawings of certain operations, etc. are conventional supplements or even form an integral part of operating instructions or manuals. In some cases it may even be convenient for the translator to try and carry out the instructions him or herself in order to check the coherence of verbal and non-verbal elements and the functionality of the text (cf. Saile 1982, who compares the German, French and English version of assembling instructions).

The analysis of non-verbal text elements usually yields some information about the aspects of text composition (e.g. paragraph markers), presuppositions (e.g. marks of omission), lexis (e.g. facial expressions which suggest an ironic meaning), and suprasegmental features (e.g. shortened lines in a poem). Of the extratextual factors it is mainly the intention of the sender and the function of the text which may be characterized by non-verbal elements.

d. The importance of non-verbal elements in translation

Non-verbal text elements are, like verbal elements, culture-specific. Within the framework of a translation-relevant ST analysis the translator has to find out which of the non-verbal elements of the ST can be preserved in translation and which have to be adapted to the norms and conventions of the target culture. A particular logo or name which is intended to have a positive connotation in the source culture may be associated with a negative value in the target culture; the TC conventions may not allow the graphic representation of a certain piece of information; the TC genre norms may require non-verbal instead of verbal representation, etc. What is taken for granted as regards linguistic text elements (that they have to be "translated"), is not always accepted for non-verbal elements, because initiators are often unwilling to commit themselves to the extra expense involved in adapting non-verbal material.

It is not difficult to identify the non-verbal elements of the source text, as they are usually fairly obvious and often predictable in certain media or text types. But it is important in each case to analyse the function of these elements. Quotation marks, for example, can point to an ironical meaning (in which case they represent a suprasegmental feature, i.e. a certain intonation) or to a neologism introduced ad hoc and explained in the text or to a reference to somebody else's utterances (in which case the text producer may want to express a mental reservation, which would have been marked by a wink of the eye in spoken discourse).

e. Checklist

The following questions may lead to a functional interpretation of non-verbal elements:

1. Which non-verbal elements are included in the text?
2. Which function do they perform with regard to the verbal text parts?
3. Are they conventionally bound to the text type?
4. Are they determined by the medium?
5. Are they specifically linked to the source culture?

3.2.6. Lexis

a. General considerations

The characteristics of the lexis used in a text play an important part in all approaches to translation-oriented text analysis. The authors underline the importance of the semantic, stylistic and formal aspects. Based on a semiotic concept of syntax, Thiel (1974a, 1978b) and Wilss (1980a) stress the interrelation between lexis and syntactic structures, while the other authors discuss several individual examples regarding particular aspects of lexis, such as the affiliation of a word to stylistic levels and registers (Thiel 1974b, 1978a, Reiss 1974a, 1984, Koller 1979), word formation (Wilss 1977, Thiel 1978a, 1978b) or certain rhetorical figures, e.g. metaphors or repetition of lexical elements (Wilss 1977, Thiel 1978b).

The choice of lexis is determined by both extra and intratextual factors. Therefore, the characteristics of the lexical items used in a text often yield information not only about the extratextual factors, but also about other intratextual aspects. For example, the semantic and stylistic characteristics of lexis (e.g. connotations, semantic fields, register) may point to the dimensions of content, subject matter, and presuppositions, whereas the formal and grammatical characteristics (e.g. parts of speech, word function, morphology) refer the analyst to predictable syntactic structures and suprasegmental features.

b. Intratextual determinants of lexis
The selection of lexical items is largely determined by the dimensions
of subject matter and content. Depending on the subject matter, certain
semantic fields will be represented by more items than others, and the
textual connection of key words will constitute isotopic chains
throughout the text. Referring to the short story of Günter Grass which
she has analysed for translation, Fröland (1978: 275ff.) speaks of "thematic words" containing hidden clues to the real subject matter of the
text. In literary texts, such clues are often given indirectly, e.g. in proper names (cf. example 3.2.3./2), especially in descriptive names (e.g.
Aguecheek or *Malvolio*).

      In this context, morphological aspects (suffixes, prefixes, com-
positions, acronyms, etc.), collocations, idioms, figurative use (meto-
nymy, metaphor), etc. have to be analysed from the point of view of
textual semantics. Componential analysis (cf. Newmark 1981: 30),
etymological investigations, and comparative lexicological studies can
also be helpful when the meaning of certain words, especially of neologisms, is not clear.

c. Extratextual determinants of lexis
The field of lexis, on the other hand, illustrates particularly well the
interdependence of extratextual and intratextual factors (cf. Figure 7).
In any text, the stylistically significant characteristics of lexis clearly
reflect the extratextual factors of the situation in which the text is
used, including the participants using it for communication (cf. Crystal & Davy 1969: 81f.). The extratextual factors not only set the frame
of reference for the selection of words, but they are themselves often –
directly or indirectly – mentioned in the text. I will therefore deal with
the extratextual factors one by one in order to explain the impact these
factors can have on the choice of lexical items.

      The first question is whether or not the expectations deriving
from the external information and clues as to the general character of
the sender (time, geographical and social origin, education, status,
etc.) or his/her particular position regarding the analysed text (e.g.
communicative role) are verified by the text. This also applies to any
internal sender who may be mentioned or presupposed in the text, e.g.
in the case of quotations or in fictional texts. If the analysis confirms
the expectations, such characteristics can be assumed to be non-intentional; if not, it seems likely that by disappointing the receiver's expectations the sender wanted to produce a certain effect. If there is

little or no external information on the sender, the analysis of the pragmatic aspects of lexis may provide some clues to the person of the sender.

The second question is whether the author is mentioned in the text as sender. In such a case, the use of the first person, of expressions like *in my view* in contrast with other persons' opinions, etc. gives the readers the impression that the sender is addressing them directly. In non-fictional texts we can assume that the first person really does refer to the author. For some text types, there are even conventions as to how authors should refer to themselves, e.g. the use of the first person plural or the third person singular (*the author*, cf. Sample Text 1, chapter 5.1.3.) in scientific texts.

Example 3.2.6./1
In English texts, *the author* can refer to a male or a female person. In German or Spanish, the translator must use the marked form *Verfasserin* or *autora*, if the author is a woman. This may be difficult to decide in cases of large cultural distance. Recently, I read a review published (in English) in a Chinese journal, in which the author referred to me using the masculine pronoun *he*.

In fictional texts, we have to assume an "implicit narrator" who is not identical with the author.

Example 3.2.6./2
In Juan Goytisolo's short novel *La isla* (cf. example 3.2.4./5) the reader is confronted with a narrator who speaks in the first person singular. Conventions seem to lead the reader to the assumption that a male author "normally" creates male narrators (though it is not as "normal" the other way round). There is no hint as to the speaker's sex in the text until almost at the end of the first paragraph, where the expression *yo misma* tells the reader (of the Spanish version) that the narrator is a woman. In a German or English translation there would be no possibility of introducing a gender marking (*ich selbst, I myself*). Fortunately, the speaker is addressed as *misis* [sic] by a taxi driver in the next paragraph, so that German and English readers get the necessary information after all.

As far as the impact of the sender's intention on lexis is concerned, we have to ask whether and how the intention is reflected by the selection of words or, if there is no external information, what intention can be inferred from the use of words in the text. It is the pragmatic aspect of intentionality in the sense of "concrete interest" underlying the text production which is being analysed in this context.

This intentionality is reflected by those characteristics of lexis which are *not* due to the specific situational conditions or to norms and conventions, as well as by those features which appear to signal an intentional "violation" of any norms and conventions valid both for the genre in question and for the conditions of medium, place, time, and motive of communication characterizing the situation of the text. This means that a feature of lexis can be assumed to be intentional if the translator has to analyse the interest and the purpose which induced the author to use precisely this expression, this figure, this word.

Example 3.2.6./3
Language can be used, for example, to camouflage the real significance of an event, as is shown in the following paragraph from an article on "double-speak": "Attentive observers of the English language also learned recently that the multi-billion-dollar stock market crash of 1987 was simply a *fourth-quarter equity retreat*; that aircraft don't crash, they have *uncontrolled contact with the ground*; that janitors are *environmental technicians*; that it was a *diagnostic misadventure of a high magnitude* which caused the death of a patient in a Philadelphia hospital, not malpractice; and that Ronald Reagan wasn't really unconscious while he underwent minor surgery, just in a *non-decision-making form*." (*THE SUNDAY TIMES*, 7 January 1990)

In order to elicit the sender's intention it seems advisable to analyse the "degree of originality" of the lexis used in the text. This is common practice with similes and metaphors. Newmark, for example, distinguishes four types of metaphor: fossilized, stock, recently created and original (1981: 32). But it can also be applied to other figures of speech, such as the adoption of words from other areas of lexis (e.g. language for special purposes in a general text), other registers (e.g. slang words in a formal text), or from regional or social dialects, and to the metonymic use of words (e.g. *the Pentagon* for the US Ministry of Defense). In all these cases the translator has to examine whether the choice of words is common or at least standardised for certain text types or whether it can be regarded as original or even extravagant.

The analysis of various lexical items in a text can often show that a particular stylistic feature is characteristic of the whole text. If the translation skopos requires the preservation of such features, individual translation decisions (in the field of lexis as well as content, composition, sentence structure, etc.) have to be subordinated to this purpose. The translator has to plan the translation strategies with this overall purpose in mind, looking for the stylistic means which serve to achieve this purpose in the target language and culture instead of translating metaphor by metaphor or simile by simile.

Similarly, the translator should also assess the stylistic implications of the author's "semantic intentionality" (Schmidt 1971: 41). Semantic intentionality refers to the reasons which have induced the author to select one particular piece of information for his or her text from the wide range of all possible information, and to the effect that this choice has on the audience. This can be of particular importance in fictional texts since it may be assumed that the number of informational details which the author may choose from is limited only by the situational conditions. The decision to take one specific detail rather than another constitutes an important clue to the author's (stylistic, literary) intention (cf. the mosaic-like assembly of details in example 3.2.3./5).

A text may not only contain implicit clues to the sender's intention, but also explicit expressions or (often conventional) clichés by which the sender's intention is announced.

Example 3.2.6./4
"Our aim is therefore to replace a sporadic approach with a systematic one; to minimise – we can never remove – the intuitive element in criteria of analysis." (From the *Introduction* to Crystal & Davy 1969: 14).

The audience orientation of a text, too, is mainly reflected by the choice of lexis, e.g., by the use of words from particular registers, lects, and styles which are not determined by the sender (cf. Bühler 1982: 429, and Wilss 1977: 637) or by inserted explanations, as in example 3.2.6./5.

Example 3.2.6./5
Compare the following extract from the brochure *York Minster Told to Children* with the texts reproduced in example 4.1.4./2:
"On the left-hand side of the doorway you will notice a list of Archbishops of York, beginning with St. Paulinus and including such names as St. Chad and St. Wilfrid, and continuing in unbroken succession to that of our present Archbishop, Dr. Michael Ramsey. On the other side of the doorway is the list of Deans.
The Archbishop is the chief Bishop in the Province of York, and his CATHEDRA or throne gives the name CATHEDRAL to the mother church of the Diocese.
The Dean is the chief of the Minster clergy, and he, together with the Chapter, is responsible for the upkeep of the building and for the services held in it."

As is shown by the example, the receiver may also be mentioned or addressed in the text. There are direct forms of address in the second person, e.g. *you* (note that in many cultures the translator has to distinguish between formal and informal forms of address: German *du/ihr* vs. *Sie*, Spanish *tú/vosotros* vs. *Vd./Vds.* or *vos/Vds.* vs. *Vd./Vds.* in

Argentina, French *tu/vous* vs. *vous*, etc.). Form and frequency of explicit addressing is culture and genre-specific.

The medium mainly influences the level of style of the lexical elements (colloquial, formal), word formation (e.g. abbreviated words or acronyms as used in mobile phone messages) and deictic expressions (e.g. operating instructions, which come to the receiver together with the machine).

Example 3.2 6./6
Just a few examples of typical newspaper abbreviations and compounds, collected from one page of *THE SUNDAY TIMES* (7 January 1990, p. E1); £215m fraud, pre-tax profits, RAF, ISC, CSF, GEC, GrandMet, Bond Corp, a pubs-for-breweries swap, the UK dairy-produce company, cash-rich institutions, PR group.

The influence of the aspect of space on lexis is evident not only in deictic elements and references to the internal situation, but also in lexical items referring to the cultural background, such as proper names, institutional and cultural terms (cf. Newmark 1981: 70ff.), etc.

Example 3.2.6./7
In a short story with the title *El sol* (The Sun), set in Northern Spain, the author uses the following similes: *el sol blanco como de plata derretida* (white as melted silver), *sentía sobre sí los rayos del sol como un baño de plomo derretido* (like a bath of melted lead). For a North European reader, for whom *sun* is something positive, associated with warmth and life, the tertium comparationis for these comparisons ("glaring light" and "unbearable heat", respectively) seems hard to understand. In German, for example, the sun is conventionally associated with gold, whereas silver is regarded as the colour of the moon. For the Spanish author and his Spanish readers, it is normal (in the summer) that the sun is something that everybody tries to avoid.

The aspect of time is also reflected in deictic elements, in internal time references, and in temporal markings of certain lexical items. This last aspect is particularly relevant both to the translation of old texts and to that of texts whose language is marked as "modern". In old texts we would not expect "modernisms" (and vice versa).

However, the translator has to decide whether the translation skopos requires a "synchronous" or an "actualizing" translation (cf. above, ch. 3.1.6.b). As it might be difficult for a 21st century translator to render a text in the language of the 18th century, s/he should at least take care not to use typically 21st century lexis (e.g. fashion words).

Example 3.2.6./8
In Jonathan Swift's *A Voyage to Lilliput*, archaic forms like *giveth*, *mathematicks*, *physick*, *Old Jury* instead of *Old Jewry*, *my self* and words like *hosier* (in

the 1735 edition, reprinted in *Gulliver s Travels*, Everyman's Library, London 1940) mark the text as "old" without being an obstacle to comprehension. The German translation (Swift 1983), however, is written in unmarked modern German.

Certain text types, such as legal documents, are characterized by archaic lexis, as is shown by Crystal & Davy (1969: 193ff.).

The motive or occasion for communication may influence the choice of lexis by requiring a particular level of style (e.g. in a funeral address) or certain formulas or clichés. This can be an important aspect when the target text is intended to be used on a different occasion from that of the source text.

Text function (in correlation with the text type) is also frequently reflected in the choice of lexical items. Crystal & Davy (1969: 173ff.) list some examples of typical lexical features of the language of newspaper reporting: complex pre and postmodification, typical adjective compounds such as *more and faster-arriving*, sequences of adjectives; emphatic and colloquial lexis, etc. Language for special purposes and metalanguage are other function-specific fields of word use. Genre conventions point to the fact that the sender is interested in subordinating form to content, thus setting guidelines for a particular effect of the text (cf. below, chapter 3.3.d). If the function changes within the text, the use of text-type conventions or of functional style can signal a particular stylistic interest on the part of the author.

Example 3.2.6./9
In Miguel de Unamuno's Novel *Niebla* (Unamuno 1979, cf. Sample Text 2, chapter 5.2.), Eugenia's uncle, who is a supporter of Esperanto as lingua franca and phonetic spelling, gives his niece's admirer the following advice: "Cuando escriba a Eugenia, lo haga escribiendo su nombre con jota y no con ge, Eugenia." In a literal translation ("If you write to Eugenia, you should spell her name with *j* instead of *g*: Eujenia not Eugenia", cf. Unamuno 1976, 71) the advice loses its function of pointing to a phonetic spelling. In English, the uncle might recommend the spelling *Ugenia* instead of *Eugenia*, and in German, where *eu* is pronounced *oi*, he might suggest *Oigenia*.

d. Checklist
The following questions may be helpful in analysing the lexis used in a text.

1. How are the extratextual factors reflected in the use of lexis (regional and social dialects, historical language varieties, choice of register, medium-specific lexis, conventional formulas determined by occasion or function, etc.)?

2. Which features of the lexis used in the text indicate the attitude of the sender and his/her "stylistic interest" (e.g. stylistic markers, connotations, rhetorical figures of speech, such as metaphors and similes, individual word coinages, puns)?
3. Which fields of lexis (terminologies, metalanguage) are represented in the text?
4. Are there any parts of speech (nouns, adjectives) or patterns of word formation (compounds, prefixed words, apocopes) which occur more frequently in the text than would normally be the case?
5. Which level of style can the text be assigned to?

3.2.7. Sentence Structure
a. General considerations
The formal, functional and stylistic aspects of sentence structure are mentioned as an important factor in almost all approaches to translation-relevant text analysis, although they are not dealt with in any systematic way. The construction and complexity of sentences (Wilss 1977), the distribution of main clauses and subordinate clauses in the text (Thiel 1978a), the length of the sentences (Thiel 1978b), the use of functional sentence perspective (Thiel 1974b), and the cohesive linking devices on the text surface (Bühler 1984) are some of the features considered to be relevant to translation-oriented text analysis. Included here are both conventional sentence structures in certain text types (e.g. imperatives in English instructive texts vs. infinitives in German instructive texts) and intentionally selected sentence structures which are meant to produce a particular effect on the reader.

In spite of the transcultural repertoire of syntactic figures of speech, such as parallelisms, chiasms, rhetorical questions, etc., the effect of these figures may vary slightly according to the different language structures. Complex hypotactic sentences are generally regarded as an appropriate means to describe complex facts. However, in German, hypotactic sentences are much more likely to look complicated and intricate (partly because the verb has to be put at the end of subordinate clauses) than, for instance, in Spanish, where the syntax has a principally linear character and where isolated non-finite constructions (gerund, participles, infinitives) are often preferred to subordinate clauses.

The analysis of sentence structure yields information about the characteristics of the subject matter (e.g. simple vs. complex), the text composition ("mise en relief", order of informational details), and the suprasegmental features (stress, speed, tension), and some syntactic figures, such as aposiopesis, may indicate presuppositions. Among the extratextual factors it is primarily the aspects of intention, medium and text function that are characterized by particular sentence structures.

b. How to find out about sentence structure
The translator gets a first impression of the typical sentence structure of a text by analysing the (average) length and type of the sentences (statements, questions, exclamations, ellipses) and the other constructions which replace sentences (infinitives, past and present participles, gerunds), the distribution of main clauses and subordinate clauses - and inclusions – in the text (paratactical vs. hypotactical sentence structures), and the connection of sentences by connectives, such as conjunctions, temporal adverbs, substitutions, etc. (cf. Crystal & Davy 1969: 43ff.). On the basis of such an analysis, s/he is able to find out how the information given in the text is structured. I wish to stress the point, however, that the analysis of sentence structure is not an aim in itself but must lead to a functional interpretation.

Below the level of sentences and clauses it is the order of the constituents (such as Subject-Predicator-Complement/SPC) or words (e.g. the position of adverbials) that may lead to a further structuring. Depending on their respective norms of word order, intonation, pitch patterns, etc., different languages use different means of focussing certain sentence parts or of giving a "relief" to the text (e.g. tense and aspect in Spanish). By analysing the different aspects of syntax (e.g. distribution of main and subordinate clauses and non-finite constructions, "mise en relief" by tense and aspect) the translator may achieve a solid basis for text interpretation, as is demonstrated in detail in Sample Text 2 (ch. 5.2.).

In addition to the classical figures of speech it is (mainly, but not only, in literary texts) the deviation from syntactic norms and conventions which is used in order to produce a particular stylistic effect. In these cases, the translator has first to find out what kind of deviation is used and how it works before s/he can decide, whether or how to "translate" it (in the widest sense of the word) in the light of the translation brief.

Example 3.2.7./1
In his short story *Los cachorros* ("The Little Dogs"), the Peruvian author Mario Vargas Llosa plays with syntactic structures, boldly mixing narration, direct speech and stream-of-consciousness technique: "Y un día, toma, su mamá, corazón, le regalaba ese pic-up, ¿para él solito?, sí...". By a syntactic analysis, we can separate the narrative sentence, which conforms to the syntactical norms ("Y un día su mamá le regalaba ese pic-up"), from the inserted elements of direct speech (*toma, corazón, sí*) and interior monologue (*¿para él solito?*). Reversing these steps of analysis, the translation is easy: "And one day, here you are, his mummy, darling, gave him that record-player, just for him?, yes..."

The syntactic features, too, depend on various other intratextual features, especially content and composition (e.g. distribution of informational details both in the text and in the sentences), lexis (e.g. verbal or nominal constructions), and suprasegmental features (especially focus, intonation). Among the extratextual factors it is mainly the aspects of intention, audience, medium (e.g. speech vs. writing), and function (e.g. conventional structures), which affect the syntactic features.

c. Checklist
The following questions may be helpful in analysing sentence structure:

    1. Are the sentences long or short, coordinated or subordinated? How are they linked?

    2. Which sentence types occur in the text?

    3. Does the order of sentence constituents correspond to the theme-rheme structure? Are there any focussing structures or deviations from normal word order?

    4. Is there any text relief?

    5. Are there any syntactic figures of speech, such as parallelism, chiasm, rhetorical question, parenthesis, aposiopesis, ellipsis, etc.? What function do they perform in the text?

    6. Are there any syntactic features which are determined by audience orientation, text-type conventions, or by the medium? Does the translation skopos require any adaptations?

3.2.8. Suprasegmental features
a. General considerations
The suprasegmental features of a text are all those features of text organization which overlap the boundaries of any lexical or syntactical

segments, sentences, and paragraphs, framing the phonological "gestalt" or specific "tone" of the text.

The particular framing of a text depends, first and foremost, on
the medium by which the text is transmitted. In written texts, the suprasegmental features are signalled by optical means, such as italics,
spaced or bold type, quotation marks, dashes and parentheses, etc.[38]

In spoken texts, the suprasegmental features are signalled by
acoustic means, such as tonicity, modulation, variations in pitch and
loudness, etc. (cf. Crystal & Davy 1969: 24ff., who confine "non-
segmental" features to spoken texts). This applies both to spoken texts
which are produced spontaneously (e.g. a contributions to a discussion, a statement by the witness of an accident) and to written texts
which are presented orally (e.g. lectures, radio and television news,
etc.).

In my view, written texts, which are read silently by the receiver, can also be assumed to have a phonological gestalt, which becomes evident to the careful reader and gives further information
about the intention of the sender and other factors. As far as poems
and certain pieces of literary prose are concerned, this assertion is
hardly likely to be contradicted, but I would venture to suggest that it
is applicable to any written text. It depends, among other things, on
stylistic and genre conventions.

It is important to distinguish suprasegmental features, in their
function as features of verbal text organization, from the non-verbal or
para-verbal elements accompanying the text, such as facial expressions, gestures, etc. On the other hand, habitual psycho-physical and
physical features of speech (such as quality of voice or excitement) as
well as features resulting from biographical factors (such as origin,
age, status, e.g. social or regional dialect) must be distinguished from
"controllable" functional features, i.e. features depending on the sender's intention or on other situational factors such as the relationship
between sender and receiver etc. (cf. Nord 1997b).[39]

---

[38]The layout of the text (e.g. the combination of text and photos, type area, or the
choice of types for titles or paragraph headings), which sometimes has an effect on
the suprasegmental features (e.g. representation of long pauses by wider spaces between paragraphs) is assigned to the category of non-verbal elements. (cf. chapter
3.2.5.), since the phonetic realization is only affected indirectly.

[39]Any "non-verbal vocal affects" or "background noises" (cf. Gutknecht & Mackiewitz 1977: 96), such as the quality of voice a person is identified by or physiological
reflexes like coughing or sneezing belong to the dimension of sender pragmatics
(chapter 3.1.1.), if they are independent of the analysed text. Though they usually

In the existing articles on translation-relevant text analysis, supraseg-mental features are not explicitly dealt with, although Koller's "form-al-aesthetic characteristics" (Koller 1979: 214), which comprise rhyme, rhythm, etc., seem to point in this direction.

b. Prosody, intonation, and stress
The concept of intonation refers to "the totality of prosodic qualities of utterances which are not linked to individual sounds" (Bussmann 1983: 219, my translation). It includes the general features of tonicity and pitch, modulation, rhythmicality, speed, loudness, tension and pauses (cf. Crystal & Quirk 1964: 44ff.).

Intonation as a means of text organization (as opposed to into-nation indicating psychical states, habitual characteristics of the sen-der or even psycho-pathological phenomena) serves mainly to mark the information structure and to divide the speech stream into tone units separated by pauses. The tone units usually correspond to infor-mation units. Another function of intonation is to mark the semantic nucleus of the sentence.

Moreover, intonation helps to disambiguate the various possible meanings of a sentence (e.g. serious vs. ironic meaning in the sentence "That was very clever of you!"). The "meaning" conveyed by intona-tion is independent of, i.e. not subordinated but coordinated to, that of lexical and semantic units. Intonation signals the attitude of the speak-er towards the message and, in this respect, its function can be com-pared with that of the stylistic function of lexis and sentence structure. It can be analysed only in connection with the other two factors.

In certain texts, intonation comprises the particular "tone" a text is spoken in. Taking the translation of the parable of the prodigal son as an example, Stolt (1978: 38ff.) shows that by choosing the tone of a fairy tale instead of that of a didactic text, the translator not only re-duces the credibility of the text but also alters the following factors in a fairly radical manner: the way the text is assessed by the readers, and the intention as well as the personality and authority of the sender, in so far as they are expressed by the text.

---

yield some information about the sender, his physical or psychical state, etc., they cannot be regarded as intentional or functional (as contrasted with an intentional cough which is used to draw the attention to something). If such voice qualities are feigned, however, they must be considered to be "elements of an alternative code" (Thürmann 1977: 24), which are assigned, if they are found to complement a verbal text, to the category of "non-verbal elements".

Although, as Crystal & Davy (1969: 34) rightly point out, they are not really suprasegmental because they occur in sequence with the verbal side of the utterance and not simultaneously with it, I include pauses in the category of suprasegmental features. For as far as the function is concerned, the position, length and variations of pauses within a text cannot be separated from intonation, since their influence on melody and speed, for example, is undeniable. However, we have to distinguish between pauses as a suprasegmental feature and pauses with a purely phonological function (as in *beflagged* vs. *be flagged*) or pauses with a paralinguistic function (as in to say nothing because there is nothing to say vs. to say nothing in order to conceal the truth (cf. Vermeer 1972: 111f., 122).

The analysis of prosodic features is of particular relevance to the interpreter. It facilitates the comprehension of content and text composition, since stress markings are a textological instrument for making the relations of coherence between sentences explicit. For example, the stress on the substituendum in the sentence "John found some *money* today" points to the substituent in the following sentence: "But he spent *it* immediately." In simultaneous interpreting, the analysis of intonation therefore can make it easier for the interpreter to anticipate how the text will continue. The pauses between the informational elements, whether "empty" or "filled" by sounds such as *ah*, *hum*, etc., divide the stream of speech and give a breathing space to the interpreter.

On the other hand, "contrastive" stress may reveal the speaker's intention. In the sentence pair "John found some *money* today" and "Peter found *happiness*", the stress on *money* forms a paradigmatic contrast with the stress on *happiness*. Syntagmatic contrast is produced by the two stress points in the sentence "John found some *money today*" if the following (or preceding) sentence is "He found *happiness yesterday*". In English, contrastive stress is often combined with certain syntactic structures, such as clefting: "It was John who found some *money* today, but *Peter* was the one who found *happiness*." Contrastive stress, too, can be very helpful to the interpreter because it limits the variety of possible "next sentences" and thus makes anticipation easier. Of course, the procedures for source text analysis have to be automatized or internalized in interpreter training, since there is not much time to start thinking about contrastive stress in the process of simultaneous interpreting.

Word stress can serve to differentiate meaning, e.g. in *cónduct* vs. *condúct*, whereas tone-unit stress sets focus points (e.g. "a *clever* child" vs. "a *stupid* child"), and sentence stress often signals emphasis. Some forms of sentence intonation or "intonation contour" (cf. Gleason 1969, 40ff.) are linked by convention with certain sentence types (e.g. question, inclusion, incomplete sentences, etc.) or rhetorical intentions. Essen (1979: 209 ff.) distinguishes between "terminal intonation" (in statements, requests, exclamations, and supplementary questions), dissolving tension, "progredient intonation" (in incomplete utterances), keeping up tension, and the "interrogative type" (in questions demanding a decision), increasing tension. Although many publications on suprasegmental features are not expressly confined to a particular language, most of them seem to be based on language-specific phonological features, and as far as I know, the supralinguistic validity of these findings has not yet been proved.

Certain genres, such as a radio commentary of a football match (cf. Crystal & Davy 1969: 125ff.) or the arrival of a train being announced by loudspeaker at a railway station, are characterized by a specific intonation which we would be able to identify at once even if we did not understand the information or if we heard the text in another place.

c. The "phonology" of written texts

In this context, the importance of sound and rhythm for the interpretation of a poem need not be stressed. It is a favourite subject in literary studies (cf. Kayser 1962: 241ff. and many others). Kayser also points to the importance of analysing rhythmical forms in prose texts, but since his subject is the "work of art", his considerations are confined exclusively to literature. Factors such as rhythmicality, melody, alliterations, rhyme, etc. have always played an important part in the analysis of literary texts, and indeed, their relevance in literary translation has certainly never been denied (cf. Basnett-McGuire 1978: 165, who speaks of "undertextual rhythms").

In my view, however, the aspects of prosody and intonation which can be observed in spoken texts and literature can also be valuable factors in the analysis of any kind of written text. We often find that a sentence which we have understood in one particular way may have quite a different meaning when we take a different view of it, i.e. when we read it with a different intonation or put the stress on another element. Though physically mute and inert on the printed page, the text may speak and "act" eloquently by itself for the inner ear and the inner eye of the reader. The receiver of a written text seems to activate some kind of "acoustic imagination" which suggests a particular "phonology" of the text. In this context, we have to distinguish between a "normal intonation" and any deviating forms of intonation which are evoked in the acoustic imagination by the specific choice of lexis, by certain syntactic structures, by signals such as punctuation marks, and by the reader's situational knowledge. However, it may well be that acoustic imagination is not equally developed in all readers, so that a particular text will not necessarily evoke the same phonological images in every reader.

d. The representation of suprasegmental features in writing

The phonological organization of a text is represented in writing by the selection of particular words, word order, onomatopoeia, certain features of typeface such as italics or spaced words, orthographic deviations (cf. the examples from Nathalie Sarraute's works given by Tophoven 1979: 129, e.g. *le soooleil, les vaaacances*), quotation marks, underlining, or even – at least where the rules allow a certain latitude – by punctuation. The possibilities of intentional use of punctuation vary according to the language-specific norms. For example, in German (as in English) the formal-syntactic punctuation rules (especially for commas) used to be rather strict. Thus, there is less opportunity for using the comma as an instrument of stylistic differentiation than, for example, in Spanish, where commas are put mainly according to semantic or prosodical and rhythmical criteria. Here, a comma signals the end of a certain stretch of discourse rather than the end of a formal syntactic unit (clause, sentence). After the recent reform of spelling and punctuation rules in Germany, people seem to feel rather insecure since they have never learnt to use a comma for stylistic reasons.

Nevertheless, even in languages with a complicated system of rules, punctuation can still be regarded principally as a stylistic feature. Behrmann (1982: 30) points out that the punctuation and even the orthography found in the works of Klopstock or Stefan George produces an "orthographical physiognomy" of the text.

In this sense, we can distinguish between "syntactic" or "discoursive" punctuation marks (full stop, comma, question and exclamation marks), which serve to guide comprehension by conventional signals, and "stylistic" punctuation marks which give "elegance and expressivity" to the sentence (cf. Stenzel 1966: 6f.). Thus, punctuation, whether conventional or stylistic, is used principally as a means of representing intonation and prosody in writing.

The analysis of suprasegmental features often yields information about the content (e.g. irony) and the subject matter (e.g. the "solemn" tone of a funeral address), as well as presuppositions (e.g. an interruption of the intonation contour in allusions) and composition (e.g. pauses, stress on the rhematic parts of the utterance). Of the extratextual factors, it is the aspects of sender, intention, place and motive/occasion and text function which are mainly characterized by suprasegmental features.

e. How to elicit suprasegmental features in a written text
Affectivity and expressivity are mainly reflected in the choice of lexis. Certain affirmative words, such as *actually* or *in fact*, and emphatic evaluations like *fantastic* or *great* seem to attract sentence stress, while others, such as modal particles like *doch* and *ja* in German, produce particular intonation contours by diverting the stress into a certain direction and explicating the illocutionary potential of an utterance.

In syntax, it is mainly focussing structures, such as clefting (e.g. *It was John who kicked the ball*), inclusions, which are spoken in a lower tone and at a higher speed than the embedding sentence, ellipses, or aposiopeses which seem to suggest special intonation patterns. Asyndetic enumerations, for example, are characterized by a higher speed than polysyndetic enumerations (*John, Peter, Mary, Paul were there* vs. *John and Peter and Mary and Paul were there*).

If not supported by lexical or syntactic means, contrastive stress is usually produced by the context. If the context is not sufficiently clear, the reader has to be guided by graphic features, such as underlining, spaced or bold type or italics, quotation marks, etc. Where these means are also used for purposes other than stress, language-specific difficulties may arise (see Sample Text 3, ch. 5.3.4.e).

Example 3.2.8./1
In European Spanish, quotation marks are used not only to indicate ironic meaning or stress etc., but – at least in some conservative media or by language purists – also to indicate neologisms not (yet) acknowledged by the Royal Academy of Language. Therefore, the function of quotation marks should be analysed carefully whenever they are used.

Finally, the phonological image of a text is also determined by theme-rheme structures. Since the thematic element normally links a sentence to the preceding utterance, it is often put in initial position with the rheme forming the end of the sentence, which is, of course, the appropriate place for the elements which the sender wants to stress. A deviation from this pattern causes surprise or leads to a certain tension between the two sentences, which is also reflected in the intonation contour.

For the translator, these considerations on phonology and intonation are of particular importance because the reader's acoustic imagination is determined by language-specific patterns. Each receiver reads a text against the background of their own native knowledge of intonation and stress patterns. Since in most cases this is an intuitive knowledge, they may not be able to adapt themselves to strange patterns even if they are told that they are reading a translation. After analysing its functions, the translator should therefore adapt the ST intonation to TL patterns.

Example 3.2.8./2
The final chapter of Juan Goytisolo's short novel *La isla* (cf. examples 3.2.4./5 and 3.2.6./2) begins with the following sentences: "El día siguiente amaneció *desvaído, gris*. Las nubes escurrían como churretes sucios sobre la playa de la Carihuela y los pájaros atravesaban el cielo en bandada y giraban de vez en cuando al compás del viento, igual que un remolino. Herminia me subió el café *a las doce* y dijo que Rafael *se había marchado*." (The underlining shows the assonances, and the italics mark the focus points.) "The next day was dawning faded and grey. The clouds swept like filthy frazzles over the beach of La Carihuela, and flights of flushed birds crossed the sky, whirling to and fro with the wind. Herminia brought me the coffee up *at twelve o clock* and told me that Rafael *had gone*." (Transl. C.N.) The story of a summer ends with the beginning of autumn, whose first unpleasant symptoms are described by means of onomatopoeic sounds and a rather monotonous rhythm signalled by assonant [u] and [a] in stressed syllables, interlaced with [i] which shifts from unstressed to stressed position. In my translation, I had to replace most of the (Romance) assonances by (Germanic) alliterations. The onomatopoeic sequence of dark vowels has been changed into a sequence of sibilants. Since dark vowels seem to correspond with melancholic feelings, especially when they are in focussed position, I have chosen *gone* instead of *left*. The position of *a las doce* at the end of the clause seems to intensify the monotony of the rhythm, although it does not conform to the theme-rheme structure: time is the only element which has been mentioned before (in the first sentence) and therefore has to be regarded as thematic. The same criteria can be applied to the English version.

d. Checklist
The following questions, referring to prosody and intonation in spoken texts and their graphic representation in written texts, may be helpful in analysing suprasegmental features:

1. Which suprasegmental features are present in the text? How are they represented graphically?

2. Are the suprasegmental features genre specific?

3. Do the suprasegmental features provide any clues to the habitual characteristics or to the emotional or psycho-pathological state of the sender?

4. Can the text be divided into prosodic units? Does the intonation contour indicate the sender's intention to clarify, stress or focus any elements of the utterance?

5. Do the suprasegmental features correspond to the theme-rheme structure of the text?

6. Does the translation skopos require any adaptations of suprasegmental features to TL patterns?

3.2.9. The interdependence of intratextual factors

Like the extratextual factors, the intratextual factors are closely related to one another, and so the recursive character of the model of analysis has to be stressed yet again. Since the information and clues elicited about each factor generally yield information about the characteristic features of other factors as well, we cannot always keep to a linear progression in the process of analysis.

In order to illustrate the interdependence of the intratextual factors I shall use the same story as I used to illustrate the interdependence of the extratextual factors in chapter 3.1.9. and which has been translated for this purpose (!). The interrelation of the factors will be shown in Figure 6.

Example 3.2.9./1
Bertolt Brecht: Measures Against Violence
When Mr. Keuner, the Thinking Man, pronounced himself against violence in front of a large audience, he noticed that his listeners backed away from him and left the room. He turned round and saw behind him – Violence.
"What did you say?" asked Violence.
"I pronounced myself in favour of violence."
After Mr. Keuner had also left, his disciples asked him where his backbone was. Mr. Keuner replied: "I haven't got a backbone. It is me who has to live longer than Violence."
And he told the following story:

> One day, in the time of illegality, there came to the house of Mr. Egge, a man who had learned to say no, an agent who presented a document signed by those who held sway over the city, which stated that to him should belong any house in which he set foot; similarly any food should be his for the asking; and any man that he set eyes on should serve him.
> The agent sat down, demanded food, washed himself, went to bed, and said, with his face to the wall, "Will you be my servant?"
> Mr. Egge covered him with a blanket, shooed away the flies, and watched over him while he slept; and, as he had done on the first day, so did he obey him for seven years. But for all that he did for him, there was one thing he took good care not to do, and that was to say a word. And when the seven years had passed and the agent had grown fat by all the eating, sleeping and giving orders, the agent died. And then Mr. Egge wrapped him in the tattered, old blanket, dragged him out of the house, cleaned the bed, whitewashed the walls, breathed a sigh of relief and replied: "No."

As the title suggests, the subject matter of the text is what can be done against violence. Mr. Keuner is a fictitious person who also appears in some other of Brecht's stories. Therefore he can be introduced by his name as somebody "known" to the reader. It may be assumed that the name Keuner is a distortion of *keiner* ("nobody"). Mr. Keuner, who is characterized by the epithet *the Thinking Man*, exhibits a particular behaviour towards violence: having pronounced himself to be against violence in public, he denies his conviction when personally confronted with violence. By means of the parable of Mr. Egge he tells his disciples, who wonder why he shows so little backbone, that it is more important to outlive violence than to become its victim. Mr. Keuner (and Mr. Egge) apparently submit to violence in order to outlive it.

The content of the story points to the subject matter suggested in the title: *measures* (i.e. "non-measures", in an ironic meaning) against violence, and determines the composition of the text. It is a frame text embedding a parable. The frame does not appear again at the end of the story because the readers are supposed to draw their own conclusions. The narration consists of two parts which are formally linked by the cataphoric element *following story*.

The subject matter and the content have a strong influence on lexis. In the first part the word *violence* is mentioned four times, twice as an abstract and twice as an allegory (indicated by the capital letter in the English translation). In the second part the word *violence* is not mentioned, but the concept is paraphrased in different forms. The document *signed by those who held sway over the city* states that the "agent" is a representative of violence, which is supported by the story (things *belong* to him, he *demands*, *gives orders*, and his behaviour in Mr. Egge's house shows his superior position). The isotopy of *serving* (*belong to*, *serve*, *servant*, *obey* and Mr. Egge's activities: *covered him*, *shooed away*, *watched over him*) characterize the contrasting semantic field.

The coherence between both parts of the story is based on the presupposition that violence emanates from those in power and that this is something "bad" or "immoral", to which a critical citizen (= somebody who has learned to think or to say no) ought to be opposed. Without this knowledge the reader will not be able to understand why the disciples ask about Mr. Keuner's *backbone* or why the period is called *time of illegality*.

The paraphrases characterizing the lexis require a particular sentence structure (e.g. the parallel sentences describing the powers of the agent) which, in turn, clarifies the content. The repetition of the same words and similar structures reminds the reader of the formulaic language of legal documents and lends authority to the content. While in the German original the stylistic level is marked mainly by syntactic means (e.g. an archaic word order), the English translation has to shift these markers to the lexis. The expressions *held sway over* and *set foot in* are intended to give an antiquated touch to this part of the text, which contrasts with the everyday language used to describe the actions of the agent.

The sentence structure also determines the suprasegmental features. In the parallel sentences, the key verbs *belong* and *serve* are placed in focus position. The relationship between sentence structure and suprasegmental features shows up even more clearly in the last paragraph in the rather awkward construction "there was one thing he took good care not to do, and that was..." and at the end of the first paragraph where the norms of word order have been ignored in order to place the thematic key word *violence* in a focus position. Thus, the suprasegmental feature of stress again refers the reader to the subject matter. The same applies to the expression "it is me who has to outlive...". It is the thinking people, those who have learned to say no, who have to outlive violence and must therefore refrain from futile sacrifice.

Figure 6: The interdependence of intratextual factors

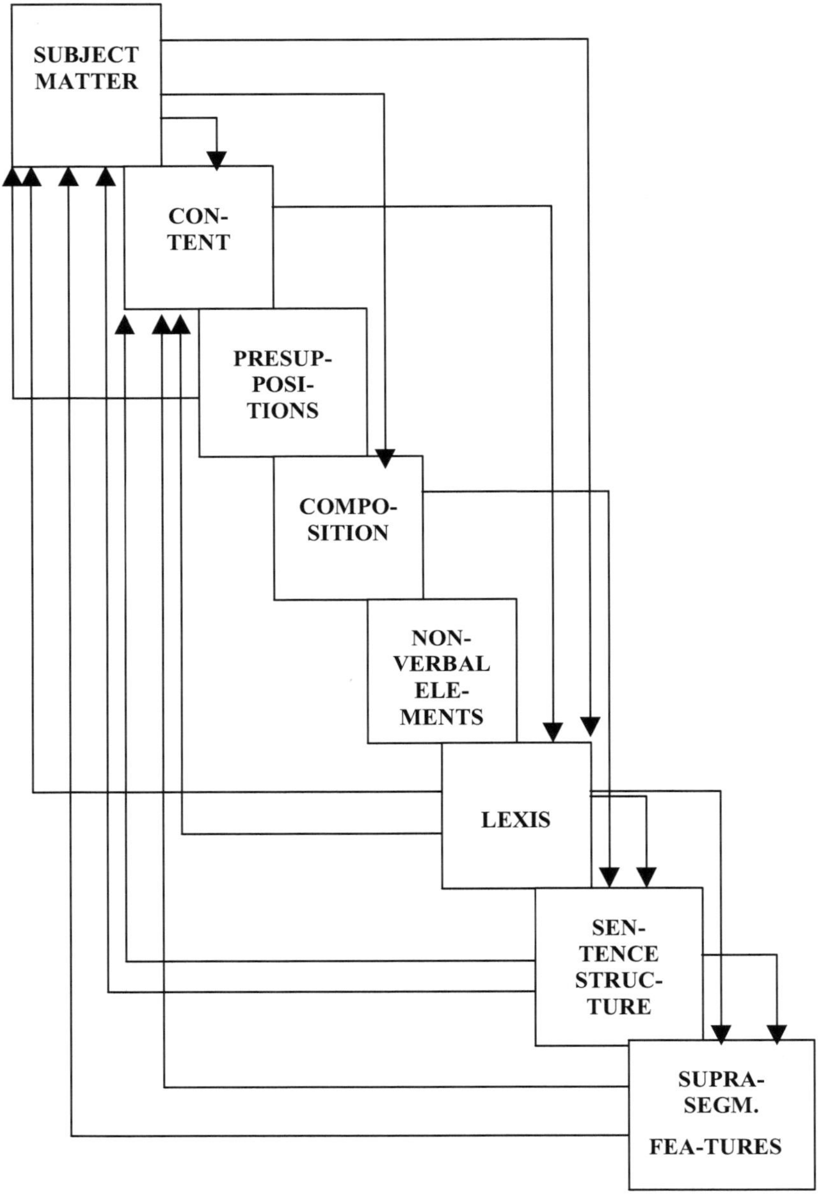

I have discussed only a few examples of the interdependence of intratextual factors, which has been represented in the diagram of Figure 6. As in Figure 5, the arrows refer only to the relationships discovered in the sample text and should not be applied generally.

3.3. Effect

a. General considerations

Effect, as I understand it, has to be regarded as a receiver-oriented category. The readers or listeners receive the content and form of the text against the background of their expectations deriving from the analysis of the situational factors and from their background knowledge. They compare the intratextual features of the text with the expectations built up externally, and the impression they get from this, whether conscious or unconscious or subconscious, can be referred to as "effect". The category of effect is therefore neither totally extratextual nor exclusively intratextual; it is an overlapping category linking the text (in the narrower sense) with its situation. The category of effect refers to the relationship between the text and its users, and, therefore, the analysis of effect belongs to the area of interpretation and not to that of linguistic description.

The effect that a text has on the receiver is the (provisional or definite) result of the communicative process. In a dialogue, both partners are affected by this result, whereas in a unidirectional process it is the receivers on whom the effect works. Their social relationship towards the sender will have changed as well as their level of knowledge or their emotional state, and even their future actions may be influenced by their reception of the text. None of these aspects (social relations, emotions, knowledge, actions) remain the same, but depending on the function of the text, one of them can, of course, be affected more strongly than the others.

The category of effect also includes the medium or long-term consequences that the reception of the text will have on the audience, even though these may be even more difficult to anticipate than the immediate effect. For example, after listening to a sermon, the churchgoers may be seized by emotion (immediate effect); some of them may be so deeply moved that they make a generous donation to an appeal for famine relief the next day (short-term effect); and a few may even decide to change their way of life (long-term effect). Accordingly we have to distinguish various degrees and types of effect.

This category does not, however, include the historical effect of a text, i.e. the history of its reception, including the reception of earlier translations, which translators of ancient texts, such as the Bible or the works of Shakespeare, Dante, or Goethe, cannot ignore when they translate the text again. These aspects belong to the category of time (cf. ch. 3.1.6.b).

For a text to have an effect at all it is an essential prerequisite that the audience can be influenced in the course of, and by, the communication process. They must be impressionable, capable of taking decisions and of being motivated to act. At the same time, the category of effect is based on the premise that words or texts indeed have an effect on the reader, and is therefore, basically, a pedagogical category.

The effect of a text is determined both by extratextual and intratextual factors as well as by a combination of particular extratextual factors with particular intratextual features. All intra and extratextual factors can play a part in producing text effect. In the following paragraphs I shall discuss only the three most important relationships between the factors that are possible in a communication process: the relationships between intention and text, between receiver and text-world, and between receiver and style.

b. Relationship I: Intention/text

One of the most important factors in text effect is the intention of the sender. We may safely assume that all senders, if they expect their text to be read at all, actually intend to produce a certain effect on the receivers and do not just leave it to chance. The intention of the sender is a teleological anticipation of the effect. Since the effect is the purpose they want to achieve, the sender or text producer will orient the intratextual elements they are going to use in the text towards the intended effect. But the effect will, in fact, only be produced if the anticipation has been considered sufficiently and if the text producer is able to employ adequately the intratextual elements she has at her disposal.

It is therefore the text producer (or, where the target text is concerned, the translator) who has to think about the possible effect of the text, irrespective of whether s/he is the sender or whether s/he produces the text for somebody else, whose intention has to be realized by the text. The translator has to anticipate the effect which the target text is intended to produce on the target audience – whether or not the

TT effect is supposed to be the same as the effect that the ST has, or had, on the ST receiver, is defined by the translation skopos.

Adequate anticipation of the intended effect requires not only great proficiency on the part of the text producer (and where the text producer is the translator, this must include cultural proficiency) but also practical imagination concerning the possible consequences of linguistic actions, the ability to put oneself "in the shoes" of the prospective receiver, as well as a great sense of responsibility towards the successful outcome of a social process.

Eliciting the intention of the sender is a phenomenon of great social and ethical importance, in which the future social position of the text producer (i.e. also of the translator) is at stake. A successful outcome to a social process depends mainly on how much thought has gone into eliciting the intended effect, and how well this has been achieved.

In translation-oriented text analysis, the question as to whether and how the intention of the sender is realized by the intratextual factors (particularly with regard to content and style of lexis and sentence structure) leads to an interpretation of the text.

c. Relationship II: Receiver/text-world

The receivers will compare the representation of the text-world, i.e. that section of the extralinguistic world which is verbalized in the text, with their expectation, which is determined by their knowledge, horizon, and "mood". The concept of mood refers to the influence of situational factors such as medium, time, place, and occasion, which make the receiver susceptible or insensitive to the particular effects of a text. This phenomenon is well known in mass communication, but it must also be assumed to be present in any other form of communication.

The choice of subject matter, when contrasting with a particular expectation, may in itself be enough to produce a certain effect. A subject that is normally taboo might shock the receivers, a popular subject might please them, a strange subject might require concentration or arouse dislike or merely disinterest, etc. The stranger the subject, the more likely it will be that the receiver reacts uncomprehendingly and is unwilling to continue reading. This aspect is of particular importance to the translator, for in order to rouse the receiver's interest in a strange subject, s/he may have to build a bridge, using a familiar subject, in order to facilitate access to alien worlds. Since the subject matter is often mentioned in the title or heading, this may be the place to build such a "bridge" (cf. chapter 3.2.2.).

Similar considerations apply to the aspect of content. The effect of the text depends partly on the selection of informational details which serve to illustrate the subject matter. The effect of a report about a political event, for example, will depend on whether more positive or more negative details are described. Sometimes, the selection of details is the result of a particular interest on the part of the sender (e.g. when s/he wants to manipulate the reader's opinion), but it may also depend on the individual perspective from which the sender has observed the event, causing them to stress some details and neglect others (e.g. when a witness is giving evidence).

The selection of informational details is particularly important in fictional texts. The sender is free to choose from an infinite variety of possible detail concerning persons, events, actions, etc. and any (intuitive or intentional) choice s/he makes throws some light on the effect (i.e. the interpretation) which s/he intends to evoke.

Example 3.3./1

In the text discussed in example 3.2.8./2 the information "end of the summer" is given by means of the description of certain details of the autumnal atmosphere (clouds, flights of birds, whirling wind, etc.), even though the narrator is lying in her bed at home, having just woken up. The excursions to the beach had been a favourite pastime of the protagonists in the story, so these details are a signal for the reader that the end of the summer is at the same time the end of a certain way of life. The last sentence, in which she is told that Rafael, who had been a frequent companion in this way of life, "is gone", seems to mark the final break with everything that this summer had meant to her.

Presuppositions can also determine the effect a text produces on the reader. The greater the amount of knowledge presupposed by the sender, the more "compact" seems the text. The translator should take this into account if s/he decides to verbalize information that cannot be presupposed to be part of the TT receiver's background knowledge, as illustrated in example 3.2.3./1. If the colour of flowers and butterflies, which Neruda presupposes to be known to his readers, is mentioned explicitly in the text, the effect will be quite different (all the more so since "blue", for example, is in no way an objective quality, and a description cannot be equivalent to personal experience). This is probably a problem peculiar to literary translation and less important in the translation of non-literary texts.

In translation, the relationship between the world represented in the text and the expectation of the receiver is of particular importance because there is always a cultural, as well as a possible spatial and temporal distance, which has to be overcome. If this distance is greater for the TT receiver than for the ST receiver, we can assume that the effect will be different for each of them. The exact level or degree of strangeness or familiarity which is intended for the TT receiver has to be fixed by the translation skopos.

d. Relationship III: Receiver/style

If the choice of the intratextual means of expression is determined by the anticipation of the effect, the category of effect – as far as its intra-textual component is concerned – must be regarded as a category of rhetoric in the classical sense, in which the effect-producing qualities of a text are assigned to certain stylistic principles ("virtutes elocutio-nis"), such as aptness ("aptum"), perspicuity ("perspicuitas"), or orna-ment ("ornatus"). These comprise the figures of speech ("figurae elo-cutionis") and registers ("genera elocutionis") as well as stylistic "for-mats" characterizing the whole text, e.g. "solemnity", "folksiness", "hastiness", "conversationality" etc.

It is the text producer who has to master these instruments of rhetoric. As far as the receiver is concerned, a theoretical knowledge of rhetoric is neither necessary nor desirable since once we know how the effect has been produced, we may be partly "immunized" against manipulation by the "hidden persuaders". The translator-as-a-receiver, however, must have a sound knowledge of rhetorical figures and know how they function in a particular culture. First, the analysis of the rhetorical qualities of the source text may, as has already been pointed out, provide the translator with some information about the sender's intention. Second, translators cannot rely exclusively on their own intuitive reaction to the text, which is of necessity subjective and determined by the conditions of their own situation, but must check the impression the text makes on them by analysing the intratextual rhetorical features of the text.

The effect of one stylistically relevant intratextual factor cannot be analysed in isolation from that of the others, particularly in the are-as of lexis, sentence structure, and suprasegmental features, where the interaction of effects is so strong that it is sometimes very difficult to identify the effect of a single stylistic device. Anaphora, for example, increase the "tension" of the text not only through the repetition of a word or expression at the beginning of a sentence (lexis), but also through the parallelism (sentence structure) and the particular intonation contour (suprasegmental feature) which it produces.

Example 3.3./2

"No sé cómo acabó el día. No recuerdo cómo transcurrió la cena, ni de qué habló Borja, ni qué dije yo. No recuerdo, siquiera, cómo ni cuándo nos despedimos del Chino. Sólo sé que al alba, me desperté." (Matute 1979: 242)

There are three parallel negative sentences (*no sé...*, *no recuerdo...*) leading to a climax, which is supported by the increasing length of the sentences and culminates in the positive contrast (*sólo sé...*). Between the first and the second sentence, there is a formal variation in the initial elements (although the two verbs are used synonymously), whereas the second and the third sentence are linked by the anaphoric repetition of *no recuerdo*. In the last sentence the initial element of the first sentence is taken up again, varying only the continuing elements (*cómo* vs. *qué*). The combination of sentence structure, lexis and intonation with increasing speed produces a particular rhythmical effect which is difficult to reproduce in the English translation. In order to preserve the rhythmical effect, the content had to be changed slightly.

"I don't know how the day ended. I don't remember how we had dinner or what Borja said or what I talked about. I do not even remember how or when we said goodbye to Chino. I only know that I woke up at dawn." (Transl. C.N.)

It cannot necessarily be assumed that the effects of various stylistic elements in a text point in one and the same direction, or even that they form part of a pattern as in example 3.3./2. If we want to elicit the global effect of a text, we have to analyse the whole spectrum of possible effects for each factor. Only by comparing the possible effects of all features are we able to identify the dominant effect intended by the sender. In most cases, even divergent effects of individual text features are encompassed by the global effect.

For example, if the effect of a metaphor in a particular text could be either *docere*, i.e. to transmit knowledge, or *delectare*, i.e. to produce aesthetic pleasure, or *movere*, i.e. to produce a particular reaction in the reader, we have to ask what effect might be intended in the same text with a climax, a simile, an alliteration or a rhetorical question. If with all these figures the effect of *movere* dominates, then this same effect will also be produced, for instance, by a periphrasis which on its own or in a different text might have had the effect of *docere*. This consideration is of particular relevance to translators, since they need not – and indeed must not! – transfer every single effect-producing feature as such, but, if this is required by the translation skopos, should transfer the global effect achieved by the particular combination of effect-producing features.

In intercultural communication, the relationship between receiver and style has to be seen against the background of the culture-specific stylistic code. Every stylistic feature should be analysed with respect to its rank in the hierarchy of stylistic usage in the particular culture, since the effect which a stylistic feature has on the reader depends on its predictability according to culture-specific conventions, aesthetic norms, etc.

The conventionalization of a great number of common text functions in text types often implies the conventionalization of effects. Thus, when choosing conventional features for a particular genre, the text producer will expect them to be recognized by the receiver as indicators of a particular text function and to produce the corresponding conventional effect. At the same time, the receivers, realizing that the text conforms to the norms they expect, will indeed be prepared for this effect. Text function is, therefore, the most appropriate factor to compensate for or "counteract" intratextual divergences from the norm, so that in the end it is the conventional effect linked with the respective text function that is successful.

Let us look at an example from everyday life. Although operating instructions are very often defective, we can assume that in most cases, in accordance with the intention of the sender to "instruct s.o. to operate X" and having the function of "instruction to operate X" assigned to the text by the receiver, they still have the conventional effect of "enabling s.o. to operate X".

d. Types of effect
Bearing in mind the relationships described above, we can distinguish types of effect which allow us to systematize the analysis of effect(s). In order to avoid the drawbacks of a rigid typology which might tempt the analyst to "straitjacket" a text, I shall try to characterize the types by simply marking the two poles between which the effect derived from the relevant relationship can be placed.

Type I: Intentional vs. non-intentional effect
A comparison of the intention elicited by external analysis with the interpretation of the intratextual factors can have two different outcomes: a) The effect produced by the text is, in fact, the effect intended by the sender, or b) the text produces an effect which does not conform to the sender's intention. In intercultural communication, this relationship is particularly relevant because it is the ST receiver and

not the TT receiver that the ST sender or text producer had in mind
when they decided on the intention they wanted to realize by means of
the text.

Type II: Cultural distance vs. zero-distance

The effect that the "reality" described in the text has on the reader depends on the cultural distance. In intercultural communication there
are, grosso modo, three possible relationships:

(a) The text-world corresponds to the source-culture. This
means that the ST receivers can match it with their own world (= zero-
distance), whereas the TT receiver cannot (= cultural distance).

(b) The text-world does not correspond to the source-culture.
Since the ST receivers cannot match it with their own world, the sender has to describe the features of the text-world explicitly, and this
description will aid the TT receiver as well. Both have a cultural distance from the text-world, though perhaps not to the same degree. Ex-
ceptionally, the text-world may correspond to the target-culture, in
which case the TT receiver has a zero-distance.

(c) The text-world de facto corresponds to the source-culture,
but the sender has "de-culturalized" it by explicitly transposing it into
a distant time and/or place (*once upon a time in a far distant land*).
This brings about a certain degree of generalization, thereby reducing
the relevance of culture-specific details. The effect can be that of zero-
distance for both the ST and the TT receivers.

Type III: Conventionality vs. originality

The types of effect linked with the relationship between receiver and
style can be characterized according to the matrix represented in Figure 7. The more predictable (according to text function) the features
of the text are, the more conventional the effect will be.

Text elements which are determined by the sender's individual
characteristics or by a particular sender intention will produce a more
"original" effect. The aspects of place, time, and motive/occasion will
gain in importance with the increasing distance between the situation
of text production and that of text reception. This applies to intracultural as well as to intercultural communication (= translation).

The effect of texts whose stylistic features are largely conventional (such as recipes or laws) is based mainly on the message they
convey, linguistic conventions serving as a pre-signal of the text function. The stylistic features of such texts gain relevance for the category

Figure 7: The relationship between extra and intratextual factors

Intratextual / Extratextual	SUBJECT MATTER	CONTENT	PRESUPPOSITIONS	COMPOSITION	NON-VERBAL ELEM.	STYLE — LEXIS	SENT. STRUCT.	SUPRAS. FEAT.
SENDER	favourite subject, special field	personal perspective, commentary; opinion	knowledge of political affiliation	chronological order if sender is a child	gesticulation of Mediterranean sender	personal deixis, idiosyncrasy	simple sentences of uneducated sender	habitual quality of voice, pitch
INTENTION	topical subject; political scandals	prettification or blurring of content	exaggerated presupp. for prestige reasons	gradual increase of suspense	misleading photographs	connotative words	indirect speech to mark mental reserv.	rhythmical calls for democracy
AUDIENCE	reference to the addressee's own life	taking the addressee's view of things	*As you all know perfectly well...*	footnotes with explanations	illustrations adequate for children	direct forms of address	imperatives	"baby-talk" intonation
MEDIUM	special subject in scholarly journal	not too complicated in spoken text	knowledge of topical events in newspaper	order of questions in blank form	diagram instead of long statistics on TV	acronyms in newspaper language	simple structures in spoken texts	high-pitched voice in microphone talk
PLACE	culture-specific subjects	information from the parish council	local deixis (*in this country*)	culture-specific conventions of composition	arms, seals, emblems, logos	elements of regional dialect in lexis, grammar and intonation, Americanisms in English or Spanish		
TIME	season-specific subjects	news of the day	temporal deixis (*last night*)	composition of classical drama	symbols, such as swastika	temporal markers in lexis and sentence structure		hexameter, blank verse
MOTIVE	season's greetings for Christmas	biographical details in obituary	knowledge of rituals	protocol	sad face	baptismal formula	aposiopesis because of emotional upset	solemn tone
FUNCTION	no personal subject in operating instructions	no personal comments in news text	no presuppositions in sales contract	separation of ingredients and instructions in recipe	illustrations in operating instructions	terminology in scientific texts	impersonal constructions in legal documents	singing intonation in liturgy

of effect only if they do not conform to genre conventions and thus indicate a different (or additional) non-conventional function.

Example 3.3./3
A law written in verse would probably lose its binding character and might be
regarded as an amusing persiflage. Operating instructions in verse, however,
can still work, even though the effect on the reader may be unconventional. A
combination of conventions belonging to different text types can produce surprising effects (cf. Sample Text 1, chapter 5.1.5.). If used for a particular genre, the boxes of the matrix in Figure 7 would be filled with all the typical features. Since the philological disciplines have not yet come up with descriptions of genre-specific features, the entries in Figure 7 serve simply as examples.

In other texts, such as tourist information leaflets or newspaper commentaries, the stylistic organization may not be entirely conventional,
but is still subordinate to the intended text function. The effect of
these texts, too, is based mainly on the information conveyed, whereas
the individual stylistic features have a subsidiary function as a pre-signal for the receiver.

However, in some texts the stylistic elements have to be seen as
rather independent text components which, as far as the intended effect is concerned, are just as important as the information (e.g. in short
stories, advertisements, etc.). In these cases, the effect is not only produced by what is said but also by the way in which it is said (cf. Sample Text 2, chapter 5.2.4.).

Texts where the factors do not correspond to each other can produce quite special effects. A lack of correspondence between content
and form may, for example, indicate irony (cf. Sample Text 2). Parody
and travesty, to quote another example, are also characterized by a discrepancy between content and form or between the text-function and
the expectation of the receiver (cf. Reiss & Vermeer 1984: 182).

There are also texts whose effect is based almost exclusively on
the stylistic and rhetorical devices the author has used, while the content aspect is pushed right into the background. The poem *Das
aesthetische Wiesel* by Christian Morgenstern (cf. Morgenstern &
Knight 1975: 8f.) may serve as an example here:

Ein Wiesel	A weasel
saß auf einem Kiesel	perched on an easel
inmitten Bachgeriesel.	within a patch of teasel.
Wisst ihr	But why
weshalb?	and how?
Das Mondkalb	The Moon Cow
verriet es mir	whispered her reply
im Stillen:	one time:
Das raffinier-	The sophees-
te Tier	ticated beast
tat's um des Reimes willen.	did it just for the rhyme.

If the translation is supposed to reproduce the effect, the content is practically interchangeable as long as the formal principle of structure is preserved, as the American translator Max Knight demonstrates with the following alternative translations of the first three lines (cf. Levý 1967: 1178):

(a) A ferret	(b) A mink
nibbling a carrot	sipping a drink
in a garret...	in a kitchen sink...

(c) A hyena	(d) A lizzard
playing a concertina	shaking its gizzard
in an arena...	in a blizzard...

The types of effect based on these three fundamental relationships can be found in any text. This shows again that equivalence (in the sense of "equal effects of ST and TT") is not a very practicable criterion for a translation. The translator needs to know exactly which type of effect is required to remain unchanged, since the preservation of cultural distance (receiver/text relationship) often precludes the preservation of the interpretation (intention/text relationship). Moreover, the effect of the target text depends largely on whether the translation skopos requires a documentary, or an instrumental, translation.

4. Applications of the model in translator training

4.0. General considerations

a. Translation as a skill and as a classroom exercise

As was mentioned at the beginning, the model of translation-oriented text analysis described above is intended to be applicable to translation teaching. It is also designed to provide criteria for the selection of text material for translation classes, the systematization of translation problems and procedures, the monitoring of learning progression, and for the evaluation and assessment of translations.

First though, we must distinguish between the teaching of translation in the training of professional translators, where translating is regarded as an aim in itself and as a skill that is acquired on the basis of an existing proficiency in both languages, and translation as a classroom exercise. The latter is used in foreign language teaching in order to test reading comprehension (L2-L1 translation) or to acquire performance skills in the foreign language (L1-L2 translation) and certain technical skills, such as the use of dictionaries, etc. Moreover, translation is supposed to provide metalinguistic insights into the structural differences and similarities of two languages. Indeed, it is firmly established as a compulsory or optional requirement in the foreign language curricula of several German regional states.

In my considerations on the applications of the text-analytical model I shall refer mainly to the training of professional translators, as practised at (academic and other) schools or departments of interpreting and translating. I shall, therefore, concentrate primarily on the development of transfer competence. The acquisition and testing of language competence (and performance) will be of secondary importance here. Transfer competence can, of course, only be acquired if there is a high level of proficiency in both source and target languages and source and target cultures.[40]

---

[40]Below a certain level of language proficiency, acquisition of transfer competence is not possible, as is clearly shown by the examples from a Thinking-Aloud experiment quoted by Königs 1986). If the test persons had had sufficient command of Spanish to realize that the unidiomatic expressions and the inconsistent mixture of German and Spanish institutional terms was due to the fact that the Spanish ST they had to translate into German was a translation, they would certainly have handled certain "problematic" passages of the text in a different way (e.g. using a literal back-translation!).

Nevertheless, translation as an exercise in the foreign language class need not be ignored altogether. Whether translation is regarded as a type of exercise or as a professional skill is of little importance as long as teachers and students have a clear concept of what they are trying to achieve. If the teaching objective is clearly defined, then the following considerations on the application of translation-oriented text analysis may be equally relevant to the training of translators as to foreign language teaching, especially where translation skills form part of the foreign language syllabus.

However, the application of pre-translational text analysis in foreign language teaching can only be useful if it is not confined to a linguistic analysis of the text, consisting of marking "difficult" passages and analysing the author's intentions and their subsequent realization in the text (cf. Ettinger 1977: 70, who vividly describes the realities of text analysis in language classes). When translation students ask their teachers "How literal or free do you want my translation to be?" (cf. Reiss 1977: 544), it becomes evident that they have no idea of what translation is really about. However, this is due to the fact that, as Königs rightly points out, "translation learners have all been foreign-language learners first" (Königs 1986: 11, my translation). Thus, one of the first tasks of an introduction to (professional) translation must usually be to make the students revise the concept of translation that they have acquired in the foreign-language class (cf. Reiss 1980b: 149)!

b. Text analysis and translation skopos

In the translation class, the text-analytical model should be combined with "translating instructions", which define the translation skopos, i.e. the intended function of the target text, as unambiguously as possible. I explain in more detail later how these instructions can be formulated.

In a pre-translation course, the students should be introduced to the model of translation-oriented text analysis, which should then be applied systematically to every translation task. The model can easily be taught and practised using L1 texts for intralingual translation, e.g. expressing a news text in the form of a personal letter, an article from an encyclopedia in the form of a short lecture, etc.

Figure 8 (for the data see example 4.0./2a and 4.0/2b) shows how the model can be formalized in line with the first phase of the looping model of the translation process (see above, Figure 4). First, the students analyse the target-text profile on the basis of the translation brief, using the same chain of WH-questions as was suggested for ST analysis. The elicited data are entered in the right-hand column of the form. In a second step, the source-text analysis leads to the identification of the translation-relevant elements and features, which are then put down in the left-hand column.

The relevance of the various factors is determined by the translation brief. If, for example, the initiator asks for a target text whose lexis and sentence structure conform to the target-cultural genre conventions, then the lexis and sentence structure of the source text need not be analysed in detail. The analysis may then be confined to deciding which of the ST elements can be preserved (where SC norms are identical with TC norms) and which have to be adapted to TC conventions.

If the translation skopos requires an equifunctional or "equivalent" translation (this is, of course, one possible translation skopos, though it is rarely formulated explicitly), the translator first enters the results of an exhaustive text analysis in the left-hand column and then fills in the corresponding data for each of the factors in the right-hand column. The same procedure applies to those situations in which the translator has to fix the translation skopos him or herself. After both the left-hand and the right-hand column have been filled in, the contrast between the ST material and the requirements of the target situation reveals the translation problems. These problems are then entered in the middle column together with the procedures leading to a functionally adequate solution. This method allows a systematic handling of translation problems throughout the text and avoids inconsistent ad hoc solutions. What this procedure also shows is that preserving the factors or functions is the most difficult translation skopos.

Example 4.0./1
In a particular translation class taught in Heidelberg in 1986, the task was to translate the first few paragraphs of the text *La subversión contemporánea* (Pabón 1971) without any translating instructions. The ST analysis produced the following result (in brackets, the designation of the factors):
The Spanish History professor Jesús Pabón (Sender), first publications in 1925 (Sender: age), had read (MEDIUM$_1$) a lecture (TEXT FUNCTION$_1$) on the subject "Subversion today" (SUBJECT MATTER$_1$), as one of a series of lectures (MOTIVE$_1$), to students and professors at the military academy *Escuela Superior del Ejército* (AUDIENCE$_1$) in Madrid (PLACE$_1$) in 1969 (TIME$_1$). It was published in 1971 (TIME$_2$) along with a number of essays (TEXT FUNCTION$_2$) on modern Spanish history (SUBJECT MATTER$_2$), in the paperback series *Biblioteca del estudiante* (MEDIUM$_2$) in order to address a larger readership (AUDI-

ENCE$_2$). The text of the lecture was printed unchanged; it contained features of spoken discourse, such as short and simple sentences and 1. person singular (SENTENCE STRUCTURE), colloquial metaphors and redundancies (LEXIS). The composition of the text (COMPOSITION) was marked by composition signals, such as headings and paragraph numbers (NONVERB. ELEMENTS).

Asked to produce an "equivalent" translation, the students did not know, for example, whether to "think back" to 1971 (when they were about 6 years old!) or to translate the text for their own contemporaries (TIME$_3$), whether to translate it as a lecture or as a printed essay (MEDIUM), whether to address their translation to a German counterpart of the Spanish officers in 1969 (!) (AUDIENCE$_1$) or of the Spanish readers of the paperback edition in 1971 (AUDIENCE$_2$) or in 1986 (AUDIENCE$_3$), and whether to reproduce the effect the text probably had on Audience$_1$ or Audience$_2$ or Audience$_3$ (EFFECT$_{1-3}$). And without a decision on these factors the linguistic translation problems could not be solved satisfactorily.

The example shows that, not only in practice, but also (and perhaps particularly) in the classroom, translators need a detailed description of the translation skopos if they are to deal with the translation task in a responsible way.

c. Formalizing the translating instructions
Using the same chain of WH-questions as for source text analysis, the translation brief or instructions can be formalized as follows (cf. Nord 1997g):

Who	*On what subject matter*
is to transmit	is s/he to say
to whom	*what*
what for	*(what not)*
by which medium	*in which order*
where	*using which non-verbal elements*
when	*in which words*
why	*in what kind of sentences*
a text	*in which tone*
with what function?	*to what effect?*

The questions can also be used as a checklist if the translator has to ask the initiator for details with regard to the translation brief.

Not all the information on these factors has to be given explicitly in the translating instructions; some may also be given implicitly. For example, the information about the intended medium also gives the translator a clue to the addressed audience, and the specification of the text function or genre implies that certain conventions of lexis or sentence structure will have to be taken into account, etc. In the introductory phase of translation teaching, however, the description of the factors, particularly the extratextual ones, should be as unambiguous and as detailed as possible.

Example 4.0./2a

The instructions for the translation of an information leaflet might read as follows. The town administration of Sagunto, Spain (1) intends to publish an English version of its tourist information leaflet (2) in 1986 (3), because of the increasing number of visitors from Britain (4). The text by Santiago Bru y Vidal (5) describes the history and the sights of Sagunto (6). The English version, which will be available to visitors at the Sagunto Tourist Information Office (7) in order to provide information and increase the attraction of the town (8), should reproduce all the information contained in the original (9), preserving layout, photos, etc. (10).

The information for the translator that can be derived from these instructions is listed in the right-hand column of Figure 8, using the numbers for cross-reference. The arrows indicate other factors which may be affected by the information. The example shows how much information on the TT situation is provided by the translating instructions. The more detailed the instructions, the less the "freedom of choice" – which is more a "pressure of choice" while the student is still at the stage of acquiring competence.

Example 4.0./2b

If the ST is analysed from the angle of the TT skopos (see Figure 8, left-hand column), it becomes evident that its effect is mainly due to a set of simple facts being presented in a rather pompous form: extremely long sentences (an average of 40 words, participle and gerund constructions, appositions, etc.) and a redundant, connotative lexis on a relatively high stylistic level (e.g. frequent use of adjectives placed in front of the noun: *feraces tierras, glorioso pasado*). The target text has to be adapted to target-cultural conventions (cf. example 3.1.4./2). Since the TT is only received in Sagunto (as opposed to the ST, which is distributed all over Spain), the informative function will have priority over the "advertising" (= appellative-persuasive) function. Since all the information has to be reproduced without changing the layout, and as there will be some additional explanations in order to compensate for presuppositions, the translator will have to reduce the stylistic redundancies, even if the target-cultural conventions allow a similar style.

In translation teaching the instructions need not be "realistic" in the sense that they have to be borrowed from the area of professional translation, but the motivation of the students will be heightened if the translating instructions can be as close to reality as possible.

Figure 8: Source-text analysis and target-text profile

	SOURCE-TEXT ANALYSIS	TRANSFER	TARGET-TEXT PROFILE
	A. EXTRATEXTUAL FACTORS		
SENDER	S: Ayuntamiento de Sagunto TP: S. Bru y Vidal	Include **name of translator** as text producer in imprint	S: Sagunto town administration (1) vs. TP = TRL (5)
INTEN-TION	Publicity and information (→ text type), service for tourists	Is the **information suitable for publicity**? (e.g. description of heavy industry)	Increase attraction of the town/ achieve publicity by way of in-formation → Lexis, Content (8)
AUDI-ENCE	Spanish-speaking tourists, normal knowledge of Spanish geography, history etc.	**different background knowl-edge** of Span. geography, his-tory etc. → compensate defi-ciencies	English-speaking tourists, little or no background knowledge, but interested (4), (7)
MEDI-UM	Folded leaflet (6 pages), glossy paper, very small type, coloured photographs	**space restrictions** for text, title page (English?), captions of photos	Like ST, no change in layout possible (2)
PLACE	Reception: Sagunto (tour of the town), rest of Spain	**TT function: instrumental** (guide function) → **proper names** of sights in Spanish	Reception: mainly Sagunto, tour of the town (7)→ Lexis, Syntax, hierarchy of text func-tions
TIME	Production: before 1977 Reception: after 1977	**Information up to date**? (check)	Production: summer 1986 Reception: after summer 1986 (3) → Content
MOTIVE	(perhaps re-opening of the castle after restoration)	Factor irrelevant	More tourists from GB (4) → Audience, Content, Function, Lexis, Syntax, Presuppositions
FUNC-TION	same as INTENTION: information + publicity	HIERARCHY OF FUNCTIONS **(information above publicity)**	MAINLY INFORMATION, since receivers are already in Sagunto
	B. INTRATEXTUAL FACTORS		
SUBJ. MAT-TER	History and modern sights of Sagunto	subject belongs to S-culture, **Cultural distance** no problem for effect (see Function)	History and modern sights of Sagunto (6) → Presuppositions
CON-TENT	Geogr. situation, Sagunto today, historical sights, port&industry, festivals	Number of inhabitants and dates: UP TO DATE? Information on **heavy industry** PERSUASIVE?	Complete information (9), according to intention and text function
PRESUP-POSI-TIONS	history (Arab period), Catholic Church (Saints), geography (landscape)	CULTURAL TERMS (explain!), NAMES OF PLACES (Spanish + explanation?)	Knowledge of geography from experience (7)
COMPO-SITION	10 paragraphs (not corresponding to content), composition → content	**change division into paragraphs** according to contents	According to text function. as clear as possible!
NON-VERB. ELEM.	photos, coat of arms, text in 3 columns below photos, large spaces between paragraphs	**compensate for expansions** (presuppositions) by reducing redundancies and spaces!	Layout as in ST, not smaller type (→ Function) (10)
LEXIS	Castilian Spanish, partly "literary", redundant, connotative vocabulary	**adapt to target-culture con-ventions** (less pathos, fewer redundancies)	British English (4), according to text-type norms, more informa-tive than eulogizing
SEN-TENCE STR.	Long hypotaxes, parentheses, appositions, enumerations	**simplify sentence structure** (divide long sentences, watch focus!)	Not too complicated (→ place of reception), conforming to text-type conventions
SUPRA-SEGM.	none	**proper names** (mark by bold type?)	Readability first and foremost!
	C. EFFECT		
EFFECT	According to text function: Visitors are attracted, come again, recommend Sagunto	**Conventional effect** according to intention: cultural distance intensifies effect	Visitors shall feel at home, come again, recommend Sagunto to friends, etc.

Even a translation that is intended to serve as an aid to comprehension or to monitor learning progress can be justified if the aim is made explicit by some sort of translating instruction (e.g. "Translate the text in such a way that I can see whether you are able to apply the rules for indirect speech in English!"). Only then will the students know exactly what is expected of them, and they can't pretend to have "thought that the translation was for some other purpose". In this sense, the perspective adopted by this model is neither purely "learner-centrated", nor exclusively "teacher-centrated". With their greater knowledge and experience teachers should guide the learning process, but take account of the needs and potential of the students.

4.1. Planning the process of translation learning

4.1.0. Fundamentals

"Translation is learned by translating, which does not allow any reduction whatsoever." This behaviourist approach (cf. Zalán 1984: 200) appears to be confirmed by the fact that 54.4 per cent of all classes offered at a typical school of translating and interpreting are practical translation classes.

However, this figure gives an inaccurate picture since it is not only translation that is taught and/or practised in these classes. They develop and enhance not only translation competence in the narrower sense, i.e. transfer competence, but also, wherever necessary, other translation-relevant competences, such as (a) linguistic competence in the native language (L1) and in the foreign language (L2) with regard to formal and semantic aspects of vocabulary and grammar, language varieties, register and style, genre conventions, etc., (b) cultural competence (e.g. areal studies about the target culture ranging from everyday life to social and political institutions), (c) factual competence in sometimes highly specialized fields (e.g. knowledge of matrimonial law, economic policies, balance of trade, information technology, etc.), and (d) technical competence for documentation and research (use of dictionaries, bibliographical methods, storage of information, etc.).

This list gives some indication of the important part practical classes play in the training of professional translators. It might be useful here to look at how some of these teaching aims can be dealt with quite separately from translation proper. Linguistic competence in the native language, for example, whose inadequacy is often deplored, could easily be taught as a separate course independent of the combination of foreign languages chosen by the student. Classes in which cultural studies or specialized fields are taught could be coordinated from a topic point of view with translation classes. Translation teaching should be preceded by an introductory course, in which students are taught the technical skills of research and documentation, methods of translation-oriented text analysis etc. in non-contrastive language classes, as well as comparative grammar, stylistics, and text linguistics in language-pair-specific classes. All these procedures would take the pressure off translation classes, which could then concentrate on the teaching of transfer competence (cf. Nord 1987b, 2005).

Even so, a translation class will nearly always include more than just the development of transfer competence. However, in view of the great variety of teaching aims it would appear to be essential to structure and systematize translator training more clearly, including a differentiation in content over and above the rather dubious distinction between the translation of general texts and the translation of texts for special purposes. This might lead to what Wilss (1982: 183) calls one of the three most important sub-targets of translation teaching, namely

> the expansion of transfer competence into operative transfer patterns or transfer formulae with the ultimate aim of building up text- and context-dependent and at the same time optimally standardizable transfer techniques (not just one transfer technique).

In the case of these transfer techniques (although not in the purely linguistic sense that Wilss has in mind), the factors in our text-analytical model could serve as focal points for translation teaching, and could be used not only to systematize translation problems and their satisfactory solution, but also as a basis for selecting text material for translation classes.

4.1.1. Selecting texts for translation classes

Selecting texts for translation classes is not a matter of adhering to rigid principles – particularly if one is looking for authentic material, which has not been produced for didactic purposes and which therefore often resists schematization. Nor is it a matter of mere intuition.

It is a fundamental requirement in translation teaching that only authentic texts should be used as material, i.e. real texts-in-situation. These texts have to be presented to the students in such a way that as much information as possible is provided on the situation in which the text "functioned" (in the original medium, as a photocopy, with additional details on sender, intention, time and place of production etc. etc., for examples see Nord 2001d). This is why collections of texts which do not specify the sources and even of isolated sentences for translation are completely pointless (cf. Nord 1987c).

Of course, it is often difficult to find authentic texts which are not too long and have exactly the degree of difficulty appropriate for the students at a particular stage in their studies. But if a text is too long and/or too difficult, the task can be made easier by a specific type of translating instructions: e.g. translation only of certain text parts combined with cursory reading and a TL summary (another form of translation that can be justified by the translating instructions).

The use of authentic texts-in-situation must, then, be a basic principle for translation classes but there should also be some form of classification.[41] Such a classification can be achieved in a variety of ways. Using the model of text analysis as a guideline, we could, for example, introduce a classification according to extratextual factors: a typology of senders (e.g. with regard to status and role or factual knowledge), of intentions (e.g. various texts by one author representing different intentions), of addressees (e.g. texts by one author with the same intention addressed to different audiences), etc. It is perhaps useful to note that it is easier to spot the factor-specific differences if the variation is kept as small as possible, matching, as it were, "minimal pairs" of texts or text types.

Example 4.1.1./1

If we compare two recipes, written by the same author under equal conditions of time and space and published in two recipe books, one for children and the other for experienced housewives, the audience-specific features of content (including presuppositions), style (including conventions) and non-verbal elements can be discovered much more easily than if we compare two recipes, written by two different authors under different conditions of time and space and published one in a recipe book for children and the other in a women's magazine.

---

[41]For translation in the training of foreign language teachers, Reiss recommends consideration of the following aspects: text type, subject matter (with regard to the motivation and the level of knowledge of the learners), direction of transfer (with regard to translatable text types), and degree of difficulty of the text (with regard to complexity of expression and argumentation, degree of culture-boundness, and peculiarities of the text specimen) (Reiss 1977: 541ff., my translation). These are very heterogeneous aspects, which may become relevant to the selection of training material in various ways.

Intratextual factors can also be used as a criterion for classification. For one translation course, the teacher may choose several texts dealing with the same subject matter (cf. example 3.1.4./2), or texts with similar sets of presuppositions (e.g. texts on certain culture-specific realities of either the source or the target culture), or texts with similar features of lexis and sentence structure (e.g. texts on the same subject, which belong to different genres – or vice versa) etc. Secondary teaching aims, such as the imparting of a specific cultural, factual or linguistic knowledge (e.g. the educational system of the source culture, literary works, terminology) can also be taken into account.[42]

This rough classification can be further refined by selecting texts with specific combinations of intratextual and extratextual factors. If the analytical model is applied consistently to all texts chosen for the translation class, the teacher will be able to coordinate the material according to similar or different text features. After working in class on a text embodying a particular combination of factors the students may be able to intensify their training by translating other texts with the same combination of factors individually or in small groups at home. On a lower level of transfer competence, this method of text selection does, of course, involve a certain amount of schematization and methodological reduction to types of translation problems. This just has to be accepted. The benefit here is that the learners do not get confused and demotivated by the plethora of problems they have to solve. Too many different problems will make success impossible to achieve.

The spectrum of possible translation strategies should therefore be kept to a minimum in the beginning. But it must definitely be expanded at an advanced stage in translation learning. Of course, van den Broeck (1978: 96) is absolutely right when he says:

> Translation didactics may consider it its proper task to give useful directions and to outline possible strategies as to the way in which such adaptations will advance the production of optimum translations. Teachers of translation may be tempted to fulfil this task by imposing stringent rules which they assume will lead to the right solutions for apparently uniform problems. But it seems more reasonable to leave the door open to a more diversified number of possi-

---

[42]Some of these factors have been considered by Arntz (1982: 111 or 1984: 206), who suggests a classification of texts according to the degree of specialization. 1. general texts, i.e. texts for non-technical communication; 2. technical texts in the wider sense (popularizing texts), in which experts speak to a lay readership about a particular field of knowledge; 3. technical texts in the narrower sense, i.e. texts for the technical communication between experts.

ble strategies, even so much so that the translator can manifest his freedom in choosing alternative strategies according to norms he judges most suitable to his purpose.

These last considerations on text selection already raise the question of learning progression (i.e. the sequence of texts used in class). Translation practice books usually grade texts in three or four levels from "easy" to "difficult", but most of them do not justify their classification. In the examinations at the Heidelberg School of Translating and Interpreting, for example, the texts presented for translation in the C-language[43] have to be "easier" than those presented in the B-language. Translators' fees are also scaled according to the "degree of difficulty" of the translation. Thus, the fee for a highly specialized texts is higher than for a general text, the translation of a text written in one of the "minor" languages (e.g. Vietnamese) will cost more than one written in French or Spanish, and the translation into the foreign language is more expensive than that into the native tongue, etc. But what has this got to do with "difficulty"?

In my view, "difficulty" is not an inherent quality of texts. For somebody with a perfect knowledge of Vietnamese and a poor knowledge of French, translation from German into Vietnamese will not be more difficult than from German into French (so, the higher price is just a matter of supply and demand). In the following chapter I will outline the factors determining the degree of difficulty of a translation task, using the factors of analysis as a frame of reference.

4.1.2. Grading the difficulty of translation tasks

In translation practice, we have to assume that the professional translator is fully competent in the three fields of language, subject matter, and transfer procedures. In this case, the degree of difficulty presented by a translation task derives from the particular features of the source text-in-situation[44]. In translation teaching, however, we have to take

---

[43]According to the standards of international institutions for translation and interpreting (AIIC, FIT), languages are classified in the following way. **A:** The native language (or another language strictly equivalent to a native language), into which the interpreter/translator works from all her or his other languages, **B:** A language other than the interpreter's native language, of which she or he has a perfect command and into which she or he works from one or more of her or his other languages, **C:** Languages, of which the interpreter/translator has a complete understanding and from which she or he works (cf. www.aiic.net).

[44]Reiss (1974b: 5) distinguishes three dimensions: a) linguistic difficulties (e.g. concerning the syntactic and semantic structure of the text), b) factual difficulties (e.g.

account of the level of proficiency the students have at a certain level of training, regarding not only their transfer competence but also their command of SL and TL. Therefore, the degree of difficulty presented by a translation task is often measured by linguistic criteria.[45]

A purely linguistic description of the phenomenon, though, does not shed a great deal of light. Difficulties in translation do not only result from the nature of a source text and its situation in relation to all the possibilities of the target language. They also depend on the level of knowledge and competence of the translator, on the translation skopos (i.e. the stylistic, functional, and pragmatic qualities required of the target text), as well as on the (technical) working conditions which the translator has to cope with. The translator-dependent factors are of particular importance from the didactic point of view since they are the ones to be influenced by teaching. But they also affect the practice of professional translation, e.g. as far as the different assessment of translations into the native language and translations into the foreign language are concerned. Working conditions, too, have a considerable effect on both practice and teaching. For example, technical details such as the lack of dictionaries or documentation material, pressure of time, poor remuneration, high standards demanded for the presentation of the target text (camera-ready manuscript, electronic storage in a particular format, etc.) – all determine the degree of difficulty of a translation task.

It would appear necessary, therefore, to distinguish between translation difficulties and translation problems (cf. Nord 1987a). A translation *problem* is an objective (or inter-subjective) transfer task

---

concerning the content of the text), and c) technical difficulties (e.g. concerning the formal presentation of the text), but she does not specify the determinants of difficulty. Thus, in the dimension of linguistic difficulties, she lists the following aspects: "stylistic level" (which is an intratextual feature of ST), "ST function" (which is an extratextual feature of ST), "direction of transfer" (which is a translator-dependent factor), and "TT function" (which is a transfer-related factor). Reiss does not mention any aspects related to the target text.

[45]On the basis of an ST/TT comparison, Thiel (1975: 24) states "a posteriori", that "a translation difficulty occurs whenever the translation of an ST segment requires a compulsory change in semantics and/or in formal means" (my translation). And Wilss, who distinguishes "transfer-specific translation difficulties (TD)", "translator-specific TD", "text-type-specific TD", and "single-text-specific TD" (1982: 161), limits the didactic applications to L2-L1 translations. Thus, he arrives at a purely linguistic definition of translation difficulty: "TD occur whenever a lexical or syntactic one-to-one correspondence between SLT and TLT cannot be practised, because literal translation would inevitably entail a negative transfer" (ib.: 164).

which every translator (irrespective of their level of competence and of the technical working conditions) has to solve during a particular translation process. There are four categories of translation problem, which will be discussed in more detail below: (a) pragmatic translation problems (PTP) arising from the contrast between the situation in which the source text is or was used and the situation for which the target text is produced (e.g. the audience-orientation of a text or deictic references to time or place), (b) convention-related translation problems (CTP) arising from the differences in behaviour conventions between the source and the target culture (e.g. text-type conventions, measurement conventions, translation conventions), (c) linguistic translation problems (LTP) arising from the structural differences between source and target language (e.g. the translation of the English gerund into German or of German modal particles into Spanish), (d) text-specific translation problems (TTP) arising from the particular characteristics of the source text (e.g. the translation of a play on words).

Translation *difficulties*, on the other hand, are subjective and have to do with the individual translator and the specific working conditions. A particular translation problem which seems very difficult to the beginner will remain a translation problem, even when the student has learned to cope with it. It can turn into a difficulty again, though, if the translator has to solve it without the necessary technical resources (cf. Nord 1997d).

A particular textual phenomenon, e.g. a pun, is a (text-specific) translation problem. The translator has to find out its function in and for the source text in order to decide whether or not the translation skopos requires the transfer of the pun to the target text. If it does not, the translation problem "pun" is solved, for instance, by translating the general sense of the passage and omitting the pun (= zero equivalence). If the translation skopos requires the transfer of the pun, the translator will have to analyse first the (culture-specific) general use and the normal effect of puns in this particular genre, then the structural possibilities of making a TL pun in this or some other passage of the text, and, lastly, the (pragmatic) consequences which the transfer of the pun will have for the intention of the sender or for the effect of the whole text. The degree of difficulty which this problem presents to the translator depends on the text type, on the language pair, and on the cultural distance between SC and TC, as well as on the factual, linguistic, and transfer competence of the translator.

In order to specify the degree of difficulty of a translation task in translation teaching, we have to take account of the following parameters, which belong to different phases of the translation process: (a) the "absolute" degree of difficulty of the source text (in the phase of ST analysis), (b) the level of knowledge and competence of the translator (factual knowledge, SL competence, transfer competence, TL competence, in all three phases), (c) the translating instructions and the pragmatic, cultural, and linguistic translation problems they involve (in the phases of transfer and TT production), and (d) the technical and working conditions (in the phases of ST analysis and TT production).

These parameters lead to four categories of translation difficulty (text-specific difficulties, translator-dependent difficulties, pragmatic difficulties, and technical difficulties), which can be identified using the model of translation-relevant text analysis.

a. Text-specific difficulties

Text-specific difficulties are related to the degree of comprehensibility of the source text and can be discovered by going through the intratextual factors of text analysis, ignoring translator-dependent criteria as far as is possible. The degree of difficulty of a source text can be measured by analysing the quantity and complexity of content, the number of presuppositions (degree of redundancy), the degree of consistency and clearness of text composition (including theme-rheme structure), the complexity of ST structures in lexis and syntax, including any defects, the number of suprasegmental features which make comprehension easier, and the number and nature of non-verbal elements.

The degree of difficulty presented by the intratextual factors is determined by the amount of information the translator has on the extratextual dimensions. To put it simply: the more the translator knows about the situation in which the source text is, or was, used, the better the comprehensibility of the text. Thus, the teacher can control the degree of difficulty of the translation task by the amount of information she provides on the situation.

b. Translator-dependent difficulties

Text-specific difficulties exist, to some extent, even for the "ideal" translator with full competence (even though experience has taught her or him how to overcome or get around such difficulties). In translation teaching, these difficulties usually have to be related to the level of the learner's knowledge and competence. This applies not only to thematic or factual difficulties (e.g. the high level of abstraction of a particular source text), or to the cultural background knowledge, but also to any other intratextual factor, if they make excessive demands on the students' abilities at a particular period in their training).

It is fair to say, I think, that in translation teaching deficient linguistic competence in SL or TL is usually the biggest stumbling-block. The teacher should therefore take great care to ensure that the (source) text is not too difficult for the learner. Although, in principle, a full command of all lexical, syntactic and suprasegmental structures of SL and TL must be regarded as the basic requirement in translation courses, it may well often be impossible to stick to this principle in translator training, especially where the SL or TL is not included in the school curricula and has to be learned from scratch. Even in their native language the students cannot be "fully competent" in all possible text types and fields of knowledge. Translation teaching must therefore start at a certain "minimum level" of competence, which should be extended in special courses that are coordinated with the practical translation classes, until competence has reached the desired level.

From this point of view, the difference in degree of difficulty between direct translation (into the native language) and prose translation (into the foreign language) has to be regarded as being mainly translator-dependent. The active command of the native language will normally be higher than that of any foreign language, but the translator's proficiency in the foreign language can, of course, reach a very good standard for highly specialized translation tasks. In translation teaching, the translating instructions can take this into account. If the instructions ask for a draft translation which will then be revised by a native speaker who is not a translator but an expert in the field, a certain level of "interlanguage" can be tolerated temporarily, provided that the text is at least comprehensible for such an imaginary revisor. There are faults which do not affect comprehensibility, and formal incorrectness is not necessarily prejudicial to the overall communicative effect.

c. Pragmatic difficulties
Pragmatic difficulties are related to the nature of the translation task. Authentic texts are produced for a native-speaker audience who re-

ceives the text in a particular situation which will often facilitate comprehension. Such texts are not however addressed to a future translator (possibly belonging to another culture), whose level of knowledge (regarding the subject matter discussed in the text) may be limited. Therefore, the teacher has to "adjust" the authentic text to the teaching situation, not by simplifying (and thus falsifying) it, but by reducing the difficulty of the translation task using a specific kind of translation brief, which I call "didactic" translating instructions.

Accompanied by appropriate instructions, which, for example, exclude or reduce certain linguistic, cultural or factual difficulties, a text that is inherently difficult may be used in a translation task which can be accomplished even by a beginner. The factors of translation-oriented text analysis can again serve as a frame of reference. Difficulties regarding content, for instance, can be reduced by asking for a summarizing translation, whereas difficulties in the field of presuppositions can be reduced by a translation skopos which does not require any compensations.

Translator-dependent difficulties, too, can be reduced by the translating instructions. To give just one example: it is relatively easy for the students to translate a text whose addressee is very similar to themselves, e.g. students at a school of translating and interpreting!

If the translating instructions require a target text corresponding to target-cultural conventions, difficulties in the field of SL competence assume less importance. There are even cases where relatively little TL competence is required. Translating a driving-licence, for instance, the translator often only has to fill in a pre-existing target-cultural form with certain data (name, date of birth, nationality, etc.) provided by the source-cultural form.

Of course, the teacher could also use the translating instructions as a method of increasing the degree of difficulty, e.g. by asking either for a change in certain situational factors, especially text function, or for an equivalence of effect despite a great cultural distance. This may present additional problems of translation which the learners cannot cope with unless they have been prepared specifically for such a task. This procedure is not to be recommended for translator training.

d. Technical difficulties
In those cases where the translation task presents too many difficulties or if the difficulties are too complex in relation to the level of the learner's knowledge and competence, the task can be made easier by

reducing the technical difficulties of research and documentation. In the introductory phase, the teacher may, for example, provide additional material in SL and/or TL. Such material might be "parallel texts" (i.e. TL texts on the same subject matter, belonging to the same genre as the ST), "model texts" (same subject matter, same genre, and even same genre variety, which allows the parallel text to be used as a model in lexis, sentence structures, and register features), "comparative texts" (same subject matter, different genre), or "background texts" (texts containing background information on the subject matter, e.g. encyclopedic texts) etc. In a second phase, the students would have to try and find this material themselves. This method allows the translation not only of texts belonging to the students' sphere of personal experience, but also of those texts which at a very early stage of their training appear to be rather difficult from the linguistic and factual point of view. The interesting thing is that by using these auxiliary texts the students manage to accomplish the translation task very well without recourse to bilingual dictionaries or other reference works (cf. Nord 1997f).

These are measures which affect the working conditions of the trainee translator, since the degree of difficulty of a translation task can also be controlled by altering the technical details. For instance, the availability of documentation material, terminologies and data banks, comparative, parallel, or model TL texts make the task easier, whereas the lack or restricted availability of auxiliary material increases the degree of difficulty. To translate a specialized text into a foreign language with nothing more than a monolingual TL dictionary to hand is terribly hard – and yet this is precisely what is still asked of students in certain examinations at certain translator-training institutions.

In my view, the students must learn to use any means of documentation and research available, including electronic tools and memory systems, and they must learn to use them efficiently, that is, within a certain time limit (which is a very important, if not the most important, factor in the practice of professional translation). The same applies to technical aids, such as typewriters, computers, dictating machines, etc., which are also components of the translator's working situation and which they must familiarize themselves with during the training period.

4.1.3. Grading the difficulty of translation texts

Reiss (1975: 46f.) classifies the degree of difficulty of a particular text by means of index numbers. The level of knowledge and competence of the group of learners plays no part in this classification. However, in the course of a teaching unit (e.g. a thirty-hour translation course over one semester) or a particular phase of study (e.g. a basic course in translation from Spanish to English over two years) the students' knowledge of certain components (e.g. vocabulary or genre conventions) can be built up and extended in a continuous process. Thus, at the end of a teaching-unit, and after careful and systematic preparation, the relative degree of difficulty of one and the same text will be lower than it was at the beginning.

This means that the learning progression has to be carefully planned for the whole unit or course. At the same time, all the other subjects taught throughout the training of professional translators should be coordinated with the translation classes in the form of a syllabus, whether they affect content (e.g. factual or cultural knowledge), linguistic competence (e.g. grammar and style of the languages involved) or transfer competence (e.g. theories and methods of translation). Only then will it be possible to establish a logical progression in translation teaching.

Let me give just a rough outline of such a progression. At the basic level, we start working with highly conventionalized, transcultural or universal text types, whose constellation of factors allows little variation, and whose intratextual features are conventional (text-specific difficulties). These texts should deal with subject matters belonging to the students sphere of personal experience, and the ST genre conventions should be familiar to the students. The conventions of the target culture should be rather rigid and known to the translators (translator-dependent difficulties). The translation skopos should be defined in detail by unambiguous translating instructions, and require the preservation of situational factors (pragmatic difficulties). The source-text should be free of faults and presented in its original form, and the teacher should provide sufficient TL auxiliary material (parallel and model texts) (= technical difficulties).

If the task is prepared in this way, the beginners will be able to cope with it easily, having to produce a TT by more or less copying an existing TL model. Difficulties arising from lack of proficiency in the languages will be largely non-existent. The learners soon experience a feeling of success and, what is more, realize what professional translation is all about. They will not even think of translating SL words, phrases and sentences, as was normal practice in foreign language classes at school.

As this basic level is left behind, the difficulties are gradually increased. The teacher chooses source texts which are less conventionalized, which are no longer fault-free, or which contain appellative language (text-specific difficulties). In my view, the text-specific difficulties should never put too great a strain on the linguistic competence of the learner group concerned, as otherwise the translation class inevitably turns into a foreign-language class. If necessary, linguistic competence can be extended in coordinated preceding or parallel language courses.

As the transfer competence of the learner increases with every text that is analysed and translated in the classroom, so the translator-dependent difficulties keep diminishing, as it were, from text to text. Accordingly, the degree of difficulty of the translation task can be raised step by step, as regards both the extratextual and the intratextual factors. The requirement to change certain factors (e.g. audience orientation, dimensions of time and place) or to establish equivalence on various ranks of the text will present additional difficulties. However, establishing equivalence is one of the most difficult tasks in translator training. The teacher should, therefore, take great care that from one translation task to the next certain aspects of the translating instructions remain the same in order to achieve a slow teaching progression. We must never forget that, even though "persistence spells success", only success spells encouragement.

In my experience, an instrumental translation is not generally more difficult than a documentary translation. Indeed, the tasks I have suggested for the basic phase of translation teaching all involve instrumental translation. However, a documentary translation can be easier in those cases where the translator is allowed to give the necessary information on the original situation (sender, time, place, medium, etc.) outside the text (e.g. in an introductory lead) and does not have to integrate it into the target text (cf. the Spanish-German translation course proposed in Nord 2001d).

It is interesting to note that the translation task is not necessarily made any easier by reducing the unit of translation (as Königs, 1981: 83f., seems to suggest). On the contrary, the equifunctional translation of a morpheme, which the author has used intentionally as a "relevant feature" in order to achieve a particular stylistic effect (cf. the example of a grapheme as a translation unit given by Toury 1983) is much more difficult than the equifunctional translation of a conventionalized text which has to be transferred as a whole into an equally conventionalized target situation.

4.2. Classifying translation problems

As has already been mentioned before, the middle column of Figure 8 describes the transfer of the "material" provided by the source text (listed in the left-hand column) to the (prospective) target situation (defined by the right-hand column). It also refers to any considerations arising from the transfer as such, outlining the translation task (What translation problems have to be solved?), the translation strategy or method (What are the potential procedures of translation and adaptation?), and the translation procedure itself (By which procedure will the required purpose be best achieved?)

In contrast to the concept of "translation difficulty", which, as described in the preceding chapter, allows a grading of the texts selected for a particular teaching-unit, the concept of "translation problem" is useful for structuring teaching and learning aims in the field of transfer competence. By classifying the translation problems presented by a particular text, or all texts chosen for a particular teaching unit, the teacher has a guideline as to which aspects of translation are to be dealt with in the course. At the same time, the students learn to distinguish the objective translation problems from their (subjective) translation difficulties, and in so doing can judge the level of competence they have achieved at a certain stage.

If we want to classify translation problems, we can use the factors in the model of translation-relevant text analysis as a frame of reference, as shown in Figure 8. As has been indicated above, translation problems can also be classified in four categories, which are listed below according to their "generalizability" from those problems which occur in any translation task to those which are only present in one concrete translation task (for more details cf. 1992a: 45-47, 1993: 205ff., 1997a: 64-67).

a. Pragmatic translation problems
Every source text can be translated into different target languages aiming at different translation purposes. Thus, the first set of translation problems arises from the particular transfer situation with its specific

contrast of ST vs. TT receivers, ST vs. TT medium, motive for ST production vs. motive for translation (= TT production), ST function vs. TT function, etc. Since these problems are present in any imaginable translation task, they can be generalized irrespective of the languages and cultures involved or of the direction of translation (into or out of the foreign language), etc. The examples show that pragmatic translation problems can be identified using the extratextual factors of the text-analytical model. In the introductory phases of translation teaching, I would recommend checking every single extratextual factor for potential pragmatic translation problems.

b. Convention-related translation problems[46]
Translating from one particular culture into another, certain translation problems may arise which would not occur between two other cultures. These problems are a result of the differences in culture-specific (verbal or non-verbal) habits, norms and conventions. To give an exhaustive list of these kinds of translation problem, we would need some kind of "comparative culture studies", which, as far as I know, does not yet exist. Therefore we have to resort to the eclectic procedure of collecting cultural translation problems as we find them, e.g. genre conventions, general style conventions, measuring conventions, formal conventions of marking certain elements in a text (e.g. in metalinguistic contexts), etc.

Basically, these problems are also present in every translation task, but in depending on the particular cultures or culture groups they may have to be dealt with differently.

c. Linguistic translation problems
The structural differences between two languages, particularly in lexis and sentence structure, give rise to certain translation problems which occur in every translation involving this pair of languages, no matter which of the two serves as source and which serves as target language. Contrastive grammar and some approaches to a kind of "didactic translational grammar" (cf. Raabe 1979) provide valuable help in solving these problems.

---

[46]The term "(inter)cultural translation problems", which was used in earlier publications, has given to misunderstandings because students thought that the category included problems related to culture-specific realities. I therefore replaced it with the less ambiguous term "convention-related translation problems".

In this context we have to distinguish clearly between problems of language performance and translation problems proper. The specific stylistic value of Latinisms in German texts (cf. Reiss [1976b] 1981: 132), although it may cause difficulties "in translation", is not, as such, a translation problem, but an intralingual problem of language performance. But since in Spanish the apparent (etymological) equivalents of these German latinisms are not stylistically marked, the translation of etymologically related words (so-called cognates) appears to be a general stylistic and semantic problem that arises in every Spanish-German and German-Spanish translation (and similarly between German and other Romance languages). The same applies, for example, to the use of the subjunctive in German indirect speech (cf. Poulsen 1984) or of auxiliary verbs in Italian (cf. Arcaini 1984). Only when contrasted with a target language which presents more, or fewer, or other semantic or stylistic differentiations, do these intralingual phenomena turn out to be translation problems. Since there are no general rules for their solution, the teacher can only raise the students' awareness to these problems by stressing their relationship to text function, register, audience orientation, etc.

d. Text-specific translation problems

Any problem arising in a particular text specimen which cannot be classified as pragmatic, convention-related or linguistic, has to be regarded as "text-specific", which means that its occurrence in a particular text is a special case. Figures of speech and individual word creations are examples of such problems. Since these problems do not fall under any one general heading and a solution found for one of them in a particular translation task does not allow for generalization, they should be avoided in the basic phase of translation teaching.

So, then, for the student as well as for the teacher, the middle column of the schema serves as a record of the translation problems dealt with when translating a particular text in class. The schemata filled in for all the texts translated during a particular course give an indication of the frequency and distribution of certain translation problems. Thus, the schemata provide a list of subjects in the field of transfer competence, which might then be used as a frame of reference when learning progress has to be tested at the end of a translation course.

We should bear in mind, however, as Wilss (1982: 192) rightly points out, that even the most sophisticated TT (translation teaching) checklist is only of partial help. This would compel the translator to take refuge in non-generalizable creative thinking and rather unique transfer procedures.

Nevertheless, if we want to achieve a solid foundation for translation teaching we have to seize any opportunity, however small, which allows some degree of systematization. By identifying translation problems in the very first phase of the translation process, the model of translation-oriented text analysis can help to make translation teaching more efficient.

4.3. Testing transfer competence

After every phase of training, before a new phase begins, the competence of the learners should be tested. In the following chapter I shall discuss some methods of testing transfer competence.

At universities which run courses for translator training, the only method of monitoring learning progress appears at present to be the translation of a text. The source-text material used for exams is selected almost exclusively according to the degree of text-specific difficulty. The evaluation and assessment of what the students have learnt so far is based on the result of the process of translation (both in the native language and in the foreign language) even in intermediate examinations, although there is often no means of verifying whether the solutions the teacher expects the students to produce have, in fact, been taught. (This is especially true with the translation of non-specialized texts.) This practice is not satisfactory for several reasons.

(a) In order to translate a complete text, the students require not only transfer competence, but also linguistic competence in SL and TL, cultural competence in SC and TC, as well as factual and research competence. In a translation task, all these competences are tested at once, and a translation error does not allow to identify the kind of competence that was deficient. Some errors may even be due to a "technical translation difficulty", e.g. lack of reference material during the exam.

As long as translation teaching continues to start before a certain level of linguistic, cultural etc. competence has been acquired and as long as texts for examinations are selected according to the degree of text-specific difficulty they present, instead of adjusting them to the predictable level of the learners' knowledge, students will continue to be in the invidious position of not being able to demonstrate their transfer competence because the source text is just too difficult for them to analyse or understand!

(b) If the only criterion that the examination regulations provide for the selection of test material is that it has to be either a "general" or a "specialized" text, then practically any conceivable translation problem can occur in such a text. This may well make sense in the final examinations, since a professional translator should be in a position to cope with any conceivable translation problem. However, in intermediate examinations teachers should clearly state what they expect the learner to know at this particular stage. The student can only solve adequately those problems that have been dealt with in class or whose solution can be found by analogy. This principle is normal practice in any other professional training, whereas trainee translators can only achieve the best mark if they present a perfect solution to all the problems present in the text (irrespective of whether they have worked on them before or not).

(c) In an examination, students are not normally allowed to comment on the solutions they have chosen in their translation. It is up to the teacher to decide whether to mark any information which is not reproduced in the TT as an "omission" or to regard it as a functional reduction (which may even deserve a "plus mark" for pragmatic adequacy) of some information which can be expected to belong to the TT receiver's culture-specific horizon. Also, if a student knows in theory how to solve a certain problem, but has TL difficulties in putting theory into practice, s/he might briefly outline the procedure for the solution. Then, the teacher could give a mark for "partial success".

In my opinion, by using the model of translation-oriented text analysis and the translating instructions as a frame of reference we might arrive at a more objective way of testing the actual progress a student has made in the course of training. First of all, the systematization of translation problems in a schema similar to Figure 8 enables the teacher to identify those problems which have been dealt with in class and those which have not. If a certain set of translation problems is established as compulsory in the training syllabus, the examiner can make sure that the examination text does not present any new or unfamiliar translation problems or – and this seems more realistic – that such problems, at least, are not included in the evaluation.

The systematization of translation purposes in class leads to clearer methodology in translation teaching and gives the learners more self-confidence with regard to the expectations of the teacher or

examiner. The learners must get accustomed to receiving clear translating instructions or to formulating their own translation skopos, which
will then serve as the frame of reference against which the functionality of the translation can be evaluated.

Both in the classroom and in the examination, the students
should be encouraged to comment on their translations and/or to justify certain solutions, using the concepts and terms of translation theory
and methodology. Holz-Mänttäri (1984b: 180) even suggests that, for
examinations, students should hand in (together with, or instead of, a
translation) a "work log" with annotations on every translational decision, stating what tools have been used in the translation. Such a log
would allow the examiner to analyse the process and not the resultant
translation and to assess the adequacy of methods in a given working
situation.

Other forms of testing transfer competence would be to ask the
students to fill in a middle column of the schema of text analysis and
translation skopos (Fig. 8) or to comment on a translation produced by
themselves or somebody else (cf. Reiss 1984: 79) using the schema as
a frame of reference. Such exercises would make it easier for the
translation teacher to give a diagnosis of the students' competence,
telling them which areas are deficient and which not. Error therapy
would benefit enormously from this procedure.

4.4. Assessing translation quality

4.4.0. Forms and functions of translation criticism
Book reviewers rarely comment on the quality of a translation because
normally a translated book is reviewed as if it were an original. If
there is any reference to the book being a translation, the assessment is
usually based entirely on a rather superficial analysis of the translation
in relation to the target-cultural norms of language and literature. In
other words, what is being reviewed is the product of the translation
process. Therefore, this form of translation criticism (or rather, target-
text assessment, because there is no way of judging the ST/TT relationship from only looking at the target text) is more relevant to the
didactics of linguistics or literary studies than to translation teaching.
For our purposes it could only be used as an indirect means of sensitizing the students to any contraventions of lexical or syntactical
norms or of cultivating linguistic awareness, especially regarding the
native language. Since most translations have to prove their function-

ality independent of the source text in a target-cultural situation, both
Reiss (1971) and Koller (1979) suggest that this form of target-text
assessment could be a first step in translation criticism.

My model of translation-relevant text analysis might be used for
such an analysis of the target text, and the results can be compared
with the general idiomatic, stylistic, literary and textual norms of the
target culture. Target-text assessment should not, however, be used as
a means of error prevention, because if presented in black and white,
typical mistranslations (e.g. the literal translation of English clefting
constructions into German or of "false friends") might easily become
irradicably fixed in the mind.

A more objective form of translation criticism should be based
on a comparative analysis of both the source and the target text and
should provide information about the similarities and differences of
SL and TL structures represented in both texts, as well as about the individual process of translation and the strategies and methods used. It
should also show whether the target text is appropriate for the required
translation skopos. This type of translation criticism is mainly concerned with the factors and constituents determining the process of
translation and the translation process itself.

The mere comparison of structures between source and target
text cannot, strictly speaking, be regarded as translation criticism. It
belongs to the sphere of language or text comparison, which is used in
contrastive linguistics and stylistics in order to ensure that no extra or
intralinguistic variables come into play. This procedure can be of little
use here since translation didactics has to take account of the extralinguistic conditions of the translation process (such as the purpose and
methods of translation serving as a frame of reference for the translator) as well. Translating is much more than a mere linguistic code-
switching operation.

If translation criticism is to be relevant to translation teaching, it
has to integrate both methods: the analysis and assessment of the
translation process and its determinants (including translation skopos
and brief) and the evaluation of the target text and its functionality for
a given purpose.

Such translation criticism is important for both teachers and
learners. Whereas in translating the learners are themselves part of,
and involved in, the translation process, in translation criticism they
can watch the process from outside and analyse its constituents at a
distance. They can then describe the product of this process and, by

contrasting it with the source text, reconstruct the process and compare it with the frame of reference provided by translation theory. Such an analysis can yield valuable insights into translating activities. This is why Reiss (1974c: 36; 1977: 540) suggests that translation comparison and translation criticism should have their place in an introductory phase of translator training.

Later on, in their professional life, the students may also require the ability to assess the quality of a translation, since in industry or administration translators are often employed as translation revisors. In such a position they should be able not only to assess and/or correct the translations of their colleagues but also to justify their corrections by reasoned arguments (cf. Reiss 1986: 3).

For translation teachers, translation criticism mainly means identifying, classifying and evaluating translation errors in order to develop methods of error prevention and error therapy. They may also want to find criteria for the marking of particularly successful solutions – how are they to be accounted for in the evaluation of a translation?

4.4.1. Translation criticism vs. translation comparison

If translation criticism is to be more than a mere target-text assessment, it must be based on a comparison of the source text with the target text, which is sometimes called "translation comparison" (cf. Koller 1979: 219f.). Since the term is ambiguous and blurs the distinction between the comparison of one ST and its TT, on the one hand, and the comparison of different translations of one ST, on the other, I shall speak of ST/TT comparison.

Reiss (1981a: 312) distinguishes various forms of ST/TT comparison which will be briefly discussed in the following paragraphs.

Intralingual ST/TT comparison (i.e. comparing various SL versions of one original, or various TL versions, in one particular target language, of one original) has its place in the area of the development of L1 and L2 competence in a pre-translation course, whereas interlingual ST/TT comparison (i.e. comparing the different translations in one or various target languages with the original) can serve as a good introduction to, or first step in, translator training.

Interlingual ST/TT comparison starts by comparing the source text and the target text(s), which will give some information about the translation process. The students can analyse and describe translation types, translation strategies or methods, and translation procedures

without themselves having to enter into the complex task of translating. In a second step, when the learners' theoretical and methodological knowledge has been consolidated, the ST/TT comparison is complemented by translation criticism.

Translation criticism requires a theoretical frame of reference,
i.e. a set of criteria for the assessment of the translation. There are several ways of establishing such a frame of reference. The translator
may have commented on her or his theoretical principles of translation
in a preface or in a postscript at the end of the book, but in most cases,
translation critics must infer or reconstruct these principles as a kind
of "tertium comparationis" between the source and the target text and
check whether they have been consistently applied in translation, before they can use them as a frame of reference. Another standard for
translation quality assessment could be the translation critic's own
view of the translation skopos. In each case, the ST/TT comparison as
well as the translation critique can be based on the model of translation-oriented text analysis, as will be shown in more detail in the following chapter.

4.4.2. A didactic model of translation criticism

Translation critics proceeds, as it were, in an anti-clockwise direction;
they must work back from the result to the beginning. If this principle
is applied to the process of translation as represented in Figure 4, the
process of translation criticism (cf. Figure 9) has to begin with an analysis of the target text-in-situation which is based on the model developed in this study. In the course of TT analysis the translation critic
will have to check whether the target text is coherent with the situation
in which it is "functioning" and whether it is in fact suitable for per-
forming the function derived from the constellation of extratextual
factors. The results of this TT analysis are then entered into the right-
hand column of the schema represented in Figure 8. This first part of
the process of translation criticism more or less corresponds to the TT
assessment suggested by Reiss and Koller. However, it is not confined
to a mere intratextual analysis of grammatical, lexical, and stylistic
normativity and semantic coherence, since it includes extratextual factors such as the pragmatic dimensions of receiver, time, place, etc.

Example 4.4.2./1
The first paragraph of a notice in Spanish, French, and German, distributed on
the beach of Cullera/Valencia, Spain, reads as follows:

ATENCION BAÑISTAS: Presten atención en todo momento a las banderas de señalización colocadas en las torres de vigilancia de las playas y obedezcan los consejos de los salvavidas. El significado de las banderas es el siguiente: [...]
ATTENTION BAIGNEURS: Faites attention à tout moment aux drapeaux de signalisation installés dans les tours de surveillance des plages et suivez les conseils des agents de sauvetage. La signification des drapeaux est la suivante: [...]
VORSICHT BADENDER: Passen Sie auf die Regelungsfahnen, die auf der Aufsichttürmen am Strand sind und gehorchen Sie die Ratschläge der Retter. Die Fahnenbedeutung ist folgende: [...]

As far as normativity is concerned, the translations, particularly the German version, would not be acceptable, of course. But the situation was clear: everybody could see the observation posts with their flags in the "international" colours red, green and yellow, and the lifeguards kept walking up and down the beach, calling people back who were swimming too far out into the open sea. In this situation, the texts could accomplish the intended function (information + warning) in spite of the linguistic and stylistic defects. Although the immediate effect that the text had on the bathers may have changed from "being impressed by the authoritative notice" to "being amused by the unidiomatic translation", the effect "complying with the instruction" must also have been achieved, since German and French visitors were not seen to be more daring than the readers of the Spanish original.

Neither this first step not the other phases of the process of translation criticism are concerned with error analysis of small segments of the text. While not wishing to defend any "pseudo-translations" such as those quoted in the example, which are, of course, a result of deficient TL and transfer competence, I would like to stress the view that it is the text as a whole whose function(s) and effect(s) must be regarded as the crucial criteria for translation criticism.

The next step in the process of translation criticism depends on whether there is any explicit information about the transfer phase, i.e. about the intended translation skopos, the methods and procedures of translation, the handling of certain translation problems, etc. If such information is available from the translator him or herself, the editor, or the initiator, perhaps in a preface or postscript or in a blurb, it can be entered in the middle column of the schema. If there is no such information, the second step in the process of translation criticism will be source-text analysis (documented in the left-hand column of the schema). In this case, the critic has to reconstruct the implicit princi-

ples of transfer by contrasting target and source text and then filling in
the middle column in a third step.

Like the TT-in-situation, the ST-in-situation is analysed according to the model of translation-relevant text analysis. If the translation
skopos is known, the ST analysis can be confined to the skopos-rele-
vant factors. In any case the critic has to pay particular attention to
those factors which have been stated as "problematic" during TT assessment (e.g. coherence deficiencies, inconsistent terminology, inter-
ferences in lexis or sentence structure, ambiguous audience orientation, etc.). The combination of ST analysis with the explicit information on the transfer principles results in a TT profile (cf. House 1981b:
52), which may then serve as a frame of reference for the assessment
of the actual translation result.

Reconstructing the implicit principles and methods of transfer
by ST/TT comparison also leads to a TT profile. In this case, translation critics can check the consistency of strategies only against the inferred transfer principles and cannot use their own methodological
standards as a frame of reference for translation criticism. If, however,
the translation brief has been formulated explicitly and is known to the
critic, it can be used as a basis for establishing a TT profile. But whatever the case, actual translation criticism consists in comparing the TT
profile and the target text itself. If the TT profile is congruent with the
target text, the translation can be regarded as functionally adequate.

After analysing and interpreting the source text, on the one
hand, and the target situation, on the other, the translation critic may
come to the conclusion that the method chosen by the translator was
not adequate. In this case, it is not enough to judge the target text on
the basis of ones own transfer principles; fair criticism would require a
"comparison of methods". This means that two middle columns of the
schema have to be filled in, one representing the method used by the
translator, and the other representing that of the critic. Two right-hand
columns, one representing the target text which is being criticized, and
the other representing a target text produced according to the critic's
method, can then be compared. They will show which of the two methods is more suitable for achieving the required TT function.

As has already been mentioned, the direction of the process of
translation criticism runs counter to that of the process of translation.
Where the translator has stated her transfer strategies explicitly, then
the starting point for the translation critic will be the analysis of the
TT-in-situation, and where the transfer strategies have to be inferred

from an ST/TT comparison, then the process of criticism starts with the analysis of the ST-in-situation.

The diagram shows that translation criticism is not concerned with comparing single ST elements or segments but with contrasting two texts-in-situation. Although each of the two texts is a text in its own right, there is, as it were, a certain relationship of coherence between them, which is defined by the translation skopos. The "units" to be translated are not linguistic units as such, but they are units which are established by translation-oriented text analysis.

Figure 9: Translation criticism

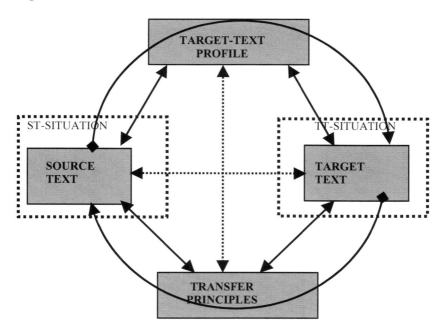

This means that a translation critique, which judges a text as a whole, is able to take account of compensatory solutions, such as inserting a completely different TL pun at another point in the text rather than trying to transfer the ST pun in its original position. According to my model, translation units are not "individual" units which depend on the translator's transfer competence, as Königs (1981: 90f.) suggests, but are units which in any given translation task can be identified right at the start. Unlike Königs (1981: 89), who distinguishes between

"analytical" and "processual" translation units, I do not consider it necessary, for the process of translation criticism, to work with translation units different from those used in the process of translation itself.
"Translation units" are, in my opinion, neither words not sentences,
but "relevant features" (cf. Toury 1983), ranging from the isotopic
level (cf. Poulsen 1981: 302f.) via the theme-rheme structure or a
metaphor to the grapheme (cf. the example given by Toury 1983).
This concept of translation unit has considerable consequences for the
definition of what is a translation error (for a more detailed discussion
of my concept of a "functional translation unit" see Nord 1997e).

4.4.3. Defining translation errors
In traditional philology, in foreign language teaching, and in other disciplines of applied linguistics, such as contrastive linguistics and psy-
cholinguistics, the question of how to define a (linguistic) error, how
to detect an error and, above all, how to develop efficient error therapy
has been under discussion for quite some time, whereas in translation
studies error analysis has been dealt with only peripherally so far (e.g.
Wilss 1982: 196 ff.).

It is fairly common practice to define an error as a deviation
from a certain norm, convention or a system of rules (cf. Cherubim
1980: 126f.). Applied to verbal utterances, such a deviation is often
specified as a "deviation from the selected model of grammar" (Presch
1980: 229). Accordingly, a translation error is defined as "an offence
against a norm in a linguistic contact situation", which, as Wilss
points out, may be the result of deficient linguistic competence or of a
lack of comprehension due to deficient factual knowledge (Wilss
1982: 201). What we have here are two completely different types of
error: a "lack of comprehension" is a part linguistic and part pragmatic
error linked to the phase of text reception, whereas an "offence against
norms of usage" may occur either in the phase of transfer, due to deficient transfer competence, or in the phase of TT production, due to deficient TL competence.

In contrast to this concept of error analysis I would like to suggest a functionalist view, namely that a particular expression or utterance does not in itself have the quality of being incorrect, but that it is
assigned that quality by the receiver in the light of a particular norm or

standard.[47] Translation errors show up against the overriding criterion of translation skopos and are linked to the factors listed in the analytical model. This is why the definition of translation skopos is so important for each individual translation task. If, for example, the translation skopos requires the reproduction of the whole of the content, the smallest omission, as long as it is not due to a TT receiver-specific presupposition, is a translation error. The same omission is not marked as an error if the translation skopos requires only a rough summary of the relevant information contained in the text. Seen in this light, an "offence against a norm" may indeed be an adequate translation, if it is intended to be of informational or stylistic value.

A translation error, then, is a failure to carry out any one of the translating instructions. Slightly altering the linguistic definition given above, we may say that a translation error is "a deviation from the selected (or rather, prescribed) model of action", from the translator's standpoint, or a "frustration of expectations" concerning a certain action (cf. Keller 1980: 40), as seen from the receiver's point of view. This definition is of great advantage in translator training, where the trainee cannot be expected to possess full SC, TC and transfer competence. By formulating specific translating instructions, the teacher can adjust the degree of difficulty of the translation task to the level of the learner's competence. Thus, it is the teacher who decides what s/he is going to mark as a translation error in a particular situation of competence testing. Of course, this procedure only works if there is a sensible systematization and logical progression of teaching aims, as far as linguistic and transfer competence are concerned.

It is current practice in translation teaching for the students to be asked to produce a "functionally equivalent" text (cf. also House 1981a: 37ff.). This aim seems to me to be asking too much of a learner in the early phases of translation teaching, and on looking at the results the teacher will not be able to discover whether a particular translation error is due to (a) lack of SL competence (in which case the student should translate an easier text or not yet translate at all), (b) lack of TL competence in the subject in question (in which case the student should not be made to translate a text dealing with this sub-

---

[47]As far as I know, Kupsch-Losereit was the first to introduce a functional view into the discussion of error analysis in translation studies. She defines a translation error as an offence against 1. TT function, 2. textual coherence, 3. text-type norms, 4. linguistic conventions, and 5. culture-specific and situational constraints (1986: 16).

ject), or (c) lack of the transfer competence expected at this stage of training.

4.4.4. Evaluating translation tasks

The functional definition of a translation error has considerable implications for the assessment of translation quality, which is a matter not only of locating and marking errors but also of their grading. Also, it should take account of what Newmark (1980: 127) calls "the elegant and subtle use of your own language, and with it, the resourcefulness, the daring, the 'Fingerspitzengefühl', the lateral thinking".

In distinguishing the various degrees of difficulty in source texts one might come to the conclusion that there is a correlation between the difficulty of a translation problem and the grading of the corresponding error, in that inadequate handling of a very complicated problem is marked as a "slight", whereas the wrong solution of a simple problem is marked as a "serious" error. Such a correlation, however, does not appear to make sense.

Let me briefly restate: the degree of difficulty of the source text should bear some relation to the learner's level of competence. Moreover, the translation task should be formulated in such a way that it does not ask too much either of the learners' command of TL or of their transfer competence, and the formulation should make clear which transfer skills are to be tested in the task. Only under these conditions can both errors and 'Fingerspitzengefühl' be assessed in relation to the level of performance which might be expected of the learners.

If the translation task conforms to the global or partial teaching aims established for a particular stage of the training, a learner should be able to accomplish it fully (= 100 per cent) when he or she has reached this stage. Since it is unlikely that there will be any texts which present only a specific set of translation problems, this means that a competence test should take into account only those errors which are due to an inadequate solution of the translation problems with which the student is familiar. Moreover, I think it would be much more encouraging for the learner if the examiner were to count the adequate solutions rather than the errors. This can be done if the translation problems contained in the text have been listed systematically.[48]

---

[48] I use the following procedure: the sum of all occurrences of the translation problems which have to be counted in a particular translation task marks the 100-per-cent limit of possible points. The different types of translation problems can be counted equal-

Also, if students have solved any problems which have not yet been taught, they may be given a "plus" mark.

In the final examinations, however, trainees should be able to solve any translation problem present in the text. Since the optimum solution should always be the standard required, giving marks for "particularly elegant" solutions seems superfluous. Anyway, such "plus" marks are usually dictated by the subjective stylistic intuition of the examiner. On the other hand, "creative" errors, which show particular resourcefulness in difficult situations, may be taken into consideration in the assessment of a translation exercise.

The overwhelming importance of the TT function sets the standard for establishing a hierarchy of errors. The extratextual factors are of primary importance since they guide the receivers' expectations and sometimes permit them to tolerate or even to overlook slight offences against intratextual norms. Therefore, pragmatic errors can be considered to be more serious than linguistic errors. Since in "normal" (= intralingual) text production, too, the extratextual factors are more important than the intratextual factors, we can even assume that this hierarchy of errors might have a positive effect on the strategies of TT production applied by the students.

The hierarchy of extratextual factors depends on the text function required by the translation brief. Different tasks lead to different grading of sender and audience, time and place, medium and motive, etc. An important requirement for developing a satisfactory model of translation assessment would be to discover the regularities in the relationship between a particular text function and the relevance of certain extratextual factors.

The dimensions of sender, intention, audience, place, time, medium and motive raise serious problems for the translator not only when they are explicitly mentioned in the text (e.g. specific source-cultural realities), but particularly also in those cases where they are implied or presupposed, or where the text refers to them (e.g. by deictic expressions). It is in such passages of a translation that it is most

---

ly or on a graded scale according to the hierarchy of relevance, e.g. pragmatic problems = 3 pts., convention-related problems = 2 pts., linguistic problems = 1 pt., etc. The examiner marks the corresponding number of points for every translation problem which has been solved satisfactorily (including varieties and repetitions of the same problem). The percentage of adequate solutions is the basis for the assessment of "transfer competence".

appropriate to check whether the pragmatic factors have been taken account of adequately.

The hierarchy of intratextual factors is also determined by the translation skopos (e.g. primacy of content over sentence structure or lexis over suprasegmental features). However, I would venture to make the prognosis that grammatical and stylistic errors, for example, would be reduced considerably if the entry requirements for translator training were strictly laid down (and adhered to) and also if translation tasks were geared to the level of competence of the learners. There is still much to be done in the field of translation pedagogy or didactics, an area which is still rather young.

5. Sample texts

5.0. General considerations

The application of the model of translation-relevant text analysis will be demonstrated by means of three sample texts, which will also show how the model can serve as a basis for translation criticism since, where possible, I have included translations of the sample texts into various target languages.

In order to support the claim that the application of the model is not confined to specific language pairs or to one direction of the translation process, I have tried to include as many languages as possible. Of course, such a venture is limited by the author's command of foreign languages! In those cases where German was not the target language, I have consulted native speakers who were familiar with the model and its theoretical foundations. Since Sample Text 3 is more concerned with methodological questions than with the practical side of translation, it was not necessary to make concrete suggestions for each of the different target versions.

The translation of Sample Text 1 into Dutch is an indirect or relay translation, which was produced on the basis of the German version, using the Spanish original and the results of the ST analysis as an additional frame of reference. To judge from the target text we may, I think, state that, with the help of an ST analysis according to our model, even a relay translation can achieve a high degree of functional adequacy.

The sample texts were selected to illustrate the way in which ST analysis, concentrating on two or three crucial aspects, helps to identify the translation-relevant features of an ST in order to achieve a functional target text without jeopardizing the translator's loyalty. The three texts belong to genres which are common in the practice of professional translation. Two of them are literary texts, but this does not, in my opinion, impair their didactic value, as the selected aspects of analysis can be applied to other text types as well. Therefore the results of ST analysis and the conclusions regarding translation strategies and methods can to a certain extent be generalized.

5.1. Text 1: The relationship between intention and function –
Alejo Carpentier: Acerca de la historicidad de Víctor Hugues

The postscript of the novel *El siglo de las luces* by the Cuban author Alejo Carpentier (Carpentier 1965) will serve to illustrate the relationship between the sender's intention and text function and its significance for translation.

5.1.0. Text
ACERCA DE LA HISTORICIDAD DE VÍCTOR HUGUES

Como Víctor Hugues ha sido ignorado por la historia de la Revolución Francesa – harto atareada en describir los acontecimientos ocurridos en Europa, desde los días de la Convención hasta el 18 Brumario, para desviar la mirada hacia el remoto ámbito del Caribe –, el autor de este libro cree útil hacer algunas aclaraciones acerca de la historicidad del personaje.

Se sabe que Víctor Hugues era marsellés, hijo de un panadero – y hasta hay motivos para creer que tuviese alguna lejana ascendencia negra, aunque esto no sería fácil de demostrar. Atraído por un mar que es – en Marsella, precisamente – una eterna invitación a la aventura desde los tiempos de Piteas y de los patrones fenicios, embarcó hacia América, en calidad de grumete, realizando varios viajes al Mar Caribe. Ascendido a piloto de naves comerciales, anduvo por las Antillas, observando, husmeando, aprendiendo, acabando por dejar las navegaciones para abrir en Port-au-Prince un gran almacén – o *comptoir* – de mercancías diversas, adquiridas, reunidas, mercadas por vías de compra-venta, trueque, contrabandos, cambios de sederías por café, de vainilla por perlas, como aún existen muchos en los puertos de ese mundo tornasolado y rutilante.

Su verdadera entrada en la Historia data de la noche en que aquel establecimiento fue incendiado por los revolucionarios haitianos. A partir de ese momento podemos seguir su trayectoria paso a paso, tal como se narra en este libro. Los capítulos consagrados a la reconquista de la Guadalupe se guían por un esquema cronológico preciso. Cuanto se dice acerca de su guerra librada a los Estados Unidos – la que llamaron los yanquis de entonces "Guerra de Brigantes" – así como a la acción de los corsarios, con sus nombres y los nombres de sus barcos, está basado en documentos reunidos por el autor en la Guadalupe y en bibliotecas de la Barbados, así como en cortas pero instructivas referencias halladas en obras de autores latinoamericanos que, de paso, mencionaron a Víctor Hugues.

En cuanto a la acción de Víctor Hugues en la Guayana Francesa, hay abundante material informativo en las "memorias" de la deportación. Después de la época en que termina la acción de esta novela, Víctor Hugues fue sometido en Paris,[sic] a un consejo de guerra, por haber entregado la colonia a Holanda, después de una capitulación que era, en verdad, inevitable. Absuelto con honor, Víctor Hugues volvió a moverse en el ámbito político. Sabemos que tuvo relaciones con Fouché. Sabemos también que estaba en París, todavía, a la hora del desplome del imperio napoleónico.

Pero aquí se pierden sus huellas. Algunos historiadores – de los muy pocos que se hayan ocupado de él accidentalmente, fuera de Pierre Vitoux que le consagró, hace más de veinte años, un estudio aún inédito – nos dicen que murió cerca de Burdeos, donde "poseía unas tierras" (?) en el año 1820. La Bibliografía Universal de Didot lleva esa muerte al año 1822. Pero en la Guadalupe, donde el recuerdo de Víctor Hugues está muy presente, se asegura que, después de la caída del Imperio, regresó a la Guayana, volviendo a tomar posesión de sus propiedades. Parece – según los investigadores de la Guadalupe – que murió lentamente, dolorosamente, de una enfermedad que pudo ser la lepra, pero que, por mejores indicios, debió ser más bien una afección cancerosa[1].

¿Cual fue, en realidad, el fin de Víctor Hugues? Aún lo ignoramos, del mismo modo que muy poco sabemos acerca de su nacimiento. Pero es indudable que su acción hipostática – firme, sincera, heroica, en su primera fase; desalentada, contradictoria, logrera y hasta cínica, en la segunda – nos ofrece la imagen de un personaje extraordinario que establece, en su propio comportamiento, una dramática dicotomía. De ahí que el autor haya creído interesante revelar la existencia de ese ignorado personaje histórico en una novela que abarcara, a la vez, todo el ámbito del Caribe.

A. C.

[1]*Nota del autor*: Estaban publicadas ya estas páginas al final de la primera edición que de este libro se hizo en México, cuando, hallándome en Paris, tuve oportunidad de conocer a un descendiente directo de Víctor Hugues, poseedor de importantes documentos familiares acerca del personaje. Por él supe que la tumba de Víctor Hugues se encuentra en un lugar situado a alguna distancia de Cayena. Pero con esto encontré, en uno de los documentos examinados, una asombrosa revelación: Víctor Hugues fue amado fielmente, durante años, por una hermosa cubana que, por más asombrosa realidad, se llamaba Sofía.

5.1.1. Analysis of extratextual factors

The analysis of extratextual factors is based on the result of research in secondary literature. In order not to try the reader's patience too much, I do not intend to go through the model of analysis schematically, but I will note the factors in brackets. The arrows indicate any factors about which information can be inferred.

Alejo Carpentier (TEXT PRODUCER and SENDER), 1904-1980 (TIME), was the son of a French architect and his Russian wife, who had emigrated to Cuba. In his childhood he visited Europe, went to school in France, and grew up speaking French and Spanish. From 1921 onwards, after studying architecture, literature and music in Havana, he devoted himself increasingly to journalism, joining Cuba's intellectual and political avantgarde. He was arrested for having taken part in a protest campaign against the dictator Machado, but in 1928 succeeded in fleeing to France, where he wrote for radio and the press and published his first articles. In 1939 he returned to Havana. He continued his journalistic activities and taught the history of music at Havana University. From 1946 onwards, he lived in Venezuela for 14 years. There he started work on this novel (GENRE) *El siglo de las luces* in 1956, the year Fidel Castro began his guerilla war against the dictator Batista ($\rightarrow$ MOTIVE?). The novel was completed after his return to Cuba in 1959 (TIME and PLACE of text production), but it was not until 1962 that it was first published in Mexico. A second edition appeared in Spain in 1965 (AUDIENCE, TIME and PLACE of reception) (cf. Strausfeld 1976: 347).

In spite of his links with Europe, Carpentier remained a Cuban, or rather, Hispanoamerican writer throughout his life (cf. Vanguardia 1980). His novels deal with the contrast between European rationalism and the "magic world" of Latin America, particularly the Caribbean ($\rightarrow$ SUBJECT MATTER) (cf. Marco 1980). His work was intended to make people understand the specific situation of Latin America ($\rightarrow$ INTENTION).

5.1.2. The postscript *Acerca de la historicidad de Víctor Hugues*
The sample text is a separate postscript of three pages, added to the 350 pages of the novel (MEDIUM) in which the French adventurer Victor Hugues from Marseille, who was in fact a historical figure in the French Revolution (SUBJECT MATTER), plays an important part. In the postscript, the author relates that he happened to hear about Victor Hugues' heroic deeds when he was in Guadeloupe (MOTIVE), and explains why the author decided to make him the protagonist of his novel (CONTENT).

The postscript is intended to give greater authenticity to the novel (INTENTION) by informing the reader about the protagonist's historical background (TEXT FUNCTION). The author gives a full account of the biographical facts, which he relates to the plot of the novel (SUBJECT MATTER), and also of the sources of information he used ($\rightarrow$ INTENTION). He owns that the wrote the novel in order to perpetuate Victor Hugues' memory "in a novel which would at the same time embrace the world of the whole Caribbean" (INTENTION). In the second edition, which I used, the text is supplemented by a footnote, in which the author tells the reader about an "amazing" episode which seems to lend further confirmation to the authenticity of the story (CONTENT, COMPOSITION).

5.1.3. The reflection of the extratextual factors in the text
The author (SENDER) introduces himself in the first sentence by using the third person (*el autor de este libro cree...*). This gives the text a rather impersonal tone, assigning it to the type of informative texts in general and scientific texts in particular (→ TEXT FUNCTION). This impression is confirmed by a number of impersonal constructions in the personal function (*se sabe* although the author relates the results of his own investigations) or the passive function (*los capítulos ... se guían*), as well as by the use of the first person plural (*sabemos que tuvo relaciones con Fouché*) (→ SENTENCE STRUCTURE), which is typical of scientific texts. In some sentences (*podemos seguir su trayectoria*) this last device achieves the effect of addressing the reader, who is thus enabled to share the author's knowledge (relationship between SENDER and RECEIVER).

These four forms of sender reference are used throughout the text, the first person plural being the most frequent. An exception is made in the footnote (→ COMPOSITION), which is itself a conventional feature of scientific texts. Here, the author relates a personal experience in the first person singular, the impersonal style of the postscript being stressed even more by this contrast.

Another unusual element is the author's "signature" under the text. This characterizes the postscript as a commentary on the novel, i.e. as a metatext (TEXT FUNCTION).

The following features are characteristic of a scientific text (TEXT FUNCTION$_1$):

a) Technical terms: *historicidad, dicotomía, acción hipostática* (→ LEXIS),
b) nominal style: e.g. *algunas aclaraciones acerca de la historicidad del personaje* (→ LEXIS, SENTENCE STRUCTURE),
c) use of the present tense in the commenting paragraphs (→ SENTENCE STRUCTURE),
d) names of authorities and sources: e.g. *Pierre Vitoux, la Bibliografía Universal de Didot, los investigadores de la Guadalupe* (→ CONTENT), and
e) literal or indirect quotations: *donde poseía unas tierras , según los investigadores de la Guadalupe* (→ CONTENT, → COMPOSITION).

Contrasting with these features are others which are not in keeping with a scientific style and indicate a literary function (TEXT FUNCTION$_2$) (cf. above, 3.1.8.b).

a) General-language lexis with numerous expressive and connotative adjectives, often placed before the noun: *el remoto ámbito del Caribe, ese mundo tornasolado y rutilante, dramática dicotomía*; long, partly asyndetic enumera-

tions: *firme, sincera heroica..., desalentada, contradictoria, logrera y hasta cínica, mercancías diversas, adquiridas, reunidas, mercadas por vías de compra-venta, trueque, contrabandos, cambios de sederías por café, de vainilla por perlas* (→ LEXIS, → SENTENCE STRUCTURE)
b) verbal style: *observando, husmeando, aprendiendo, acabando por dejar...* (→ SENTENCE STRUCTURE)
c) past tenses, particularly the dynamic *pretérito perfecto simple*, in the narrative passages (→ SENTENCE STRUCTURE)
d) lack of bibliographical references, anonymity of some authorities: *historiadores, investigadores*) (→ CONTENT) and
e) sceptical metacommunicative commentary on the quotation, "(?)", instead of an exact reference of the source (→ COMPOSITION).

This combination of features illustrates the intention of the author who wants to convey the impression that he has carefully investigated the historical facts (SUBJECT MATTER). At the same time, he does not wish to bore the reader – who expects to be reading a novel and not a text book – with the typical drawbacks of a real scientific text (expectation of the AUDIENCE). These two concurring intentions are parallelled by the two concurring text functions, the purely informative function of the scientific text, and the literary function of the novel (TEXT FUNCTIONS).

Another pointer to this interpretation is supplied by the numerous inclusions, which are rather uncommon in a Spanish scientific text (→ SENTENCE STRUCTURE, COMPOSITION) and which have various functions. Most of them do not contain any information which is indispensable for comprehension, but seem to address the audience in order to court their understanding (*harto atareada..., en Marsella, precisamente*), referring to their background knowledge of, for example, the French Revolution, American history, a historian named Pierre Vitoux, etc. (→ PRESUPPOSITIONS). This last example, however, seems to illustrate that the addressee cannot really be presupposed to have this knowledge. It is a device which helps to avoid a schoolmasterly tone (→ SUPRASEGMENTAL FEATURES), the reader being treated as an equal partner (role of SENDER and RECEIVER, EFFECT), whose justifiable need of information is gladly met by the author.

The inclusion "o *comptoir*" serves to illustrate (if a knowledge of French can be presupposed) what is meant by *almacén* (→ LEXIS), providing, at the same time, a certain local colour (→ LEXIS), while the inclusion *según los investigadores...* is a mere marker of reported speech (→ CONTENT).

The medium is referred to in the text as *este libro* or, indirectly, as *esta novela* (→ LEXIS). The motive for text production is mentioned in the last sentence, where the author states that it would be interesting to describe the life of this neglected historical figure in a novel (→ CONTENT). Any political topicality, which is suggested by the communicative background, is not mentioned explicitly in the postscript, but the title of the book and the biography of the author seem to point to this. Such a thematic reference may have been expected, at least, by the Latin American readers in 1962. The question is of considerable importance for the translation of the novel, but is not particularly relevant to the translation of the postscript.

5.1.4. Analysis of intratextual factors
a. Subject matter
In accordance with the conventions for scientific texts, the subject matter is mentioned in the title. The expectation raised by the title is confirmed by the analysis of the isotopic levels in the text (→ LEXIS).

b. Content
The following analysis of content shows at the same time the macro-structure of the text.

> Title: ACERCA DE LA HISTORICIDAD DE VICTOR HUGUES
> 1. Introduction: justification and "programme" of the postscript
> 2. Biographical notes on Victor Hugues
> > 2.1. Period before the beginning of the plot: origin, career as a mariner, establishment of a *comptoir* in Port-au-Prince (short chronological account of the most important stages in his life)
> > 2.2. The plot of the novel: recapture of Guadeloupe, war against the U.S., activities as a privateer and in French Guiana (commentary and reference to sources)
> > 2.3. Period after the end of the plot:
> > > a) trial before military tribunal, acquittal, political activities in France (brief enumeration of the authentic facts);
> > > b) V.H. died near Bordeaux in 1820 or 1822 or returned to Guiana and died there later of leprosy or cancer (theories of various historians);
> > > c) V.H. was buried near Cayenne (footnote as inclusion: the personal account of an interview with a descendant confirms part of the plot – V.H. was in love with *a beautiful Cuban girl* called Sofía).
> 3. Conclusion: appreciation of V.H.'s personality (cf. Introduction) and reference to the more comprehensive subject matter of the novel.
> Signature: A. C.

c. Presuppositions

Apart from the afore-mentioned "pseudo-presuppositions" in the inclusions, the text presupposes some knowledge of the history of Haiti and the island of Guadeloupe as well as of the geography of the Caribbean (e.g. *Cayena*). Where these details (e.g. *deportación*) were mentioned in the novel, they can be presupposed even though they may not have been part of the ST receiver's horizon before. Certain events and personalities of the French Revolution are supposed to be part of the ST reader's general education, which proves (as has already been indicated by the title) that the text was written for an educated audence interested in historical and political issues. Since these presuppositions are not entirely specific to the source culture, they are not relevant for the effect which the text produces on the reader, except where they have to be regarded as being part of the horizon of the TT receiver (as the history of the French Revolution probably is for French readers (cf. example 5.1.6./17).

d. Composition

The text presents the information in almost chronological order (cf. CONTENT), as is typical of the subject matter and of TEXT FUNCTION$_1$.

Both the introductory and the concluding paragraph, which reveal the author's intention and contain an (indirect) appeal to the reader, present a rather linear theme-rheme structure. The first theme is introduced by the title, the second part of which is taken up as the theme of the first clause. The rheme of the first clause is converted into a contrastive theme in the second clause (*historia* vs. *el autor*), and the rheme of the second clause repeats the title. Thus, the introduction is a kind of expansion of the short reference to the subject matter which is presented in the title.

The concluding paragraph is also directly connected to the preceding sentence (if we disregard the footnote): (a) the question as to what became of Victor Hugues cannot be answered; (b) his activities, as far as they are known, show the importance of his personality; (c) therefore, the author has decided to write the novel; (d) it is intended to honour the world of the Caribbean. This simplifying paraphrase clearly shows the linear thematic progression of the passage.

e. Non-verbal elements

The first non-verbal feature that catches the eye is the remarkably wide spacing between the paragraphs, whose function is not immediately clear. Apart from the transition between 2.2. and 2.3. (cf. CON-TENT), the paragraphing corresponds to the thematic composition of the text. The wide spaces seem to be a feature of literary rather than of scientific texts.

In the text, a number *1* points to the footnote. The note itself is marked as *Nota del autor* (in italics) and is printed in smaller type below the text, as is the convention in scientific texts.

The literal quotation is indicated by quotation marks, the quotation itself being followed by a question mark in brackets, which seems to indicate the sceptical attitude of the author towards the information given in the quotation.

f. Lexis

Some peculiarities of lexis, which appear to depend on the author's intention, have been mentioned above (chapter 5.1.3.). The time and place of text production are not really reflected in the lexis, since there are no words marked as modernisms or Americanisms; but neither does the text contain any obsolete or specifically European lexical items. The origin (and political affiliation) of the author is only hinted at by the use of the pejorative *yanqui* instead of *norteamericano* in one of the inclusions.

There is one isotopic level which throws some light on the subject matter of the text: This level is composed of expressions of knowledge and ignorance (*saber, ignorar, no saber, saber muy poco, creer*), expressions of knowledge transfer, which characterize the transition from ignorance to knowledge (*hacer aclaraciones, narrar, nos dicen, se asegura, parece   según los investigadores, revelar*), and of expressions designating sources of knowledge (*material informativo, documentos, instructivas referencias*). The distribution of these elements over the text marks the thematic division of the text into authentic facts, dubious information, and lack of information about the stages of Victor Hugues' life.

g. Sentence structure

The long inclusions characterizing the sentence structure of the text have already been mentioned. Like some shorter insertions (e.g. *con sus nombres y los nombres de sus barcos* or *en su propio comportamiento*), they serve to shape the structure of the extended hypotactic sentences with their numerous participle and gerund constructions, adverbial expressions, etc., which make heavy demands on the reader's concentration (cf. the remarks on the education of the addressed audience). The sentence structure marks the "baroque" style of which Carpentier declared himself a follower (cf. Barral 1980). It is only in the paragraphs 2.1. and 2.3.(a) that this structural principle is abandoned in favour of a more linear sentence structure, which particularly in 2.1., with its long enumerations, gives a more dynamic effect to the text. The sentence structure of the footnote is also characterized by shorter syntactic units, as is typical of descriptions of personal experience.

Thus, the sentence structure of the text reflects the different functions of the text parts as well as the thematic structure, and it seems justifiable to interpret the syntactic features as stylistic devices illustrating the author's intention. The combination of the conventional features of different text types is clearly not conventional itself. The author plays with the conventions of scientific texts and uses them as a contrast to the typical features expected in a novel.

h. Suprasegmental features
Many of the inclusions, e.g. those in the first sentence and the one before the last, bring about a specific intonation contour, because the elements following an inclusion are stressed. Since the intensity stress also increases towards the end of the sentence, there are sentences with two or more accentuation points. This has the effect of structuring the hypotaxes, which would otherwise be too long to be acceptable for Spanish readers, and also increases the degree of comprehensibility.

As in English, long adverbials are usually separated from the rest of the clause at the beginning of a sentence. Where this is done, as in our text, even with very short adverbials (*en verdad*, *de paso*), the focussing effect cannot be overlooked (just try reading the sentence without the commas).

5.1.5. Analysis of effect
The characteristic features elicited by the analysis produce a specific effect on the audience. They accept the information presented to them in a comprehensible form as the real historical background of the novel they have read. The text elements which they recognize from scientific texts with purely informative function, assure them of the truthfulness of the information (= INTENTIONAL EFFECT), whereas the elements of literary style, which establish a connection between post-

script and novel, form a surprising contrast (= ORIGINALITY). Since the readers receive the impression that the author expects them to have a high degree of background knowledge, they never feel that they are being "talked down" to, especially as the narrative passages (e.g. those describing the adventurous life of the protagonist) appeal to their emotions and the author addresses them on a personal level (*A.C.*), and as an equal (= small CULTURAL DISTANCE).

A secondary effect (or consequence) of the text is that the reader probably regards the plot of the novel as "authentic" (perhaps more authentic than it really is!), agreeing with the author's view on Latin American reality. It is clear that the author has been able both to realize his intention by using various stylistic devices and to produce the desired effect on the audience.

5.1.6. Translation criticism

In "average Western cultures" the conventional standard of literary translation requires an exoticizing translation of the content and an equivalent translation of the style, which in the case of our sample text, whose effect is achieved almost exclusively with the stylistic devices used by the author, is tantamount to an equivalence of effect. So, a translation has to reproduce the effect described above (see 5.1.5.) on the TT receiver, which means that the stylistic devices used in the target text must be chosen for the primary purpose of effect.

Some of the problems resulting from this translation skopos, which are related mainly to the categories of intention and text function, will be discussed in this chapter using examples from the published German and English versions. To judge from the year of publication, both translations are based on the first edition of the original. Hence, the footnote, which was added in the second edition, is not included in the translations. Neither of the two translators gives any comment on their translation strategies, and so we must assume that – consciously or otherwise – they followed the convention described above and aimed at an equivalence of effect between ST and TT.

The English translation by Victor Gollancz was published as a *Penguin* paperback in 1963. According to the text printed on the cover, for copyright reasons the book is for sale only in Britain, New Zealand, and South Africa (not in the U.S.). The German translation by Hermann Stiehl was published in 1964 by Insel-Verlag as a hardback edition. The two translations were preceded in 1962 by a French version, and it is this version which probably made the book known in

Spain and Latin America, before the original, which was hard to get at the time, was able to reach its intended readership. On the occasion of Carpentier's death in 1980, the Spanish publisher Barral wrote that he had first read the book in French, before he started publishing Carpentier's works in Spanish (cf. Barral 1980).

The French version, published in the series *Folio* by Gallimard (Transl. René L. F. Durand) and marked as "Texte intégral", does not contain the postscript either. Instead, the editor, Jean Blanzat, stresses the importance of the historical figure of Victor Hugues in his foreword to the translation:

> Victor Hugues est assez obscur pour que le romancier puisse, sans abus, l'animer d'une vie imaginaire, mais ses actes sont assez nombreux et connus pour ancrer le récit dans la vérité historique qui est, ici, nécessaire (Blanzat 1985: 13).

To make things easier, the versions are marked *ET* (= English translation) and *GT* (= German translation). Where necessary, we make our own suggestions, in which we also correct defects other than those commented on (*SET* = suggested English translation, by P. Sparrow; *SGT* = suggested German translation, by C. Nord). At the end of the chapter we present corrected English and German versions of the whole text. For the Dutch relay translation I am greatly indebted to my colleague Joanna Best, Heidelberg.

a. Coherence and stress

The coherence of the text is supported by the chronological order of informational details (the stages of Victor Hugues' life are always mentioned thematically at the beginning of the paragraphs), the linear theme-rheme progression, and the accentuation of significant thematic elements within the clauses as well as by the levels of isotopy. These linking devices are not specific to Spanish, but can be found in various languages. Since the translation skopos is equivalence of effect, we can, therefore, assume that in the English, German, and Dutch versions these devices had to be preserved, using the appropriate structures specific to the languages concerned.

The clear composition has been reproduced both in ET and GT with the focussed elements in initial position. In example 5.1.6./1, ET corresponds better to the source text (ST) than GT, which refers to time instead of place, thus losing the connection with the metaphor *perderse las huellas*. As far as text composition is concerned, the accentuation of chronology in GT is also acceptable.

Example 5.1.6./1
ST: Pero aquí se pierden sus huellas.
ET: But it is here that we lose trace of him.
GT: Aber dann verliert sich seine Spur.

In example 5.1.6./2, the accentuation of the thematic elements at the beginning of the sentence is not realized idiomatically in GT.

Example 5.1.6./2
ST: En cuanto a la acción de Víctor Hugues en la Guayana francesa, hay abundante material informativo [...].
ET: As for Victor Hugues' activities in French Guiana, there is ample source material to be found [...].
GT: Was die Tätigkeit Victor Hugues' in Französisch-Guayana betrifft, so findet sich [...] ausreichendes Material.
SGT: Über Victor Hugues' Aktivitäten in Französisch-Guayana schließlich gibt es [...] reichliches Quellenmaterial.

The relevance of both theme-rheme structures and recurrence/paraphrase for text coherence can be illustrated by means of the relationship between the title and the first and last sentences. The part literal, part paraphrased reproduction of the title marks the first sentence as a typical introductory sentence of a scientific text, and in the final sentence, we find another paraphrase of the first sentence. Therefore, ST and ET (despite having changed the recurrence of *ignorado* into a paraphrase) give the impression of being consistent, well-rounded texts, whereas in GT *fast übergangen* ("almost ignored") and *unbekannt* ("unknown") lack coherence.

Example 5.1.6./3
ST: ACERCA DE LA HISTORICIDAD DE VICTOR HUGUES
Como Víctor Hugues ha sido ignorado por la historia de la Revolución Francesa [...], el autor de este libro cree útil hacer algunas aclaraciones acerca de la historicidad del personaje. [...] De ahí que el autor haya creído interesante revelar la existencia de ese ignorado personaje histórico en una novela...
ET: THE VICTOR HUGUES OF HISTORY
Since Victor Hugues has been almost completely ignored by historians of the French Revolution [...] the author feels it might be useful to throw some light on the historical background of the character. [...] That is why the author considered it would be interesting to reveal the existence of this neglected historical figure in a novel...
GT: ÜBER DEN HISTORISCHEN VICTOR HUGUES
Da die Geschichte der Französischen Revolution [...] Victor Hugues fast übergangen hat, hält es der Autor für angebracht, einiges über die historische Rolle dieser Gestalt zu sagen. [...] Deshalb schien es dem Autor interessant, das Leben dieser unbekannten historischen Gestalt in einem Roman zu enthüllen...

SGT: EINIGE BEMERKUNGEN ÜBER DEN HISTORISCHEN VICTOR
HUGUES
Da Victor Hugues von den Geschichtsschreibern der Französischen Revolution [...] bisher nicht zur Kenntnis genommen wurde, hält der Verfasser einige
klärende Bemerkungen über diese historische Gestalt für angebracht. [...] Aus
diesem Grunde hielt es der Verfasser für lohnend, das Leben dieser bisher unbekannten historischen Gestalt in einem Roman zu beleuchten...

While the theme-rheme progression between the title and the first sentence can easily be reproduced, the accentuation of certain elements,
which mark the focus of the author's communicative intention, seems
to present more difficulties.

Example 5.1.6./4
ST: [...] – harto atareada en describir los acontecimientos ocurridos en Europa,
desde los días de la Convención hasta el 18 Brumario, para desviar la mirada
hacia el remoto ámbito del Caribe –...
ET: [...] – too busy describing what was taking place in Europe between the
time of the Convention and the 18th Brumaire to divert their gaze to the distant confines of the Caribbean –... (cf. example 5.6.1./14).
GT: [...] – die viel zu sehr damit beschäftigt war, die europäischen Ereignisse
von den Tagen des Nationalkonvents bis zum 18. Brumaire zu beschreiben,
um noch einen Blick für den fernen karibischen Raum übrig zu haben –...
SGT: [...] – viel zu sehr mit den Ereignissen beschäftigt, die sich vom Natio-
nalkonvent bis zum 18. Brumaire in Europa abspielten, als daß sie noch einen
Blick auf die ach so fernen Länder in der Karibik hätten werfen können –...

The paradigmatic contrastive stress on *Europa* and *Caribe* (cf. chapter
3.2.8.), which is not accomplished by *europäische Ereignisse* ("European events") vs. *karibischer Raum* ("Caribbean area"), is of particular relevance to the effect produced on the European reader, whose
gaze also has to be diverted from Europe to the Caribbean. Although
German relative clauses, which are always marked off by commas, are
a little "heavier" than English defining relative clauses, the ET solution can be imitated in GT.

In Spanish and English, defining relative clauses have a focussing effect, which in the following example is increased by the
inclusion *en verdad*:

Example 5.1.6./5
ST: [...] por haber entregado la colonia después de una capitulación que era,
en verdad, inevitable.
ET: [...] for having lost the colony to the Dutch after a surrender which was in
point of fact inevitable.
GT: [...] weil er die Kolonie im Anschluß an die Kapitulation, die in Wirklichkeit unvermeidlich gewesen war, den Holländern übergeben hatte.

SGT: [...] weil er die Kolonie nach einer ohnehin unvermeidlichen Kapitulation an die Holländer abgetreten hatte.

While in ET the sentence stress is automatically directed to *inevitable*,
the relative clause of GT is understood as a non-defining relative
clause because of the definite article in front of the antecedent and the
use of the past perfect. The expression *in point of fact* in ET provides
the accent of intensity produced by the commas in ST. In GT, the expression *in Wirklichkeit* ("in reality") contrasts with a *scheinbar* ("apparently") not implied in the passage and attracts the focus, whereas in
SGT the focal stress is directed at the adjective *unvermeidlich* ("inevitable") by the adverb *ohnehin* ("anyway").

Another important linking device is isotopy. In the following
example, the coherence of GT is affected by the interruption of the
isotopic chain:

Example 5.1.6./6
ST: [...] se asegura que, después de la caída del Imperio, regresó a la Guayana...
ET: [...] one is assured that after the collapse of the Empire he returned to Guiana...
GT: [...] versichert man, er sei nach dem Untergang des Empire nach Guayana
zurückgekehrt...
SGT: [...] versichern jedoch, er sei nach dem Zusammenbruch des Napoleonischen Reiches noch nach Guayana zurückgekehrt...

In ST, *caída del Imperio* is an elliptic paraphrase of *el desplome del
imperio napoleónico* (ET: "when the Napoleonic Empire foundered";
GT: "als das napoleonische Reich unterging"). In German, the word
Empire (with a French pronunciation) can be used to designate the
French Empire under Napoleon I. (cf. DUW 1983, Brockhaus 1973),
but it is much more frequently used (with an English pronunciation) to
denote the British Empire (cf. DUW 1983). The context points to the
first reading, but for a receiver who is not familiar with the historical
background the second reading might be equally possible. Considering the informative function of the text, a recurrence, as in ET, would
be more adequate than the paraphrase.

As has already been mentioned, the most important isotopy is
that of knowledge/ignorance, which is verbalized throughout the text
by expressions designating knowledge transfer and knowledge
sources. A list of passages containing some of these isotopic elements
shows that GT often misses the author's intention, whereas ET succeeds in keeping closer to the ST.

Example 5.1.6./7
ST: ha sido ignorado
ET: has been [...] ignored
GT: fast übergangen hat
SGT: nicht zur Kenntnis genommen wurde

ST: hasta hay motivos para creer...
ET: there is even cause to believe...
GT: einiges spricht sogar dafür...
SGT: man darf sogar annehmen...

ST: hacer algunas aclaraciones
ET: throw some light
GT: einiges sagen
SGT: einige klärende Bemerkungen

ST: revelar la existencia
ET: reveal the existence
GT: das Leben [...] enthüllen
SGT: das Leben beleuchten

ST: documentos
ET: documents
GT: Unterlagen
SGT: Dokumente

ST: abundante material informativo
ET: ample source material
GT: ausreichendes Material
SGT: reichliches Quellenmaterial

ST: en las "memorias" de la deportación
ET: memoirs
GT: In den "Memoiren" der Deportation
SGT: in den "Mémoires" der Deportation

The examples show that coherence (→ CONTENT) and stress (→ COM-POSITION, → SUPRASEGMENTAL FEATURES) provide valuable hints as to the sender's intention.

What also became clear from this ST analysis was the fact that the combination of scientific and literary stylistic features is a characteristic device used to realize the sender's intention.

b. Scientific style

One of the features of Spanish scientific style is the reference to the author by *el autor (de este libro)* and the use of either the first person plural (*sabemos*) or impersonal constructions (*se sabe*). These features are also common in English and German scientific texts (cf. Crystal & Davy 1969: 251ff., and Sowinski 1973: 232). ET uses the conventional form *the author* and the first person plural (see, for example, *Foreword* and *Preface* in Crystal & Davy 1969), whereas GT uses *der Autor* instead of the usual *der Verfasser*, but does on the whole correctly reproduce the functional style of scientific texts (first person plural, *man*, and a large number of impersonal or passive constructions). The reference to the sender in the footnote could be translated by the first person plural both in ET and GT, and the formula *Nota del autor* should be translated, according to stylistic conventions, by *Author s Note* and *Anm.d.Verf.* respectively (below the footnote and in parenthesis).

In the following example, the formulation of GT does not correspond to the norms of scientific style:

Example 5.1.6./8
ST: Se sabe que Víctor Hugues era marsellés...
ET: We know that Victor Hugues was a Marseillais...
GT: Man weiß, daß Victor Hugues Marseiller war...
SGT: Es ist bekannt, daß Victor Hugues [...] aus Marseille war...

Another syntactic feature of scientific style is the use of the present tense to separate the commenting passages from the narration. Because of the similar use of tenses in English and German, both translations can achieve an analogous effect by simply following the model of the ST.

In the field of lexis, it seems more difficult to provide the text with the typical features of scientific style, as can be shown by the translation problems caused by the three technical terms *historicidad*, *dicotomía*, and *hipostático*. Although corresponding terms exist both in English and German (*historicity/Historizität*, *dicotomy/Dichotomie*, *hypostatic/hypostatisch*, cf. DUW 1983 and OUD 1970), these are either confined to certain terminologies (*Dichotomie*, *hypostatic/hypostatisch*) and may therefore not be familiar to every educated reader, or they differ from the ST expressions in meaning (*Dichotomie*) or in their stylistic connotations (*historicity/Historizität*). Thus, apart from *dicotomy*, which seems to be rather equivalent to *dicotomía* in both meaning and style, they cannot be used in the respective target texts and have to be replaced by paraphrases or synonyms (cf. example 5.1.6./9, where ET gives an incorrect paraphrase of *hypostatic*). In this case, the markers of scientific style should be shifted to other elements of lexis (e.g. an increased percentage of Latinisms in GT, such as *Aktivitäten* instead of *Tätigkeit*, *Deportation* instead of *Verschlep-*

pung, Rehabilitierung instead of *ehrenvoller Freispruch*, see also examples 5.1.6./7 and 10).

Example 5.1.6./9
ST: Pero es indudable que su acción hipostática – firme, sincera, heroica, en su primera fase; desalentada, contradictoria, lograra y hasta cínica, en la segunda – nos ofrece la imagen de un personaje extraordinario que establece en su propio comportamiento una dramática dicotomía.
ET: But there can be no doubt that his activities during his period of power – resolute, sincere and heroic in their first phase, wavering, mean and even cynical in their second – give us a picture of an extraordinary man, whose behaviour contains a dramatic dicotomy.
GT: Zweifellos bietet aber sein für uns greifbares Wirken – entschlossen, aufrichtig, heroisch in der ersten und kleinmütig, widerspruchsvoll, opportunistisch und sogar zynisch in der zweiten Phase – das Bild einer außergewöhnlichen Persönlichkeit, die durch ihr eigenes Verhalten eine dramatische Zweiteilung darstellt.
SET: But there can be no doubt that his activities, as far as they are known – [...] – give us the picture of an extraordinary man whose very behaviour reveals a dramatic dicotomy.
SGT: Zweifellos ist aber der historische Victor Hugues, soweit uns seine Taten überliefert sind, ein außergewöhnlicher Mann, dessen Verhalten – standhaft, geradlinig, mutig in der ersten Zeit, später schwach, widersprüchlich, machtgierig und sogar menschenverachtend – eine tragische Gespaltenheit offenbart.

The characteristics of scientific style should even be marked in passages which seem less important:

Example 5.1.6./10
ST: Algunos historiadores [...] nos dicen...
ET: Some of the very few historians [...] say...
GT: Einige Geschichtsschreiber [...] teilen uns mit...
SGT: Einige Geschichtsforscher [...] vertreten die Auffassung...

Another relevant feature which the author uses to characterize scientific style are quotations[49]. The ST contains a literal quotation in quotation marks (example 5.1.6./11), two indirect quotations (example 5.1.6./12) and a piece of information allegedly taken from a French bibliography (example 5.1.6./13).

Example 5.1.6./11
ST: [...] nos dicen que murió cerca de Burdeos, donde "poseía unas tierras" (?) en el año 1820.
ET: [...] say that he died near Bordeaux, where he "owned lands" in 1820.

---

[49]The problem of translating quotations is dealt with in detail in Nord 1990a and 1990b.

GT: [...] teilen uns mit, er sei im Jahre 1820 in der Nähe von Bordeaux, wo er
"Ländereien besaß" (?), gestorben.
SET: [...] say that he died in 1820, not far from Bordeaux where he "owned
estates" (?).
SGT: [...] vertreten die Auffassung, er sei im Jahre 1820 in der Nähe von Bor-
deaux, wo er "Ländereien" (?) besessen habe, gestorben.

The use of quotation marks suggests to the reader that the expression
in question is a literal reproduction from a certain source. In GT, the
postposition of the verb (due to the subordinate phrase) seems unlikely
in a literal quotation. It would therefore be more convenient to extra-
polate the verb from the quotation and use the question mark as a
sceptical comment on *Ländereien* rather than on *besaß*. ET omits the
question mark completely, and the missing comma before the date dis-
torts the sense of the sentence.

Indirect quotations seem to present fewer difficulties to the
translator since they reproduce only the message, not the form of the
source. Linguistic translation problems may arise, however, if different markers are used for indirect quotations in SL and TL. In example 5.1.6./12, neither ET no GT have interpreted *parece* (in connection
with the inclusion *según los investigadores de la Guadalupe*) as a signal that the first part of the sentence, unlike the second part, which
contains the author's commentary, is meant to be the continuation of
the indirect quotation given in the preceding sentence. The literal
translation by *scheint* and *it seems* destroys the coherence of the
passage. Since in German the subjunctive mode suffices to mark the
reported speech, the inclusion need not be translated in GT. As the
context (see the analysis of content, part 2.3.b) makes clear that the
impersonal construction *se asegura* does not refer to general public
opinion but to the statements of the historians, the information about
the source can be shifted to the first sentence both in GT and ET. This
procedure would also help to avoid any possible misunderstanding in
ET: since the expressions *one is assured* and *Guadeloupan historians*
are not connected by anaphoric elements (e.g. a definite article), the
reader of ET might come to the conclusion that these expressions refer
to different sources.

Example 5.1.6./12
ST: Pero en la Guadalupe [...] se asegura que, después de la caída del Imperio,
regresó a la Guayana, volviendo a tomar posesión de sus propiedades. Parece
– según los investigadores de la Guadalupe – que murió lentamente, dolorosamente, de una enfermedad que pudo ser la lepra, pero que, por mejores indicios, debió ser más bien una afección cancerosa.

ET: But in Guadeloupe [...] one is assured that after the collapse of the Empire he returned to Guiana and once more took possession of his property there. It seems, according to Guadeloupan historians, that he died slowly and painfully of a disease which could have been leprosy but which there is better reason to believe was a form of cancer.

GT: Aber auf Guadeloupe [...] versichert man, er sei nach dem Untergang des Empire nach Guayana zurückgekehrt und habe wieder von seinen Gütern Besitz ergriffen. Den Forschern von Guadeloupe zufolge scheint er eines langsamen, schmerzhaften Todes gestorben zu sein, von einer Krankheit befallen, die möglicherweise die Lepra, wahrscheinlich aber, wie bessere Indizien andeuten, ein krebsartiges Leiden war.

SET: But in Guadeloupe, [...] historians assure us that... According to them, he died slowly...

SGT: Geschichtsforscher auf Guadeloupe [...] versichern jedoch, er sei nach dem Zusammenbruch des Napoleonischen Reiches nach Guayana zurückgekehrt und habe seine Güter wieder in Besitz genommen. Er sei dann nach langem, qualvollen Leiden an einer unbekannten Krankheit, möglicherweise Lepra, gestorben. Viele Anzeichen deuten allerdings eher auf Krebs hin.

The name of the source of reference does not present any problem. The formulation of GT does not conform to the conventions of scientific style, but the obsolete spelling of the name of the bibliography (with the hyphen) seems a good device for signalling the age – and authority! – of the source.

Example 5.1.6./13
ST: La Bibliografía Universal de Didot lleva esa muerte al año 1822.
ET: Didot's Universal Bibliography gives the year of his death as 1822.
GT: Didots Universal-Bibliographie verlegt diesen Tod in das Jahr 1822.
SGT: Didots Universal-Bibliographie gibt als Todesjahr 1822 an.

c. Literary style
One of the most important features of literary style is, as I have mentioned, the use of expressive and connotative words, particularly adjectives.

A characteristic example of connotative lexis is the word *yanqui* as a pejorative synonym for *norteamericano* (cf. VOX 1979). In German, *Yankee* also has a pejorative connotation (cf. DUW 1983), and in British English it is marked as colloquial (cf. OALD 1974) or pejorative (OUD 1970). In American English, *Yankee* is used to denote the inhabitants of the Northern states, particularly those of New England (cf. RHD 1968). Since ET is not sold in the United States, the use of *Yankee* seems acceptable; an alternative with a stronger pejorative connotation would be *yanks* (cf. OALD 1974).

In Spanish, it is the adjective collocated before the noun that is mainly liable to be connotative. Translating Spanish texts into languages where the position of adjectives is fixed, the translator is confronted with the (linguistic) problem that the connotations cannot be conveyed by syntactic but only by lexical means (see ET and SGT for *el remoto ámbito del Caribe* in example 5.1.5./4; in ET, the connotative effect of *distant confines* could even be stressed by the addition of *far*).

Example 5.1.6./14
ST: Atraído por un mar que es – en Marsella, precisamente – una eterna invitación a la aventura desde los tiempos de Piteas y de los patrones fenicios...
ET: Attracted by a sea which, in Marseille especially, has been a perpetual call to adventure ever since the days of Pytheas and the Phoenician mariners....
GT: Den Verlockungen eines Meeres erliegend, das – gerade in Marseille – eine ewige Einladung zum Abenteuer ist seit den Zeiten des Pytheas und der phönizischen Kapitäne...
SGT: Dem Ruf des Meeres folgend, das – gerade in Marseille – schon seit den Zeiten des Pytheas und der phönizischen Seefahrer eine ewige Verlockung zum Abenteuer gewesen ist...

In GT, no connotation is conveyed by the noun *Einladung* ("invitation") nor by the noun *Verlockungen* ("temptations"), which used in its plural form converts the abstract notion into a concrete one, whereas *Ruf des Meeres* and *Verlockung* (in the singular) point to a literary level of style. In ET, the expressions *perpetual call* and *ever since* mark the style of the passage as literary.

The combination of two almost synonymous adjectives is another rather common means of literary intensification. In the following example, the difference between the two adjectives consists in the fact that *tornasolado* contains not only the sememe "colourful", but also a connotation of restlessness and movement and possibly even hints at the splendour of the sun (*sol*), whereas *rutilante* suggests the metallic lustre of gold (cf. Moliner 1975, VOX 1979).

Example 5.1.6./15
ST: los puertos de ese mundo tornasolado y rutilante
ET: the ports of that glittering and colourful corner of the world
GT: in den Hafenstädten dieser schillernden, glänzenden Welt
SET: the ports of that sparkling and glittering corner of the world
SGT: in den Hafenstädten jener buntschillernden, glitzernden Welt

The aspect of movement might be intensified by replacing *colourful* by *sparkling* in ET, and *glänzend* by *glitzernd* in GT. Both adjectives have an onomatopoeic effect and allow associations with both wealth (e.g. diamonds or champagne) and strong sunlight. In GT, the demonstrative pronoun in *diese ... Welt* ("this ... world") does not make it sufficiently clear that it is the "far distant confines of the Caribbean" that the author is referring to. Moreover, the pronoun *jene* belongs to a more literary style (cf. DUW 1983).

The interdependence of lexis and sentence structure and its influence on the effect of the text can be illustrated by the asyndetic enumerations of adjectives (example 5.1.6./9), verbal forms (participles, gerunds), and nouns, as in the following example.

Example 5.1.6./16
ST: Ascendido a piloto de naves comerciales, anduvo por las Antillas, observando, husmeando, aprendiendo, acabando por dejar las navegaciones para abrir en Port-au-Prince un gran almacén – o *comptoir* – de mercancías diversas, adquiridas, reunidas, mercadas por vías de compra-venta, trueque, contrabandos, cambios de sederías por café, de vainilla por perlas...
ET: Having risen to the rank of mate aboard merchantmen [sic], he travelled through the Antilles, observing, nosing about and learning, until he finally gave up the sea in order to open a large shop – or *comptoir* – in Port-au Prince, for an assortment of goods that were acquired, collected or purchased, either by trading, smuggling or exchange – silk goods for coffee, vanilla for pearls.
GT: Zum Steuermann auf Handelsschiffen aufgestiegen, befuhr er, die Augen offenhaltend und immer dazulernend, das Gebiet der Antillen und ließ schließlich die Seefahrt sein, um in Port-au-Prince einen großen Laden – oder ‚Comptoir' – für verschiedene Waren zu eröffnen, die er durch Kauf oder Schmuggel oder Tausch erwarb – man tauschte Seide gegen Kaffee, Vanille gegen Perlen –,...
SET: [...] he travelled through the Antilles, looking and learning until he finally gave up the sea in order to open a large shop, or *comptoir*, in Port-au-Prince, for an assortment of goods that were acquired, collected, purchased – by trading, smuggling or barter: silk for coffee, vanilla for pearls.
SGT: Nachdem er zum Steuermann auf Handelsschiffen aufgestiegen war, segelte er durchs Karibische Meer, schaute hier, schnupperte da, lernte alles, hängte schließlich die Seefahrt an den Nagel, um in Port-au-Prince ein großes Geschäft aufzumachen, ein Kontor oder "Comptoir" mit allen möglichen Waren, die durch Kaufen, Tauschen, Schmuggeln erworben, erfeilscht, ergattert wurden, Seide gegen Kaffee, Vanille gegen Perlen.

ET changes all the asyndetic enumerations consisting of three or four elements into syndetic enumerations of three elements, connecting the second and third element by *and* or *or*. This leads to a certain monotony of style and rhythm. SET tries to increase the "speed" of the passage by replacing the first asyndeton by an alliterating pair of verbs (*looking and learning*), reproducing the second asyndeton (*acquired, collected, purchased*), and using a dash and a colon instead of lexical connectives.

By means of connected word pairs and polysyndetic enumerations, and through the omission of the past participles, GT conveys the impression of a rather measured pace. The reader does not realize that it is not semantic quality but quantity the author is striving after, neumerating all the facets of the *glittering and sparkling* life of his character. SGT therefore tries to reproduce as many of the asyndetic structures as possible in order to give an idea of the breathtaking, almost telegraphic speed in which the author relates the story of Victor Hugues' life over a period of several years.

This last example may illustrate two more features of literary style. Firstly, verbs or verbal nouns seem to give more colour and life to the description of actions than nouns, and should be preferred in the translations as well (see SGT: *Kaufen, Tauschen, Schmuggeln* instead of *Kauf, Tausch, Schmuggel*). Secondly, the use of the past tense marks the narrative parts of the text. Since the author almost exclusively uses the forms of the *pretérito perfecto simple*, which are rarely contrasted with forms of the *pretérito imperfecto*, tenses do not in this case present a translation problem. In the sentence *Sabemos también que estaba en París, todavía, a la hora...*, the durative aspect is made explicit by *todavía*. Thus, it is not difficult to translate it even into a language without aspectual differentiations, such as German.

The author's signature, which also may be regarded as a feature of literary style, has been omitted in GT. The function of such details, which may at first sight seem insignificant and whose "translation" in no way presents any difficulties, can be elicited by text analysis.

In spite of its informative function, the postscript to the novel has to be regarded as a literary text. Apart from the stylistic features corresponding to genres and text types we therefore have to consider the characteristics of the author's personal style present in the text.

d. Personal style

One of the features of Carpentier's style which has been mentioned before is the "baroque" sentence structure, as seen in example 5.1.6./16. Long sentences are not uncommon in Spanish texts, but they are usually constructed in a linear fashion. Carpentier, however, often prefers rather complicated hypotaxes with long inclusions which produce a fairly strong tension between the beginning and end of a sentence (see also examples 5.1.6./3 and 4, 9, 12).

Example 5.1.6./17

ST: Cuanto se dice acerca de su guerra librada a los Estados Unidos – la que
llamaron los yanquis de entonces "Guerra de Brigantes" – así como a la acción de los corsarios, con sus nombres y los nombres de sus barcos, est basado en documentos reunidos por el autor en la Guadalupe y en bibliotecas de la
Barbados, así como en cortas pero instructivas referencias halladas en obras
de autores latinoamericanos que, de paso, mencionaron a Víctor Hugues.

ET: The passages dealing with the war against the United States – what the
Yankees of those days called the "Brigands' War" – together with the activities of the privateers, both their names and the names of their ships, are based
on the documents consulted by the author in Guadeloupe and in the libraries
of Barbados, as well as in brief but revealing references discovered in the
works of those Latin-American writers who have mentioned Victor Hugues in
passing.

GT: Was über den Krieg gesagt wird, den er den Vereinigten Staaten lieferte –
und den die Yankees damals „Seeräuberkrieg" nannten – ebenso die Darstellung der Tätigkeit der Korsaren samt ihren Namen und den Namen ihrer
Schiffe, gründet sich auf Unterlagen, die der Autor auf Guadeloupe und in den
Bibliotheken der Insel Barbados sammeln konnte, sowie auf kurze, aber lehr-
reiche Hinweise in Werken lateinamerikanischer Verfasser, die Victor Hugues
beiläufig erwähnen.

SET: [...] the war against the United States – or the "Brigands' War", as the
Yankees used to call it –...

SGT: Alle Angaben über seinen Krieg gegen die Vereinigten Staaten – von
den Yankees damals „Brigantenkrieg" genannt – und über die Korsarenaktionen, einschließlich der Namen von Personen und Schiffen, stützen sich auf
Dokumente aus Guadeloupe und den Bibliotheken auf Barbados sowie auf
kurze, aber aufschlußreiche Hinweise in Werken lateinamerikanischer Autoren, die Victor Hugues beiläufig erwähnen.

Hypotactic constructions are fairly common in German. The syntactic
features of personal style should therefore be changed into a nominal,
condensed sentence structure. Moreover, participle constructions like
guerra librada...., documentos reunidos... or *referencias halladas...*
are normal in Spanish, often possible in English (*documents consulted...* and *references discovered...* vs. *war against...*), but impossible in German. The relative clauses chosen in GT (e.g. *der Krieg,
den er ... lieferte*) sound extremely awkward because the verb is redundant. They have to be replaced by the normal prepositional constructions *Krieg gegen..., Dokumente aus ..., Hinweise in...*).

In ST, a condensation of style is effected by means of related
participle constructions at the beginning of a sentence (5.1.6./14, 16)
and gerund constructions (5.1.6./16). In English, these constructions
can be reproduced (6.1.6./14, 16 ET), whereas in German, the use of
the past or present participle instead of a temporal clause may mark a
literary style (5.1.6./14 GT), if used economically. However, three

participles in a row (5.1.6./16 GT) are simply indigestible and should be replaced by temporal or main clauses (5.1.6./16 SGT).

e. Audience orientation
The orientation of the text towards the addressed audience is reflected, firstly, by the presuppositions and, secondly, by the inclusions, which in this text seem to establish a feeling of solidarity between the sender and the receiver.

As explained above, most of the presuppositions are pseudo-presuppositions. In most cases, therefore, the translator can produce the same effect on the reader by using the same presuppositions. However, if a presupposition which has a merely rhetorical function for the ST reader actually belongs to the background knowledge of the TT reader or can be inferred from the text, the effect will be different. Let me give a short example.

In example 5.1.6./17, an English name (*Brigands War*) is quoted by means of a literal translation or calque. The word *brigantes* is not included in DRAE 1984, VOX 1979, Moliner 1975, Alonso 1979, Pequeño Larousse 1970. In DEA 1999, it is marked as *historical* and defined as "bandolero". Being largely unknown, the name of the war may thus be regarded by the Spanish readers as an exotism, i.e. a term belonging to the foreign culture.

In English and German, the words *brigand* (OALD 1974) and *Brigant* (DUW 1983, Brockhaus 1973) are not generally known, but at least they are included in the dictionaries. For German readers, the translation *Brigantenkrieg* (SGT) might not sound as exotic as the original, but it seems more appropriate than the explicating translation *Seeräuberkrieg* (GT). The same applies to English readers. Since in this case the name has to be translated back to its original language, we can only hope that the English reader regards *Brigands War* as a strange Americanism.

The inclusions are intended to intensify the syntactic tension (→ personal style) and to bring about a particular intonation contour (→ suprasegmental features). They are also used to address the readers directly, not only those familiar with European history (see example 5.1.6./4: *harto atareado...*, 5.1.6./14: *en Marsella...*), but also those with a knowledge of foreign languages and cultures (see example 5.1.6./16: *o comptoir*, 17: *Guerra de Brigantes*), and those who have read the novel thoroughly (see example 5.1.6./9: *firme, since-ra...*).

There are only two inclusions which do not conform to this pattern. One serves as a marker of reported speech (example 6.1.6./12: *según los investigadores*) and therefore cannot be regarded as a particular stylistic means of addressing the receiver, and the other is intended to present the author as an expert whose investigations on the subject are reliable.

Example 5.1.6./18

ST: Algunos historiadores – de los muy pocos que se hayan ocupado de él accidentalmente, fuera de Pierre Vitoux que le consagró, hace más de veinte años, un estudio todavía inédito – nos dicen...

ET: Some of the very few historians who have concerned themselves with him – purely by chance, except for Pierre Vitoux, who, more than twenty years ago, devoted an as yet unpublished study to him – say...

GT: Einige Geschichtsschreiber – einige der wenigen, die sich zufällig mit ihm beschäftigt haben, abgesehen von Pierre Vitoux, der ihm vor mehr als zwanzig Jahren eine noch unveröffentlichte Studie widmete – teilen uns mit...

SET: Historians – some of the very few who have concerned themselves with him, en passant, except for Pierre Vitoux [...] – say...

SGT: Einige Geschichtsforscher – wenige haben sich mit ihm beschäftigt, die meisten nur flüchtig, außer Pierre Vitoux, der vor mehr als zwanzig Jahren eine bisher unveröffentlichte Arbeit über ihn verfaßte – vertreten die Auffassung...

In this example, it seems difficult to avoid ambiguity. In ST, the inclusion is a complement to the subject *algunos historiadores*, while the element *fuera de Pierre Vitoux...* is a complement to *accidentalmente*. ET has reduced the inclusion in order to make the reference clear, whereas the construction in GT is ambiguous.

Inclusions are mainly used to add information or a thought related to the context without integrating it into the sentence structure or in order to stress the significance of an apposition. In many cases the dashes seem superfluous in GT because the inclusion is a subordinate clause fitting into the sentence structure (e.g. examples 5.1.6./4, 17) which is normally marked off by commas. This would apply equally to ET in example 5.1.6./17, but in this case, the wrong use of the relative pronoun *what* destroys the coherence of the sentence anyway. In the English translation, commas may be used instead of dashes if the inclusion is not too long and does not contain further inclusions (e.g. *in Marseille especially*, or *comptoir*), because, as Quirk et. al. (1972: 1071) point out, "dashes tend to give a somewhat more dramatic and informal impression, suggesting an impromptu aside, rather than a planned inclusion".

The effect which an inclusion has on intonation and focus is illustrated by the following example. GT adds an inclusion, thus stressing a detail which is not accentuated in the ST.

Example 5.1.6./19
ST: Se sabe que Víctor Hugues era marsellés, hijo de un panadero...
ET: We know that Victor Hugues was a Marseillais and the son of a baker...
GT: Man weiß, daß Victor Hugues Marseiller war – Sohn eines Bäckers –...
SGT: Es ist bekannt, daß Victor Hugues ein Bäckerssohn aus Marseille war...

In example 5.1.6./9 SGT, the word *Verhalten* is stressed by the pause immediately after it, which is indicated by the dash. Therefore, a lexical equivalent for the stress marker *propio* in the ST is superfluous. In ET, the focus should be marked by the intensifier *very*.

5.1.7. Conclusions and suggested translations
By analysing various translation problems and comparing the solutions given in the English and German versions with the original, I intended to show that my model of translation-relevant text analysis can provide a framework for a functional translation. In spite of some imperfections, the English version seems to meet the requirements of the translation skopos much better than the German version. This may be due in part to structural analogies in Spanish and English, but, as is shown by the suggested translations, the German language also provides appropriate stylistic means to solve such translation problems as "coherence and stress", "scientific style", "literary style", "personal style", and "audience-oriented elements".

To conclude this chapter, we now give in full the suggested English, German, and Dutch versions, in which the aspects discussed above have been taken into account.

a. Translation into English
(V. Gollancz, revised by P. Sparrow; Footnote: Nord/Sparrow)

THE VICTOR HUGUES OF HISTORY

Since Victor Hugues has been almost completely ignored by historians of the French Revolution – too busy describing what was taking place in Europe between the time of the Convention and the 18th Brumaire to divert their gaze to the far distant confines of the Caribbean – the author feels it might be useful to throw some light on the historical background of the character.

We know that Victor Hugues was a Marseillais and the son of a baker, and there is even cause to believe that he was remotely descended from negroes, though this would be hard to prove. Attracted by a sea which, in Marseille especially, has been a perpetual call to adventure ever since the days of Pytheas and the Phoenician mariners, he sailed off to America as a cabin-boy, and made several voyages to the Caribbean. Having risen to the rank of mate aboard merchant-ships, he travelled through the Antilles, looking and learning, until he finally gave up the sea in order to open a large shop, or *comptoir*, in Port-au-Prince, for an assortment of goods that were acquired, collected, purchased –by trading, smuggling or barter: silk for coffee, vanilla for pearls. Many such establishments still exist in the ports of that sparkling and glittering corner of the world.

His real entry into history dates from the night when his business was burned down by the Haitian revolutionaries. From that moment onwards we can follow his progress step by step, exactly as it is charted in this book. The chapters describing the recapture of Guadeloupe follow a precise chronological plan. The passages dealing with the war against the United States – or the "Brigands' War", as the Yankees used to call it – together with the activities of the privateers, their names and the names of their ships, are based on documents consulted by the author in Guadeloupe and in the libraries of Barbados, as well as on brief but revealing references discovered in the works of those Latin-American writers who have mentioned Victor Hugues in passing.

As for Victor Hugues' activities in French Guiana, there is ample source material to be found in the memoirs of the exiles. After the point in time at which this novel ends, he was tried in Paris before a military tribunal for having lost the colony to the Dutch, after a surrender which was in point of fact inevitable. Acquitted with honour, Victor Hugues again began to move in political circles. We know that he came into contact with Fouché. We also know that he was still in Paris when the Napoleonic Empire foundered.

But it is here that we lose trace of him. Historians – some of the very few who have concerned themselves with him en passant, except for Pierre Vitoux, who, more than twenty years ago, devoted an as yet unpublished study to him – say that he died in 1820, not far from Bordeaux where he "owned estates" (?). Didot's Universal Bibliography gives the year of his death as 1822. But in Guadeloupe, where the memory of Victor Hugues is still very much alive, historians assure us that after the collapse of the Empire he returned to Guiana and once more took possession of his property there. According to them, he died slowly and painfully of a disease which might have been leprosy but which we have more reason to believe was a form of cancer.[1]

What in fact was Victor Hugues' fate? We still do not know for sure, just as we know very little about his birth. But there can be no doubt that his activities, as far as they are known – resolute, sincere and heroic in their first phase, wavering, mean and even cynical in their second – give us a picture of an extraordinary man whose very behaviour reveals a dramatic dichotomy. That is why the author considered that it would be interesting to reveal the existence of this neglected historical figure in a novel which would, at the same time, embrace the world of the whole Caribbean.

A. C.

[1]*Author s Note*: These lines at the end of the first edition of the novel had just been published in Mexico, when one day, in Paris, I happened to come across one of Victor Hugues' direct descendants, who was in possession of some important family documents. From him I learnt that Victor Hugues was buried in a place not far from Cayenne. In one of those documents I made an amazing discovery: Victor Hugues had been dearly loved, for a period of many years, by a beautiful Cuban girl whose name – believe it, or not – was Sofia.

b. Translation into German
(C. Nord)

EINIGE BEMERKUNGEN ÜBER DEN HISTORISCHEN VICTOR HUGUES

Da Victor Hugues von den Geschichtsschreibern der Französischen Revolution – viel zu sehr mit den Ereignissen beschäftigt, die sich zwischen der Gründung des Nationalkonvents und dem 18. Brumaire in Europa abspielten, als daß sie noch einen Blick auf die ach so fernen Länder in der Karibik hätten werfen können – bisher nicht zur Kenntnis genommen wurde, hält der Verfasser einige klärende Bemerkungen über diese historische Gestalt für angebracht.

Es ist bekannt, daß Victor Hugues ein Bäckerssohn aus Marseille war – und man darf sogar annehmen, daß er ganz entfernte schwarze Vorfahren hatte, obwohl das natürlich nicht leicht zu beweisen wäre. Dem Ruf des Meeres folgend, das – gerade in Marseille – schon seit den Zeiten des Pytheas und der phönizischen Seefahrer eine ewige Verlockung zum Abenteuer gewesen ist, ging er, als Schiffsjunge zunächst, auf große Fahrt nach Amerika, in die Karibik. Nachdem er zum Steuermann auf Handelsschiffen aufgestiegen war, segelte er durchs Karibische Meer, schaute hier, schnupperte da, lernte alles, hängte schließlich dann die Seefahrt an den Nagel, um in Port-au-Prince ein großes Geschäft aufzumachen, ein Kontor oder „Comptoir" mit allen möglichen Waren, die durch Kaufen, Tauschen, Schmuggeln erworben, erfeilscht, ergattert wurden, Seide gegen Kaffee, Vanille gegen Perlen, so wie es auch heute noch viele Handelsunternehmen in den Hafenstädten jener buntschillernden, glitzernden Welt gibt.

In die Geschichte ging er aber erst ein, als eines Nachts sein Geschäft von den haitischen Revolutionären in Brand gesteckt wurde. Von diesem Augenblick an können wir seinen Lebenslauf verfolgen, Schritt für Schritt, so wie er im Roman erzählt wird. Die Kapitel über die Rückeroberung Guadeloupes sind nach einem strikt chronologischen Schema aufgebaut. Alle Angaben über seinen Krieg gegen die Vereinigten Staaten – von den Yankees damals „Brigantenkrieg" genannt – und über die Korsarenaktionen, einschließlich der Namen von Personen und Schiffen, stützen sich auf Dokumente aus Guadeloupe und aus den Bibliotheken auf Barbados sowie auf kurze, aber aufschlußreiche Hinweise in Werken lateinamerikanischer Autoren, die Victor Hugues beiläufig erwähnen.

Über Victor Hugues' Aktivitäten in Französisch-Guayana schließlich gibt es in den „Mémoires" der Deportation reichliches Quellenmaterial. Nach dem Zeitraum der Romanhandlung wurde Victor Hugues in Paris vor ein Kriegsgericht gestellt, weil er die Kolonie nach einer ohnehin unvermeidlichen Kapitulation an die Holländer abgetreten hatte. Nach seiner Rehabilitierung konnte er sich erneut politisch betätigen. Wir wissen, daß er Kontakt zu Fouché hatte, und wir wissen auch, daß er den Zusammenbruch des Napoleonischen Reiches noch in Paris erlebte.

Aber dort verliert sich seine Spur. Einige Geschichtsforscher – wenige haben sich mit ihm beschäftigt, die meisten nur flüchtig, außer Pierre Vitoux, der vor mehr als zwanzig Jahren eine bisher unveröffentlichte Arbeit über ihn verfaßte – vertreten die Auffassung, er sei im Jahre 1820 in der Nähe von Bordeaux, wo er „Ländereien" (?) besessen habe, gestorben. Didots Universal-Bibliographie gibt als Todesjahr 1822 an. Geschichtsforscher auf Guadeloupe, wo sein Andenken immer noch stark lebendig ist, versichern jedoch, er sei nach dem Zusammenbruch des Napoleonischen Reiches noch nach Guayana zurückgekehrt und habe seine Güter wieder in Besitz genommen. Nach langem, qualvollen Leiden sei er dann an einer unbekannten Krankheit, möglicherweise Lepra, gestorben. Viele Anzeichen deuten allerdings eher auf Krebs hin.[1]

Wie ist nun Victor Hugues tatsächlich gestorben? Darüber wissen wir genauso wenig wie über seine Geburt. Zweifellos ist aber der historische Victor Hugues, soweit uns seine Taten überliefert sind, ein außergewöhnlicher Mann, dessen Verhalten – standhaft, geradlinig, mutig in der ersten Zeit, später schwach, widersprüchlich, machtgierig und sogar menschenverachtend – eine tragische Gespaltenheit offenbart. Aus diesem Grunde hielt es der Verfasser für lohnend, das Leben dieser bisher unbekannten historischen Gestalt in einem Roman zu beleuchten, der gleichzeitig ein Bild der gesamten karibischen Welt vermittelt.

A. C.

[1]Der Roman mit diesem Nachwort war bereits in seiner ersten Auflage in Mexiko erschienen, als ich in Paris zufällig einen direkten Nachkommen von Victor Hugues kennenlernte, der wertvolle Familiendokumente besaß. Durch ihn erfuhr ich, daß Victor Hugues in einem Ort in der Nähe von Cayenne begraben liegt. Aus einem der Dokumente ging aber zu meinem großen Erstaunen auch hervor, daß Victor Hugues viele Jahre lang von einer schönen Kubanerin treu geliebt wurde, die, man kann es kaum glauben, tatsächlich Sofía hieß (Anm. d. Verf.).

c. Translation into Dutch
(J. Best)

ENKELE AANTEKENINGEN BIJ DE HISTORISCHE FIGUUR VICTOR HUGUES

Aangezien Victor Hugues in de geschiedschrijving over de Franse Revolutie tot nu toe niet voorkomt – de historici waren veel te zeer in beslag genomen door de gebeurtenissen die zich tussen de Nationale Conventie en de 18e Brumaire in Europa afspeelden om nog een blik te kunnen werpen op de verre landen van het Caraïbische gebied – acht de auteur enkele verhelderende woorden over deze historische figuur op zijn plaats.

We weten dat Victor Hugues in Marseille als zoon van een bakker geboren werd. Verondersteld wordt zelfs dat hij ver in het verleden zwarte voorvaderen heeft gehad, hetgeen natuurlijk moeilijk te bewijzen valt. Hij voelde zich aangetrokken tot de zee die sinds Pytheas en de Fenicische zeevaarders – vooral in Marseille – altijd al tot avontuur heeft gelokt en ging op grote vaart naar Amerika, aanvankelijk als scheepsjongen. Nadat hij het tot stuurman op handelsschepen had gebracht doorkruiste hij het Caraïbische gebied, nam hier een kijkje, snuffelde daar wat rond, leerde van alles en gaf er ten slotte de brui aan, om in Port-au-Prince een grote zaak oftewel "comptoir" te beginnen in allerlei waren, gekocht, gesmokkeld of geruild, zijde tegen koffie, vanille tegen parels, net zoals dat ook nu nog vaak gebruikelijk is bij veel handelsondernemingen in den havensteden van dit bontgekleurde en flonkerende gebied.

Historische betekenis kreeg Victor Hugues echter pas toen zijn zaak op zekere nacht door de Haitiaanse revolutionairen in brand werd gestoken. Vanaf dat tijdstip kunnen we zijn lotgevallen op de voet volgen, net als in den roman. Het hoofdstuk over de herovering van Guadeloupe volgt een streng chronologisch schema. Alle gegevens over zijn oorlog tegen de Verenigde Staten – door de Yankees toentertijd "Struikroveroorlog" genoemd – en zijn zeeroverijen, inclusief de namen van personen en schepen, zijn gebaseerd op documenten uit Guadeloupe en bibliotheken op Barbados. Bovendien vinden we enkele korte maar bruikbare aanwijzingen in werken van Latijnsamerikaanse auteurs die Victor Hugues terloops vermelden.

Omtrent zijn activiteiten in Frans-Guyana geven de "memoires" over de deportatie rijkelijk uitsluitsel. Na de gebeurtenissen die in de roman beschreven worden, werd Victor Hugues voor de krijgsraad in Parijs ontboden omdat hij de kolonie – na een overigens onvermijdelijk capitulatie – aan de Nederlanders had afgestaan. Hij werd in ere hersteld en ontwikkelde opnieuw activiteiten op politiek gebied. We weten dat hij contact had met Fouché. We weten eveneens dat hij tijdens de ineenstorting van het Napoleontische Rijk nog in Parijs woonde.

Dan raken we het spoor echter bijster. Enkele historici – slechts weinige hebben zich met hem beziggehouden, de meeste maar vluchtig, behalve Pierre Vitoux, die meer dan twintig jaar geleden een tot nu toe niet gepubliceerde studie aan hem wijdde – beweren dat hij in 1820 in de buurt van Bordeaux, waar hij "landerijen" (?) zou hebben bezeten, is gestorven. Didots Encyclopedisch Woordenboek noemt 1822 als sterfjaar. Historici op Guadeloupe, waar de herinnering aan Victor Hugues nog zeer levendig is, verklaren echter uitdrukkelijk dat hij na de ineenstorting van het Napoleontische Rijk naar Guyana is teruggekeerd en zijn goederen weer in bezit heeft genomen. Hier is hij volgens hen na een lange en kwellende onbekende ziekte, mogelijkerwijs lepra, overleden. Veel tekenen wijzen echter ook op kanker.[1]

Hoe heeft het einde van Victor Hugues er werkelijk uitgezien? Daarover weten we net zo weinig als over zijn geboorte. Ongetwijfeld geven zijn daden – voor zover bekend door overlevering – blijk van een tragische gespletenheid (in het begin is hij standvastig, recht door zee en moedig, later legt hij zwakheid, tegenstrijdigheid, machtswellust en verachting voor de medemens aan de dag). Om deze reden vond de schrijver het de moeite waard om het leven van deze tot nu toe onbekende figuur in een roman nader te belichten, een roman die tegelijkertijd een beeld geeft van de hele Caraïbische wereld.

A. C.

---

[1]Nadat de eerste druk van de roman met dit nawoord in Mexiko was verschenen, leerde ik in Parijs toevallig een directe nakomeling van Victor Hugues kennen die waardevolle familiedocumenten bezat. Door zijn toedoen ervoer ik dat Victor Hugues in een plaats in de buurt van Cayenne begraven ligt. Uit een van de bovengenoemde documenten bleek eveneens tot mijn grote verbazing, dat Victor Hugues jarenlang trouw bemind werd door een Cubaanse schone die inderdaad – het is nauwelijks te geloven – de naam Sofia droeg (N. v. d. A.).

5.2. Text 2: The relationship between subject matter, text structure and effect – Miguel de Unamuno: Niebla

5.2.0. Text

Al aparecer Augusto a la puerta de su casa extendió el brazo derecho, con la mano palma abajo y abierta, y dirigiendo los ojos al cielo quedóse un momento parado en esta actitud estatuaria y augusta. No era que tomaba posesion del mundo exterior, sino que observaba si llovía. Y al recibir en el dorso de la mano el frescor del lento orvallo frunció el entrecejo. Y no era tampoco que le molestase la llovizna, sino el tener que abrir el paraguas. ¡Estaba tan elegante, tan esbelto, plegado y dentro de su funda! Un paraguas cerrado es tan elegante como es feo un paraguas abierto.
(Translations in chapter 5.2.5. and 5.2.6.)

5.2.1. Analysis of extratextual factors

Miguel de Unamuno (SENDER/TEXT PRODUCER), 1864-1936 (TIME), is a "typical writer of the *generación del 98*" (Wittschier 1982: 45). He spent his childhood and youth in his native town Bilbao, then studied philosophy and literature and became a professor at the famous University of Salamanca (PLACE), where he held the position of rector for many years (except for the period of Primo de Rivera's dictatorship) (cf. Antón Andrés 1961: 198).

His literary work comprises philosophical studies, novels, several dramas and modernist poems, his favourite subjects being religion, ancient and modern Spain, people and their relationship with society, with their country, and with God (cf. García López 1968: 557). His style of writing is described as "vivid and expressive"; he avoids the hidebound traditions of literary style and seeks new ways of giving "more grace and more precision" to language (cf. García López 1968: 552).

By breaking linguistic and literary conventions Unamuno attempts to scandalize his readers, demanding an active reception of the text (INTENTION). As Anthony Kerrigan puts it in his *Introduction*, Unamuno "did not believe in any genre of writing (and of living). And if the critics insisted on judging his books according to the rules, he would invent his own genre, and did, changing existing names: he also invented 'trigedias' and 'drumas'." (Kerrigan 1974: viif.). That is why *Niebla* is called a *nivola* (playing on the semi-assonance of *niebla* and *novela*).

Niebla was published as a book in Spain in 1914 (MEDIUM, PLACE, TIME, → AUDIENCE) and was the start of a new era in Unamuno's novels. In this book it is not the plot, a simple love story

(CONTENT), but the philosophical analysis of such concepts as "time" and "identity" (cf. Antón Andrés 1961: 205) and of "fictionality" as opposed to "reality" (cf. Wittschier 1982: 45) that Unamuno is concerned with (SUBJECT MATTER).

The opposition between reality and fiction is an unusual subject for a fictional text, because it partly destroys the fiction, giving rise to an ironic distance between the author and his protagonist, which is already reflected in the title of the book. Stevens & Gullón (1979: 11) explain the metaphor in their introduction to the paperback edition of *Niebla* (Unamuno 1979):

> Niebla es la novela del absurdo existencial, del hombre perdido en la angustia de una vida sin finalidad. La vida es niebla y entre la niebla se abren los caminos por donde vagamos.

In the following chapters I am going to show how the subject matter is reflected in certain stylistic features and how the ironic effect of the text is achieved. The analysis is based on a short, but, in my view, characteristic paragraph of the book, and concentrates on one single aspect, the relation between subject matter and text structure.

5.2.2. The beginning of a text as a key to its interpretation
The beginning of a long text, particularly in fiction, can be the key to its interpretation (cf. chapter 3.2.4.c) because the way in which an author introduces the figures and the time and place of the plot provides the foundation for the comprehension of the whole text. Therefore, a thorough analysis of the beginning should be the first step in translating a novel. The sample text confirms this hypothesis in that it presents some of the most important characteristics of the composition and the internal structure of the whole book. These have to be taken into consideration if the translation is to give a correct impression of the stylistic devices which the author uses in order to realize his intentions. If the translation skopos requires equivalence of effect – as appears to be the conventional skopos of literary translation in our culture today – these stilistic devices should be reproduced in the translation.

By analysing the text structure I intend to bring out irony as the thematic thread running through the whole book. Both the protagonist Augusto and the novel as a literary product are treated with irony by Unamuno. He even ridicules himself as the inventor of a fictitious person who frees himself from his "creator", and cries defiantly: "I am to die as a creature of fiction? Very well, my lord creator Don Miguel de Unamuno, you will die too! [...] Good will cease to dream you!" (Unamuno 1976: 24). Thus, it is the thematic element of irony that gives the novel its particular effect, and I will demonstrate that it is reflected in the microstructures of the text.

5.2.3. Some considerations on ironic intention

It is generally accepted that ironic utterances have an "extra degree" of expressivity (cf. Oomen 1983: 22) which derives from the contrast between certain linguistic qualities and the pragmatic conditions of the situation. Ironic speakers offend against the rule of sincerity (cf. Groeben & Scheele 1984: 3), which is indispensable for the success of a speech act, but at the same time they give the listener a hint that they do not mean what they are saying, so that the listener can understand the correct meaning of the utterance (cf. Warning 1976: 418).

In ironic speech, the sender pretends to be sincere, while signalling that s/he is not. If the ironic contrast between what is said, and what is meant, is not clear from the situation, the sender has to use certain signals or markers of irony, so-called "interference factors" which are intended to prevent a literal interpretation of the utterance. There are verbal and non-verbal or paralinguistic irony markers, such as the repetition of words, extravagant metaphors, overlong sentences, or a wink of the eye, a particular intonation, quotation marks, or italics (cf. Weinrich 1966: 61).

Since irony is based on an understanding between sender and receiver about the discrepancy between text and situation, it does not normally present any difficulties in oral communication. A written text, however, is separated from its situation, and a fictional text even creates its own (fictitious) situation. The greater the distance between the text and its pragmatic surroundings, the greater the obligation to use irony markers. If the readers are to understand irony in a fictional text, they have to be familiar with the author's world, and this familiarity is often established by the text itself (cf. Warning 1976: 421).

The sample text contains an introductory description of the protagonist of a fictional text. The author does not intervene himself (e.g. as a personal narrator), but in his *post-prólogo* he has addressed the reader personally, commenting on the *prólogo* of a certain (fictitious) Victor Goti. In "normal" novels the description of a person lives on the fiction of being realistic, while in this case the author has already jeopardized this fiction by his comments before the beginning of the story. Breaking the convention that an author usually does not give any critical comments on a prologue written by a friend (!) together with the word-creation *post-prólogo* ("after-foreword") might already be taken as two irony markers which allow the readers some hypotheses about the relation between text and situation, sensitizing them to the possibility of irony in the novel itself.

For the reader/translator it is important not only to decipher irony and elicit the real meaning of the text; the main question is what intention the author tries to realize by his ironic utterances and what function irony has in the text. These two factors determine whether the irony in the source text should be reproduced in the target text and, if so, how this should be effected.

Irony can have several functions: it may serve to avoid the conventions of politeness, to achieve an advantage in argumentation, to express emotional detachment or cool superiority, to establish an intimate relationship between sender and receiver (who is not the object of irony) or to comment on a situation (cf. Oomen 1983: 35ff.). Irony may also be used to ridicule the addressee in the eyes of a third person in order to bolster the self-confidence of the speaker (cf. Groeben & Scheele 1984: 4ff.).

We may safely assume that in our sample text Unamuno wants to express a certain detachment, a kind of alienation effect, towards his creation, Augusto, and to establish a feeling of solidarity between author and reader (and not between the reader and the protagonist). But it does seem rather unlikely that the author creates a figure in a novel with the sole purpose of ridiculing it in the eyes of the reader (is this possible, anyway, in a fictional text?).

Unamuno's irony is neither gross nor rude, but extremely subtle (see Allemann's definition of "poetic irony", 1969: 17), and therefore rather difficult to detect. But when we analyse the structure of the sample text, the essential features become clear. Unamuno describes his protagonist with great precision, using irony as a thematic element running through the whole book, and combines critical distance with tender sympathy. Unamuno compares Augusto's existence as Unamuno's creation with his own existence as God's creation. The novel is ironic in the sense that it presents "assumptions and assertions on the fictitiousness of the world" (cf. Japp 1983: 240, my translation) in the form of fiction.

5.2.4. Analysis of text structure

The thematic and stylistic interpretation of the sample text is based on three aspects of the factor of composition, that is: theme-rheme structure, sentence structure, and the relief produced by aspect and tense. The other intratextual factors will not be considered in this analysis.

a. Theme-rheme structure
The analysis of the theme-rheme structure is based on a purely semantic interpretation of theme and rheme (cf. ch. 3.2.4.e), regardless of its position in the sentence. The information units are represented in infinitives in order to separate the semantic from the syntactic structure.

The thematic and rhematic elements are numbered so as to make clear to which theme a certain rheme belongs. For example, rheme 1/4 is the fourth rheme to the first theme.

In the first sentence, the first theme, i.e. the protagonist of the novel, is introduced to the reader only by his first name, Augusto. This device conveys the impression that the reader is expected to know Augusto, for only two people who know a third person can refer to him/her in this way at the beginning of a conversation. Thus, the readers get the impression that they are being addressed personally and that they are part of the (fictitious?) situation. This is a first indicator of the "fusion" of reality and fictional world in the novel.

The first theme is complemented by ten rhemes, before a new theme is introduced.

Theme 1:	Augusto
Rheme 1/1:	aparecer a la puerta de su casa
Rheme 1/2:	extender el brazo derecho, con la mano palma abajo y abierta
Rheme 1/3:	dirigir los ojos al cielo
Rheme 1/4:	quedarse un momento parado en esta actitud estatuaria y augusta
Rheme 1/5:	no tomar posesion del mundo exterior
Rheme 1/6:	observar si llueve
Rheme 1/7:	recibir en el dorso de la mano el frescor del lento orvallo
Rheme 1/8:	fruncir el entrecejo
Rheme 1/9:	no ser molestado por la llovizna
Rheme 1/10:	ser molestado por el tener que abrir el paraguas

The ten rhemes present Augusto, the protagonist of the novel, without saying anything explicitly about him, about his age, his appearance, his profession, his way of life, etc. Nevertheless, the reader receives a lot of valuable information from the way in which Augusto's actions (or rather, non-actions), his behaviour and his possible or actual feelings are described.

Augusto's actions and feelings are presented in a strictly chronological order (*ordo naturalis*, cf. Lausberg 1971: 27), so that the reader gains the impression that quite a long time has elapsed between Augusto's first appearance at the door and the feeling described in Rheme 1/10. The *ordo naturalis* conventionally implies clearness and authenticity, but at the same time runs the risk of being monotonous and dull, as Lausberg (1971: 27) points out. Since throughout the whole of the paragraph we find no description of a movement of the whole body, but only of some parts (arm, eyes, forehead), the long sequence of rhemes conveys the impression of a motionless, quiet scene. The readers have time to follow, one by one, the narrator's observations as if they themselves were watching Augusto at the door of his house. The time of narration is longer than the narrated time.

In this way, the reader has time to interpret Augusto's facial expressions and gestures. However, the obvious conclusions as to what Augusto may be thinking or feeling are anticipated – and immediately contradicted! – by the narrator (Rheme 1/5 and 1/9), who contrasts solemnity and triviality (Rheme 1/4 and 1/6), practical common sense and aesthetic sense (Rheme 1/9 and 1/10). By this stylistic device, Augusto is characterized as being an extraordinary person. The speed of the narration is slowed down even more by the enumeration of feelings and intentions which are only surmised, but not realized.

The second theme derives from a segment of the last rheme to Theme 1 (1/10): Augusto's umbrella. The observer's (or rather, reader's) eyes are directed away from the overall view of the scene evoked by Rheme 1/1 towards several features of the person's body (Rheme 1/2 to 1/10, moving from the general aspect of his posture and the less articulate parts of the body to the face and even the thoughts) and finally towards a particular object in the person's hand. This object, an umbrella, seems rather surprising in the Spanish setting which the reader has inferred from the extratextual situation (name of the author, place and medium of publication, etc.).

Theme 2 is accompanied by four rhemes, describing four qualities of the umbrella. Here, Unamuno's unconventional style becomes evident once again. Two of the qualities refer to the appearance (*elegante*, *esbelto*), and the other two characterize the condition (*plegado*) and the location (*en su funda*), the latter two qualities lending the umbrella the two former qualities. The author uses here the rhetorical figure of zeugma (i.e. a figure by which a single word is made to refer to two or more words in the sentence; especially when applying to

them in different senses, cf. OUD 1970), which is also regarded as an
irony marker (cf. Warning 1976: 419, and Groeben & Scheele 1984:
66). When we consider Rheme 1/10, from which Theme 2 derives, the
order of the rhemes suggests a certain climax towards *en su funda*.
The umbrella looks so elegant because it is in its cover, and that is
why Augusto hesitates to open it even though it is raining. Evidently,
Augusto is not only an aesthete, but also a pedant, who likes things to
be in their place.

Theme 2:	(el paraguas de Augusto)
Rheme 2/1:	estar muy elegante
Rheme 2/2:	(estar) muy esbelto
Rheme 2/3:	(estar) plegado
Rheme 2/4:	(estar) en su funda

The rhemes of the second theme contain no action or activity at all.
They describe a state of affairs which, as it seems, should not be
changed for important aesthetic reasons. It seems impossible to slack-
en the tempo of the narration further, but by the use of a simple device, the author succeeds in stopping the course of time completely.
He withdraws, as it were, from the scene, entering into philosophic
timelessness by generalizing. Thus, *Augusto s (folded) umbrella*
(Theme 2) becomes *a folded umbrella as such* (Theme 3) and, in contrast, *an opened umbrella as such* (Theme 4). Here, the rhematic elements accompanying these two themes imply a comparison. It is,
however, not the quality (*elegant* or *ugly*) that forms the tertium comparationis, but the degree in which these qualities are present!

Theme 3:	un paraguas cerrado
Rheme 3/1:	ser muy elegante
Theme 4:	un paraguas abierto
Rheme 4/1:	ser muy (= igualmente) feo

Here, once more, the ironic, detached attitude of the author towards
his protagonist becomes evident. He seems to be eager to share this attitude with the reader by turning a rather insignificant object, belonging to the protagonist, into the subject matter of a general philosophical consideration. The reader must be aware of the fact that the author
is not seriously concerned with the aesthetics of either folded or o-
pened umbrellas, but that the real subject of the sentence is Augusto
or, rather, the fictitiousness of reality or the realness of fiction. The
author's wink is intended to prevent the reader from becoming part of
the fictitious world described in the text.

So, let me briefly restate the results of the analysis of the theme-rheme structure. Looking at the whole catalogue of themes and rhemes, we discover two parallel developments: on the one hand, the number of rhemes accompanying a theme clearly decreases (10 – 4 – 1), and on the other hand, the themes become less and less specific, more and more general (*the individual person Augusto – Augusto s umbrella, an unspecified specimen of a certain type of object   the folded or opened umbrella as such*, as an abstract idea). The two lines of development are not opposed to each other, but complementary. The more individual an object of description is, the more specific qualities or features it will present. The accumulation of ten rhemes with one main theme ("progression with a continuous theme", as Daneš calls it, cf. 1978: 189) conveys a high degree of density and a minimum of communicative dynamics to the text, while the transition from Rheme 1/10 to Theme 2, which belongs to the type of "simple linear progression" (cf. Daneš 1978: 189), keeps the narration flowing to some degree, at any rate. The changes from Theme 2 to Theme 3 (by generalizing the theme and turning back, as it were, to Rheme 2/1) and from Theme 3 to Theme 4 (by using the antonym on the same level of generalization, linking Rheme 3/1 and Rheme 4/1 indirectly by a comparison) imply a total standstill in the narration. Indeed, the following paragraph contains a rather long stream of thought in which Augusto muses over the incompatibility of beauty and usefulness (*How beautiful an orange still uneaten!*) and the aimlessness of life. He is only released from this paralysis by the encounter with Eugenia.

The detailed analysis shows how the subject matter is reflected in the theme-rheme structure of the text. The interdependence between subject matter and structure becomes even more obvious when we try to look at the syntactic structure from a similar angle.

b. Sentence structure

The stylistic devices of sentence structure we are taking into consideration in this chapter are the length and construction of the sentences, the distribution of main clauses and subordinate clauses, the order of sentence constituents, and the linkage of clauses and sentences. The sentence structure is illustrated by a schematic representation of the sentence, in which main clauses are characterized by simple lines, subordinate clauses by dotted lines, and coordinating connectives by a +-sign.

Adverbial infinitive and gerund constructions and finite clause objects (FCO, for the term cf. Quirk et al. 1972: 832), which in Spanish – as in English – are integrated into the intonation and not marked off by commas as in German, are regarded as sentence constituents. For the sake of clarity, they are mentioned in the pattern. Punctuation marks are also included.

The representation of the sentence patterns illustrates the syntactic structures of the paragraph. The sample text consists of six sentences, five of them being of medium length (2, 3, 4, 5, 6). The sixth sentence is rather long, but is divided into two equal, almost parallel parts, which are only linked by punctuation (comma instead of full stop). The paratactical structure is obvious. The only subordinate clause (6), which from the semantic point of view is closely linked to the main clause by the comparison, is not marked off by a comma. The finite clause object *si llovía* is integrated into the main clause like a nominal object and does not interfere with the paratactical structure. The adverbial complements, some of which are quite long, are integrated into the main clauses in the form of infinitive or gerund constructions, although the grammatical system of Spanish would have allowed subordinate clauses as well.

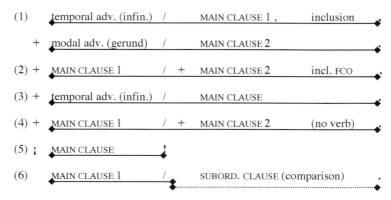

Coordinating connectives (*y* in additive and *sino que* in adversative function) between clauses and sentences produce a smooth flow of syntax without significant pauses. The expression *no era que* is not regarded as a main clause, but as a coordinating connective (cf. *es que* as a causal conjunction) introducing a negative causal clause. Causal clauses which "establish an imputed causality and thus provide a reason other than that expected" (cf. Warning 1976: 420) are conventional irony markers. The polysyndetic linkage of elements, including the beginning of a new sentence with a coordinating connective, slows down the tempo of the syntactic flow of the narration.

Sentences 2 and 4 are parallel constructions. In sentence 4, the second main clause is replaced by an elliptic noun phrase without a verb. Thus, the intensifying and slowing effect of repetition is combined with the stylistic principle of (formal) variation, which prevents monotony and at the same time increases the static impression of the paragraph. The repetition of syntactic patterns is also considered to be an irony marker (cf. Groeben & Scheele 1984: 66).

Sentence 5 has quite an original structure. A copulative verb (*estar*) is combined with four complements in the form of a syndetic enumeration which seems complete in itself. The first two complements have the same function and the same structure (two qualities are mentioned by *tan* + adjective), the third complement describes a state of the object (*plegado*), and the fourth complement refers to the place or environment of the object (*en su funda*). The unusual combination, in which the copulative verb is not repeated, sounds very short and condensed and conveys the impression of a surprising climax. Since the sentence does not open with a connective and is formulated as an exclamation, it presents a clear contrast to the preceding sentences.

Sentence 6 sounds like a slogan. With its chiastic construction, this general statement on the beauty of umbrellas appears to be a kind of punch-line to the whole paragraph and again shows the ironic undertone of the text. The marked rhythm of the sentence and the assonances between *cerrado* and *elegante*, on the one hand, and *feo* and *abierto*, on the other, can also be regarded as irony markers.

On the whole, the paratactical structure of the passage, with its numerous polysyndetic linkages, intensifies the impression of a quiet, motionless description. The difference of theme-rheme structure between sentences 1 to 4 and 5 to 6 has a counterpart in the sentence structure, since the last two sentences can be clearly distinguished in length and syntax from the first four.

c. Relief structure

The concept of relief structure (or *mise-en-relief*) is based on the idea that the importance, or weight, given to a piece of information by the author is reflected by the choice of main and subordinate clauses and their corresponding prosodic and intonation features. Thus, an utterance formulated in a main clause would be marked as foreground information, while subordinate clauses as well as non-finite infinitive, participle or gerund constructions, provide the necessary background information. Seen in this way, the distribution of rhematic information into main and subordinate clauses produces a relief structure in the text.

In languages with temporal aspects, such as Spanish, relief structure is also marked by the use of tenses. Tenses with a perfective aspect (e.g. the Spanish *pretérito perfecto simple (PPS)*, as in *extendió*) present the dynamic actions and processes of the foreground, while tenses with imperfective aspect (e.g. the Spanish *pretérito imperfecto (PI)*, as in *tomaba*, or the subjunctive tenses) describe the static conditions of the background (cf. Gili y Gaya 1967: 149).

Both the distribution of clauses and the use of tenses have a combined effect on the relief structure present in the sample text, tenses providing the decisive aspect.

Rheme 1/1: background (infinitive)
Rheme 1/2: foreground (main clause in PPS)
Rheme 1/3: background (gerund)
Rheme 1/4: foreground (main clause in PPS)
Rheme 1/5: background (main clause in PI)
Rheme 1/6: background (main clause with FOC in PI)
Rheme 1/7: background (infinitive)
Rheme 1/8: foreground (main clause in PPS)
Rheme 1/9: background (main clause in subjunctive)
Rheme 1/10: background (elliptic main clause, verb from 1/9)

In this first part of the paragraph, the foreground consists of three very small actions or even non-actions (*extendió el brazo*, *quedóse parado*, and *frunció el entrecejo*), while all the other utterances are explanations by the (omniscient) author, which provide the characterization of the person. Thus, it is the background which actually contains the most important information. Here we find the contrast between what is said and what is meant, which is characteristic of ironic speech (cf. Willer & Groeben 1980: 292). If we assume that the distribution of information into main and subordinate clauses according to its communicative significance is a literary convention, then we may characterize the particular relief structure of the sample text as an "offence" against this convention, this being another indicator of the author's ironic intention.

Rheme 2/1 to Rheme 2/4 belong to the background. They contain the justification of Rheme 1/10 in the form of an inner monologue or *stream-of-consciousness* which is marked not only by the use of PI,

but also by the exclamation marks and the use of *tan* instead of *muy*.
As Warning (1976: 410) points out, the stream-of-consciousness technique can also be regarded as an irony marker.

The last sentence is formulated in the present tense, which in
Spanish, according to Gili y Gaya (1967: 153), has a non-perfective
aspect. The present tense characterizes the sentence as a comment by
which the author, with an ironic smile, so to speak, seems to take the
side of his protagonist. Belonging neither to background nor foreground, this sentence could be called an "aside".

The analysis of the relief structure confirms the results of the
analyses of theme-rheme and sentence structures. The composition of
the sample text follows an ingenious system which is not immediately
apparent. Only a thorough structural analysis can reveal the hidden
mechanisms of irony. A translator who wants to reproduce this particular form of poetic irony, must try to reproduce the structural features
on which it is based, at least those which are not specific to the source
culture and language. In the following chapter I will discuss whether
the published translations of the text into English and German have
reproduced the ironic structures of the Spanish original, and, where it
is found to be the case, what procedures have been used.

5.2.5. Translation criticism

The English translation of the novel (*Mist*) is included in the volume
Novela/Nivola (Unamuno 1976), translated and with an introduction
by Anthony Kerrigan. The first paragraph of chapter I (= ET) reads as
follows:

> Augusto appeared at the door of his house and held out his right hand, palm
> downward; gazing up at the sky, he momentarily struck the posture of a sta-
> tue. He was not taking posession of the external world, but merely observing
> whether or not it was raining. As he felt the fresh intermittent wet on the back
> of his hand, he frowned, not because the drizzle bothered him, but because he
> would have to open up his umbrella. It made such a fine line folded in its
> case! A folded umbrella is as elegant as an opened one is awkward.

The German version of the novel (*Nebel*) was published in 1968 as a
paperback edition of Otto Buek's translation, revised by Doris Deinhard. The first paragraph of chapter I (= GT) reads as follows:

> Augusto trat aus der Tür seines Hauses, streckte den rechten Arm aus, spreizte
> die Hand, die innere Fläche nach unten gewandt, und verharrte dann, den
> Blick zum Himmel gerichtet, einen Augenblick in dieser statuenhaften und er-
> habenen Haltung. Nicht, als ob er so von der ihn umgebenden Welt Besitz er-
> greifen wollte: er wollte nur feststellen, ob es regnete. Er runzelte die Stirn, als

er die Kühle des langsam niederrieselnden Staubregens auf dem Handrücken verspürte. Und es war weniger der feine Regen, der ihn störte, als vielmehr der ärgerliche Umstand, daß er seinen Regenschirm öffnen mußte – so schlank, so elegant, so geschickt war dieser in sein Futteral gerollt. Ein geschlossener Regenschirm ist ebenso elegant, wie ein offener häßlich ist.

In the following critical analysis, ET and GT will be compared with the source text only where theme-rheme structure, sentence structure, and relief structure are concerned. Lexical translation problems will not be discussed in detail. Nevertheless, as far as possible, lexical faults or imperfections have been corrected in the suggested translations (SET and SGT) presented at the end of the chapter.

a. Theme-rheme structure

The theme-rheme structure of ET and GT are presented in the following table. Any differences between the translations and the ST (see ch. 5.2.4.a) have been marked by italics.

	ST	ET	GT
Theme 1	Augusto	Augusto	Augusto
Rheme 1/1	aparecer a la puerta de su casa	to appear at the door of his house	*aus* der Tür seines Hauses *treten*
Rheme 1/2	extender el brazo derecho...	to hold out his *hand...*	den Arm ausstrecken...
Rheme 1/3	dirigir los ojos al cielo	to *gaze up* at the sky	*die Hand spreizen*
Rheme 1/4	quedarse un momento parado...	to *strike the posture* of...	in dieser Haltung ... verharren
Rheme 1/5	no tomar posesion...	not to be taking possession	nicht Besitz ergreifen *wollen*
Rheme 1/6	observar si llueve	to be *merely* observing whether or not it was raining	*nur* feststellen wollen, ob es regnete
Rheme 1/7	recibir en el dorso de la mano...	to feel .... on the back of his hand	*die Stirn runzeln*
Rheme 1/8	fruncir el entrecejo	to frown	*auf dem Handrücken verspüren*
Rheme 1/9	no ser molestado por la llovizna	not to be bothered by the drizzle	nicht *so sehr* vom Regen gestört sein
Rheme 1/10	ser molestado por el tener que abrir el paraguas	(to expect) *to have to open up* his umbrella	von dem ärgerlichen Umstand, seinen Regenschirm öffnen zu müssen, gestört sein

	ST	ET	GT
Theme 2	(el paraguas de A.)	it (Augusto's umbrella)	dieser (A.'s Schirm)
Rheme 2/1	estar muy elegante	*make a fine line folded in its case*	so schlank, so elegant, so *geschickt*
Rheme 2/2	(estar) muy esbelto		in sein Futteral gerollt sein
Rheme 2/3	(estar) plegado		
Rheme 2/4	(estar) en su funda		
Theme 3	un paraguas cerrado	a folded umbrella	ein geschlossener Regenschirm
Rheme 3/1	ser muy elegante	to be very elegant	sehr elegant sein
Theme 4	un paraguas abierto	an opened one (= umbrella)	ein offener (Regenschirm)
Rheme 4/1	ser muy (= igualmente) feo	to be very (= equally) *awkward*	sehr (= ebenso) häßlich sein

As far as the order of rhemes is concerned, ET follows the ST, while GT converts the complement of Rheme 1/2 into Rheme 1/3 and the original Rheme 1/3 into a complement of 1/4. Consequently, the movement of the eyes does not appear in the catalogue of actions. Moreover, GT exchanges Rheme 1/7 and 1/8, thus destroying the *ordo naturalis* which gives the enumeration its characteristic steady flow, and producing an *ordo artificialis* which introduces an element of suspense that is not present in the ST.

In both translations, the four rhemes accompanying Theme 2 are blended into one. This procedure intensifies the dynamic progression of the sentence, presenting the qualities of the umbrella, which seem so important to Augusto, in an overall view, instead of characterizing them one by one (GT), or reducing the four details to two (ET) and thus missing the opportunity of forming a climax and/or a zeugma which, as has been mentioned already, is another indicator of ironic meaning. Unamuno's love of minute details is not reflected in the two translations. The narration time is not much longer than the time required by the observer to look at the person.

Although the semantic changes in Rheme 1/1 (GT), 1/2 (ET), 1/3 (ET), 1/4 (ET), 1/6 (ET, GT), 1/9 (GT), and 1/10 (ET) are not very striking, they should not be underestimated, because the stillness of the scene and the meticulousness of the description (and, thus, the ironic effect) depend on each individual detail. Augusto appears at the door of his house, he does not step out (GT), he holds out his arm, not his hand (ET), and he does not spread his hand (GT). He does not strike the posture of a statue (ET), but the posture he has adopted reminds the observer (the narrator, Unamuno!) of a statue. For Augusto, it is not a minor aim (ET, GT) to observe whether it is raining, but this is why he holds out his arm, and he does not frown because he would have to open up his umbrella (ET), but because he is bothered by the necessity of destroying the beauty of his umbrella (and not by the awkwardness of carrying an opened umbrella)!

Both translations miss a great deal of Unamuno's irony, though in different ways. The analysis of the irony markers will be represented in a table at the end of the chapter.

b. Sentence structure

The sentence patterns of ET and GT differ considerably from that of the ST, as is illustrated by the following diagrams.

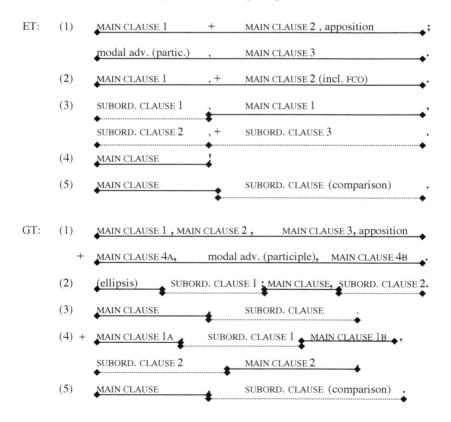

Both sentence patterns seem much more hypotactic than that of the original. The paratactic, polysyndetic character of the ST sentence structure and the parallelisms which form the basis of the steady flow of narration in ST are lost. In GT, the constant alternation of main and subordinate clauses as well as the inclusions convey the impression of great speed and breathlessness. This impression is intensified by the ellipsis in sentence 2, the replacement of coordinating connectives by asyndetic transitions (colon, dash), and by the combination of sentence 4 with sentence 5. The consequences of this last change are far more serious since it destroys the macrostructure of the passage which is characterized by the contrast between sentences 1 and 4 with sentences 5 and 6. Moreover, the distinction between the perspectives of detached description and inner monologue is blurred.

Compared with this, the combination of sentence 3 and sentence 4 in ET is a minor change which does not spoil the effect of the macrostructural features. Nevertheless, the pause between the two sentences which serves to build up an expectation in the reader (Why did Augusto frown?) has gone because the explanation follows immediately. This gives a much more factual, serious tone to the passage, weakening the ironic effect.

Neither ET nor GT have succeeded in reproducing the characteristic structure (chiasm, rhythm, assonances) of the last sentence. However, if this surprising statement is not formulated in a pointed, pathetic way, it actually loses much of its ironic effect.

c. Relief structure

In English and German, the distribution of main clauses and subordinate clauses may also give a certain relief structure to a text. Non-finite constructions, such as gerunds, participles and infinitives, can be used as a means of indicating background information, although in German they are often marked as literary.

As far as tenses are concerned, English has two sets of aspectual contrasts: perfective/non-perfective and progressive/non-progressive (cf. Quirk et al. 1972 : 90ff.). While the former refers to the difference in aspect of present perfect and simple past, which is not relevant in our sample text, the latter is a valuable tool for distinguishing between a momentary or completed action, an action in progress, and the description of a state or position.

The German language makes neither of these distinctions. But, like English, it does distinguish verbal aspects. These refer to the manner in which a verb action is regarded or experienced irrespective of the grammatical form in which the verb is used. Dynamic verbs serve to designate actions and processes with a perfective aspect (such as *appear* or *frown*), whereas stative verbs describe a state or condition (such as *stand*), a relation (such as *be, consist of*), a perception (such as *want, believe*), etc. (cf. Quirk et al. 1972: 95f.). There are verbs which can be used both in the perfective and the non-perfective aspect. This verbal aspect is normally determined by context markers, such as morphological features (e.g. *he frowned* vs. *he was frowning*), temporal adverbs (e.g. *suddenly*) or modal auxiliaries, such as *used to* or *started to*. Dynamic verbs usually mark the foreground in main clauses, but may receive a non-perfective aspect in subordinate clauses, whereas stative verbs and progressive forms are only used for background information.

In the light of these considerations we are going to analyse the relief structure of ET and GT. In the following table, main clauses are marked as MC, subordinate clauses as SC, foreground actions as F, and background actions and states as B. The verbal aspects are characterized as p (= perfective) and np (= non-perfective), respectively. The foreground actions are marked by italics.

Rh.	ET	Aspect	Rel	GT	Aspect	Rel
1/1	*appeared*	p/MC	F	*erschien*	p/MC	F
1/2	*held out*	p/MC	F	*streckte aus*	p/MC	F
1/3	gazing	p-np/MC	B	*spreizte*	p/MC	F
1/4	*struck*	p/MC	F	verharrte	np/MC	B
1/5	was not taking	np/MC	B	nicht als ob er ... wollte	np/SC	B
1/6	was observing	np/MC	B	wollte	np/MC	B
1/7	felt	np/MC	B	*runzelte die Stirn*	p/MC	F
1/8	*frowned*	p/MC	F	verspürte	np/SC	B
1/9	bothered	np/SC	B	war	np/MC	B
				störte	np/SC	B
1/10	would have to	np/SC	B	mußte	np/SC	B
2/1	made a fine line	np/MC	B	war	np/MC	B
3/1	is elegant	np/MC	B	ist	np/MC	B
4/1	is awkward	np/MC	B	ist	np/SC	B

A text beginning with two (ET) or even three (GT) foreground actions will not normally have the effect of a "slow-motion"-picture, but rather that of a film which is running too fast. The irony implied in the ST contrast of only three minute, but well calculated, foreground movements or rather non-movements against the background set by seven items which describe possible and actual reasons, thoughts,

feelings, impressions and states of mind, is lost if the reader is unable
to recognize the underlying logic of the distribution. In ST, foreground
and background items are mentioned at increasing intervals, whereas
there is no system in the distribution of F and B details either in ET or
in GT. ST, ET, and GT tell three different (foreground) stories:

> ST: Augusto holds out his arm, stands still for a moment, and frowns.
> ET: Augusto appears at the door of his house, holds out his hand, strikes a certain posture, and frowns.
> GT: Augusto steps out of the door of his house, holds out his arm, spreads his hand, and frowns.

The last two sentences are clearly assigned to the background both in
ET and GT. Since in German the inner monologue is not marked by a
particular use of tenses, the translator might include, apart from the
exclamation mark and the use of *so*, one of the modal particles (e.g.
doch) which are so typical of spoken German language (and so difficult to "translate" into other languages!), as an additional indicator of
stream-of-consciousness.

5.2.6. Conclusions and suggested translations

Neither translation gives a true impression of the ironic effect produced by the particular features of theme-rheme structure, sentence
and relief structure. In the table below, we can compare the occurrences of structural features and irony markers discovered in the ST
with those in ET and GT. Of course, there may be some additional
markers in the translations, which will not show up in the table. For
instance, in ET, the rather technical expression *the fresh intermittent
wet* produces an ironic contrast with the less technical context (*take
possession, drizzle, fine line*). But on the whole, there are few compensations for the omitted irony markers (which I feel could have
been reproduced in the target language) either in ET or in GT.

STRUCTURAL FEATURES	ST	ET	GT
ordo naturalis	+	+	-
movements of the body	0	0	1
movements of parts of the body	1	3	2
facial expressions	2	1	2
contrast triviality vs. solemnity	+	-	-
contrast common sense vs. aesthetic sense	+	-	+
narration time longer than narrated time	+	-	-
rheme progression 1/10-2	+	+	+
rheme progression 2/1-3	+	-	+
rheme progression 3/1-4/1 (contrast)	+	-	+

STRUCTURAL FEATURES (cont.)	ST	ET	GT
gradually decreasing numer of themes	+	-	-
increasing generalization of themes	+	+	+
minimum communicative dynamics in 1	+	+	+
simple linear progression in 2 and 3	+	+	+
number of sentences	6	5	5
long sentences	5	3	2
short or medium-size sentences	1	2	3
paratactical structure	+	-	-
polysyndeton	+	-	-
macrostructural "gap" between sentences 4 and 5	+	+	-
foreground items	3	4	4
background items	12	9	9

IRONY MARKERS	ST	ET	GT
climax (in trivial context)	+	-	-
zeugma	+	-	-
imputed causality	+	-	+
parallelism between sentence 1a and 1b	+	-	-
parallelism between sentences 2 and 4	+	-	-
repetition of lexical element (tan)	+	-	+
chiasm (in trivial context)	+	-	-
rhythmic qualities of punchline	+	-	-
assonances in punchline	+	-	-
violation of conventional information distribution	+	+	+
stream-of-consciousness technique	+	+	+

The accumulation of irony markers is very important for the ironic effect. Each of the structural features mentioned may have a completely different effect when it is used alone or in a different context. Together, they are unmistakable indicators of ironic meaning.

Apart from the structural irony markers, there are also quite a few lexical ones, such as the pun on the name of Augusto and his *actitud augusta* (left out in ET), the variation on the words designating rain (*llovía – orvallo – llovizna*), the use of rare or onomatopoeic words or collocations (e.g. *lento orvallo*), etc., which we have also tried to take into consideration in the following suggested translations.

SET: Appearing at the door of his house, Augusto held out his right arm, the hand palm downward, and directing his eyes skywards, he remained for a moment in this statue-like and exalted pose. He was not, however, taking possession of the outside world, but observing whether or not it was raining. And, when he felt the freshness of the light droplets on the back of his hand, he frowned. Yet it was not the drizzle that was bothering him, but the necessity of opening up his umbrella. Didn't it look beautiful and slim, elegantly folded, and in its cover? A folded umbrella is a thing of beauty – yet how ugly is an opened one. (P.S.)

SGT: Als Augusto in der Tür seines Hauses erschien, streckte er seinen rechten Arm aus, die Handfläche nach unten, und blieb dann, die Augen gen Himmel richtend, einen Augenblick in dieser erhabenen Haltung eines Denkmals stehen. Doch er machte sich nicht etwa die Außenwelt untertan, sondern stellte fest, ob es regnete. Und als er auf seinem Handrücken die Kühle des sanften Nieselns fühlte, runzelte er die Stirn. Aber ihn störte nicht etwa der leichte Regen, sondern die Notwendigkeit, seinen Schirm aufzuspannen. Der war doch so elegant, so schlank, gefaltet und in seiner Hülle! Zusammengerollt ist ein Schirm elegant, häßlich dagegen aufgespannt. (C.N.)

5.3. Text 3: The relationship between text function and audience orientation – Tourist information: SPEZIALITÄTEN

5.3.0. Text
SPEZIALITÄTEN

„Liebe geht durch den Magen". Dieser Spruch findet in München seine besondere Bestätigung. Denn es gilt als ein Teil der vielzitierten Münchner Gemütlichkeit, daß man
hier auch zu essen und zu trinken versteht. Probieren Sie deshalb zuerst, was unter
„Schmankerl" als Münchner Spezialität auf der Speisenkarte aufgeführt ist: Die Weißwurst, jene zarte Köstlichkeit, „gemixt" aus Kalbsbrat, Salz, Pfeffer, Zitrone und
Petersilie. Den Leberkäs', der weder mit Leber noch mit Käse etwas gemein hat, sondern ein aus Rindsbrat und Speck gebackener Laib ist. Den Leberknödel, die berühmteste Sorte bayerischer Knödelarten. Kaum wegzudenken sind außerdem die altbekannten Schweinswürstl mit Kraut. Kenner wissen, wo sie besonders schmackhaft am
Rost gebraten werden. Aber was wäre die gute Speis' ohne das berühmte Münchner
Bier? Der Durstige bestellt „Eine Maß" (1 Liter). Die meisten nehmen „Eine Halbe"
(½ Liter). Hell oder Dunkel? Süffiger ist, laut Volksmund, das „Dunkle". Aber immer
mehr bevorzugen das „Helle" und das „Pils". Und wie wär's mit dem obergärigen
Weißbier (Weizenbier)? Oder mit „Märzen" und „Bock" (Starkbiere)? Köstlich
schmecken sie alle. Vor allem, wenn Sie mit einem sorgsam gesalzenen „Radi" – auf
Hochdeutsch Rettich – Ihren Durst erst so recht schüren und dazu die Münchner Brotspezialitäten probieren: Brez'n, Remische, Salzstangerl, Loawen, Mohnzöpferl. Noch
vieles ließe sich nennen. Aber lassen Sie sich doch einfach vom Magenfahrplan einer
altmünchner Gaststätte inspirieren! Auch die sich ständig erweiternde internationale
Speisenkarte der Stadt darf hier nicht unerwähnt bleiben. Wer in München eine kulinarische Weltreise unternehmen will, der braucht nicht lange zu suchen, um die Gaumenfreuden Italiens, Frankreichs, Ungarns, Japans, Jugoslawiens, Mexikos, Spaniens,
Österreichs, Griechenlands, der Schweiz, der Tschechoslowakei, ja selbst Chinas und
Indonesiens zu genießen. (Translation in chapter 5.3.4)

5.3.1. Analysis of extratextual factors
The text is published on the back of a folded map (MEDIUM) of the
city of Munich, which is sold for a few cents by tourist information of-
fices in Munich (PLACE). It is edited, as the reader is told in the English version, by the Tourist Office of the City of Munich (SENDER, →
AUDIENCE), whose address is given in the imprint. The imprint also
states the names of those responsible for design, cartography, drawings, photographs, print, reproduction, and typesetting. The name of
the author is not mentioned, but the imprints of the English, French,
Italian, and Portuguese (not the Spanish) versions state the names of
the respective translators (TEXT PRODUCER). The German original is
dated 1984 (TIME).

The text can be regarded as part of a tourist information folder
(TEXT TYPE). Its appearance and format distinguishes this text type

from the more elaborate and expensive tourist brochure characterized by a larger number of photographs, glossy paper, (often) pseudo-literary texts, etc., in which the operative function plays a more important part. (There is also a Munich brochure of this type.) For our sample text, we may assume that the informative function has priority, although there may be some persuasive elements, too (TEXT FUNCTION). Since the text is printed on the back of a map of the city (MEDIUM), there is sufficient reason to believe that the text is read mainly in Munich (PLACE OF RECEPTION) by tourists (AUDIENCE) who want to find their way about the city and to see its most important sights (TEXT FUNCTION). The addressees of the German original will be German-speaking visitors from Germany or from abroad who do not know Munich other than from hearsay.

Apart from the text on *Specialities*, the folder contains several non-related texts on *History*, *The Munich Year*, *Music*, *Museums*, *Shopping*, etc. (COMPOSITION).

5.3.2. The relevance of audience orientation
Unlike the texts on *History* or *Museums*, the text *Specialities* not only provides interesting information, but is also of immediate relevance to the (physical) comfort of any visitor to Munich. Neither the tourist from North Germany nor the foreigner can manage without the explanations of the text if they want to understand, for example, a menu in a Munich restaurant. Therefore, the sample text has the important function of serving as an informative "glossary" to a Bavarian menu.

This text illustrates the immediate importance of audience orientation for the function not only of the ST, but also of any translation, since this kind of text is usually translated in instrumental function. Using the model of translation-oriented text analysis, I will show whether or not, and how, the translators have coped with the translation problems related to audience orientation. I am not going into the details here of text-type conventions, of style or of the language variety chosen for the target text (e.g. in the case of the Portuguese version).

5.3.3. Analysis of intratextual factors
If we take the informative function as having priority, we have to analyse the following factors: (a) the subject matter and its projection in the title, (b) the content and its relevance to the different types of audience, (c) the presuppositions or background knowledge which can

(or must) be assumed for them, (d) the composition, which in this type of text is an important aid to comprehension, (e) the non-verbal elements (particularly layout, illustrations, printing types, space restrictions, etc.), and (f) the lexis, particularly regarding the transfer (translation, borrowing, adaptation, etc.) of SC-specific proper names and culture-bound references.

The remaining factors are of minor relevance in a equifunctional translation of this sample text. The TT sentence structure should conform to target-cultural conventions in order to facilitate the reception of the information. Suprasegmental features (such as onomatopoeic, rhythmical and prosodic effects, focussing structures, etc.), which play an important part in persuasive texts, are of secondary importance in the translation of this type of text and should also be adapted to target-cultural norms. The following analysis will therefore be limited to the first six factors.

a. Subject matter

Where several texts combine to form a whole, however independent they may be, it is important that each component has a title or heading which clearly indicates its particular subject matter, and that the headings are formulated such that the hierarchical relationship of the texts is made clear.

The ST meets these requirements. The heading *Spezialitäten* refers to the field of gastronomic specialities (the plural of *Spezialität* is used only in this sense) and is similar in form to the other headings. Since the non-Bavarian German reader has certain stereotypical ideas about Bavarian gastronomy (e.g. about the importance of beer!), the photo of a typical waitress with a great number of beer mugs in her arms clearly indicates the subject matter above the text.

b. Content and composition

Although the text is not divided into paragraphs (probably for reasons of space), its composition is fairly clear. A short introduction stresses the importance of food and drink for our general wellbeing and for the wellbeing of Bavarians, in particular. This introduction has no informative value, but serves as a sort of phatic introduction for the following explanations (→ LEXIS).

The first paragraph of the main text mentions the famous *Schmankerl*, explaining the word and listing the most important Munich specialities. If the name alone does not provide sufficient information or is confusing, the text gives some details about the ingredients (e.g. *Weisswurst* or *Leberkäs*). Certain regional expressions, such as *Kraut* (instead of standard German *Sauerkraut*), are assumed to be familiar to the reader (→ PRESUPPOSITIONS). With regard to the *Schweinswürstl* ("pork sausages"), the reader receives the information that they are grilled, whereas the remark *Experts know where...*, seems to have less informative than persuasive value.

The second part explains certain aspects of the Bavarian beer culture, such as quantities (e.g. *Mass*) and qualities (e.g. *Dunkle, Weissbier*). The explanations describing taste (*süffig*), production methods (*obergäriges Weizenbier*), or effect (*Starkbier*) cannot be regarded as being exhaustive (→ PRESUPPOSITIONS).

The third part deals with the little snacks which are served with the beer, such as radish or the innumerable kinds of bread. Some of the typical Bavarian proper names convey at least some information to the non-Bavarian German-speaking readers (e.g. *Salzstangerl*, which may be a small stick of salty pastry), whereas others (e.g. *Remische*, which might be a distortion of *Römische*, i.e. "Roman [rolls]") leave them completely in the dark (→ PRESUPPOSITIONS). Perhaps the author did not have enough space to explain the names. The paragraph ends rather abruptly with just a few explanatory remarks about the menus of some Munich restaurants.

The text concludes with a list of European, Asian, and Latin American restaurants. The order of countries does not seem to have any logical basis (→ COMPOSITION).

c. Presuppositions

According to its primary informative function, the text contains few presuppositions. It is addressed to readers who do not know Munich and its specialities, and therefore, the information given by the text has to be as detailed as possible (see, for example, the explanations about *Weissbier* and *Märzen*, and the comment on the ingredients of *Leberkäs*.

As we have already seen, the ST does not always come up to this standard. When the lack of information is an obstacle to comprehension, the translator has to decide whether or not to add the necessary details. Local colour (e.g. Bavarian proper names) is a luxury which an informative text can seldom afford unless the end result is to confuse rather than amuse (→ LEXIS).

Along with the linguistic presuppositions about the informative value that certain proper names have for the German-speaking (but not for the English-speaking or Spanish-speaking) reader, there is at least one culture-specific presupposition that the translator should take into account. While the German receivers usually know the light or bitter taste of *Helle* and *Pils* and will therefore understand the implied contrast with the more *süffig* taste of dark beer, this background knowledge cannot be presupposed in all visitors from other countries.

d. Non-verbal elements

The layout is the same for all versions of the text. If additional information or explanations have to be inserted (→ PRESUPPOSITIONS), the translator will, therefore, be confronted with the problem of having to compensate for the expansions by reductions in other text sections, without at the same time jeopardizing the functionality of the whole. This can be done in the passages having less informative value, such as the introduction and the sentences with appellative function (*Kenner wissen...*, etc.).

Bold print is only used in the original for the headings, and italics are not used at all. These markers would have been useful for the proper names of food and drinks. If the translating instructions allow no means other than quotation marks for underlining exotisms, the translator should ensure that they are used consistently so that the readers immediately recognize the words and expressions which they may use to order a particular speciality in a Munich restaurant.

The photograph above the text indicates the subject matter, but it is only through the heading and the text itself that its meaning becomes absolutely clear.

e. Lexis

As far as lexis is concerned, I shall try to elicit any elements which reveal intentions other than informative and which appeal to the reader or to induce him to adopt a positive attitude towards the subject matter of the text.

These non-informative elements include the saying in the introduction, regional (i.e. Bavarian) words (such as *Schmankerl, Knödel, Brez n* and colloquial forms (e.g. *Speis* instead of *Speise, wie wär s* instead of *wie wäre es*, or *gemixt* instead of *gemischt*), connotative expressions (e.g. *Gemütlichkeit*), metaphors (e.g. *Magenfahrplan*), and the way of addressing the reader directly (e.g. *Probieren Sie...*).

GERMAN	ENGLISH	FRENCH

Spezialitäten

«Liebe geht durch den Magen». Dieser Spruch findet in München seine besondere Bestätigung. Denn es gilt als ein Teil der vielzitierten Münchner Gemütlichkeit, daß man hier auch zu essen und zu trinken versteht. Probieren Sie deshalb zuerst, was unter «Schmankerl» als Münchner Spezialität auf der Speisenkarte aufgeführt ist: Die Weißwurst, jene zarte Köstlichkeit, «gemixt» aus Kalbsbrat, Salz, Pfeffer, Zitrone und Petersilie. Den Leberkäs', der weder mit Leber noch mit Käse etwas gemein hat, sondern ein aus Rindsbrat und Speck gebackener Laib ist. Den Leberknödel, die berühmteste Sorte bayerischer Knödelarten. Kaum wegzudenken sind außerdem die altbekannten Schweinswürstl mit Kraut. Kenner wissen, wo sie besonders schmackhaft am Rost gebraten werden. Aber was wäre die gute Speis' ohne das berühmte Münchner Bier? Der Durstige bestellt «Eine Maß» (1 Liter). Die meisten nehmen «Eine Halbe» (½ Liter). Hell oder Dunkel? Süffiger ist, laut Volksmund, das «Dunkle». Aber immer mehr bevorzugen das «Helle» und das «Pils». Und wie wär's mit dem obergärigen Weißbier (Weizenbier)? Oder mit «Märzen» und «Bock» (Starkbiere)? Köstlich schmecken sie alle. Vor allem, wenn Sie mit einem sorgsam gesalzenen «Radi» - auf Hochdeutsch Rettich – Ihren Durst erst so recht schüren und dazu die Münchner Brotspezialitäten probieren: Brez'n, Remische, Salzstangerl, Loawen, Mohnzöpferl. Noch vieles ließe sich nennen. Aber lassen Sie sich doch einfach vom Magenfahrplan einer altmünchner Gaststätte inspirieren! Auch die sich ständig erweiternde internationale Speisenkarte der Stadt darf hier nicht unerwähnt bleiben. Wer in München eine kulinarische Weltreise unternehmen will, der braucht nicht lange zu suchen, um die Gaumenfreuden Italiens, Frankreichs, Ungarns, Japans, Jugoslawiens, Mexikos, Spaniens, Österreichs, Griechenlands, der Schweiz, der Tschechoslowakei, ja selbst Chinas und Indonesiens zu genießen.

Specialities

"The way to a man's heart is through his stomach", it is said, and this proverb is perhaps particularly true in Munich, a city where some attention is devoted to good eating and drinking. As an introduction, try some of the "Schmankerl" on the menu, that is, Munich specialities. Weisswurst, that delicate mixture of veal, salt, pepper, lemon and parsley. Leberkäs which, despite its name, has nothing to do with liver or cheese but is a baked loaf of ground beef and bacon. Leberknödl, the best-known of the Bavarian dumplings. Life would be almost inconceivable in Bavaria without the famous Schweinswürstl (pork sausages) with sauerkraut. Experts know where they are grilled to perfection. But what would good eating be without the famous Munich beer? Munich has been styled the inofficial beer capital of the world and who would contest this claim? If you're really thirsty, order "eine Mass" (a quart). Mostly you drink "eine Halbe" (a pint). Which do you prefer, light or dark? Previously, dark had the preference. But now, more and more people drink "pale" or "Pils" beer. Then there's the sparkling Weissbier made from wheat. Or "Märzen" and "Bock" (strong beers.) All of them are delicious, especially when enjoyed with a carefully salted, thirst-inducing, "Radi" – in English, radish – and some of Munich's famous bread and rolls. The "Dampfnudel", "Rohrnudel", and "Schmalznudel" are Bavaria's answer to the doughnut, each quite an individual in itself. One could go on and on. But let yourself be inspired by the menu in an old-Munich restaurant. International cooking too has made great headway in Munich. Withou t leaving the city, you can make a world tour and enjoy the culinary pleasures of Italy, France, Austria, Hungary, Yugoslavia, Czechoslovakia, Switzerland, Greece, Spain, Mexico. Or for that matter, China, Japan, Vietnam and Indonesia.

Gastronomie

»L'amour passe par l'estomac« affirme un proverbe allemand... qui se trouve à Munich amplement confirmé : l'art culinaire munichois est en effet d'une appétissante variété. Essayez donc nos »Schmankerl«, les saucisses blanches, un vrai régal fait de viande de veau assaisonnée de sel, poivre et citron; le Leberkäs' qui, en dépit son nom, ne contien ne pas de viande de bœuf accompagnée de lard; les Leberknödel, la plus renommée des nombreuses sortes de quenelles bavaroises. N'oubliez pas non plus nos savoureuses »Schweinswürstl« (saucisses de porc) aux fines herbes ; les conaisseurs savent où l'on sert les meilleures. – Mais que seraient les meilleurs plats sans la célèbre bière de Munich? Celui que a grand-soif en commande d'emblée »eine Maß«: un litre bien tassé! Le plus souvent, pourtant, on commence par »eine Halbe« (un demi-litre). – Brun ou blonde? C'est une autre question! La brune passe par plus capiteuse, mais de plus en plus nombreux sont les amateurs de blonde ou de »Pils«. Il y a même aussi la »blanche« (Weißbier), brassée au blé au lieu d'orge. Et encore la »Märzen« et le »Bock« (bières fortes). Toutes, en tous cas, son délicieuses. Sourtout lorsqu'on les accompagne d'un gros radis blanc, qui aiguise la soif. Citons aussi nos diverses sortes de pain: Brez'n, Remische, Salzstangerl, Loawen, Mohnzöpferl... Mais comment tout mentionner! Laissez-vous donc tenter par l'offre alléchante d'un restaurant de vieille tradition munichoise. – Par ailleurs les menus internationaux deviennent de plus en plus nombreux à Munich et permettent de faire, dans nos murs, un voyage »culinaire« autour du monde. Point n'est besoin de chercher longtemps pour goûter chez nous les plaisirs de la table à la française, ou ceux de nombreux autres pays: Italie, Hongrie, Japon, Yougoslavie, Mexique, Espagne, Autriche, Grèce, Suisse, Tchécoslovaquie, voire même de Chine et d'Indonésie.

ITALIAN	SPANISH	PORTUGUESE

Specialità

«L'amore passa per lo stomaco». Questo detto trova a Monaco di Baviera la sua particolare conferma, dato que é una parte della tanto citata giovialità monacense, intesa qui anche come mangiare e bere. Provate quindi per prima cosa ció che la lista delle vivande indica sotto la voce «Schmankerl» per le specialità monacensi: la salsiccia bianca, una squisitezza fatta di un «misto» di vitello, sale, pepe, limone e prezzemolo; il «Leberkäs», che nulla ha in comune né col fegato (Leber) né col formaggio (Käse) ma e un impasto di varne di manzo con lardo; i «Leberknödel» (gnocchi di fegato), la piú famosa specie di gnocchi bavaresi. Da non dimenticare inoltre le note «Schweinswürstl mit Kraut» (salsicette di suino con crauti), e i conoscitori sanno dove esse vengono arrostite alla traticola in modo particularmente gustoso. M che cosa sarebbe la buona pietanza senza la famosa birra di Monaco? L'assetato ordina «eine Maß» (1 litro); la maggioramza «eine Halbe» (mezzo litro). Chiara o scura? Piú amabile é, secondo l'opinione popolare, «das Dunkle» (la scura); ma sempre piú vengono preferite «das Helle» (la chiara) o «das Pils» (la Pils). E che dire della superfermentada «Weißbier» (birra di grano)? O della «Bock» (birra forte)? Tutte hanno un gusto delizioso, supratutto quando stimulate la sete con un «Radi» (rapa) – in puro tedesco - «Rettich» - accuratamente salato e vi aggiungete anche le specialità di pane monacensi: «Brez'n», «Remische», «Salzstangerl», «Loawen», «Mohnzöpferl» e tante altre ancora. Ma lasciatevi pure ispirare dal vasto programma culinario di una vecchia locanda monacense. Né si può qui scrodare di menzionare la sempre più ricca lista internazionale delle vivande della città. Chi a Monaco vuole intraprendere un viaggio nel mondo culinario, non ha bisgno die cercare a lungo per godere le gioue della tavola italiana, francese, ungherese, rumena, iugoslava, russa, messicana, spagnola, austriaca, greca, svizzera, cinese, giaponese e persino indonesiana.

Especialidades

«El amor pasa por el estómago» es una adagio que vale especialmente para Munich. Entender de comida y bebida forma parte de la tan citada «Gemütlichkeit», la acogedora atmósfera de Munich.Pruebe lo indicado en la lista de platos bajo la rúbrica «Schmankerl», especialidades de la cocina muniquesa: la salchicha blanca, delicioso manjar, cuyos ingredientes son ternera, sal pimienta, limón y perejil. «Leberkäs», «Queso de hígado», que nada tiene de común ni con el queso ni con el hígado, pues se compone de carne de vaca y tocino. «Leberknödel», «Albóndiga de hígado», la más famosa entre las variedades bávaras. No se pueden pasar por alto las famosísimas salchicas de cerdo con chucrut. Los gourmets saben dónde las asan mejor a la parrilla. Pero ¿qué valdrían estos deliciosos bocados sin la proverbial cerveza de Munich? El sediento pide «eine Mass», un litro. Por lo general se bebe «eine Halbe», medio litro. ¿Negra o rubia? El pueblo opina que se deja beber mejor la negra, pero cada vez se bebe más la rubia y la «Pils». Sin olvidar la «Weissbier», cerveza blanca o de trigo, de fermentación especial, la «Märzen» y la «Bock», cervezas fuertes. Todas tienen su inconfundible sabor, sobre todo si se toman con una especialidad muniquesa, que son los rábanos salados. Hay que probar también las especialidades de pan: Brez'n, Remische, Salzstangerl, Loawen, Mohnzöpferl. Habría aún mucho que decir; pero es mejor que se deje guiar por la lista de platos de un tradicional restaurante muniqués. Pero más conocidos restaurantes de este tipo los podrá encontrar en los alrededores de Marienplatz. Y no hay que olvidar el ambiente international. Si desea hacer un recorrido culinario internacional, no tendrá que esforzarse mucho. A mano tendrá las delicias que ofrecen al paladar Italia, Francia, Hungría, El Japón, Yugoslavia, Méjico, España, Austria, Grecia, Suiza, Checoslovaquia, y hasta China e Indonesia.

Especialidades

«O amor passa pelo estômago». Este provérbio encontra em Munique sua afirmação toda especial. Porque comer e beber faz parte da muito citada «Gemütlichkeit» (bem-estar) muniquense. Por isso prove primeiro os «Schmankerl» - que se encontram no cardápio entre «Münchner Spezialitäten»: a salchicha branca, aquela mistura deliciosa de carne picada de vitela, sal limão et salsa; o «Leberkäs, que nxo tem nada a ver com Leber (fígado), nem com Käse (queijo), mas é uma massa de carne de vaca e de toucinho. O Leberknödel é o mais famoso dos Knödel bávaros. Também quase não se pode imaginar o menu bávaro sem as famosas Schweinsbratwürstl (linguiças fritas de porco) com Sauerkraut (chucrute). Os conhecedores sabem onde encontrar as mais gostosas, grelhadas na brasa. Mas o que seria tudo isso sem a famosa cerveja muniquense? Quem tem muita sede pede «eine Mass» (um litro), a maioria pede «eine Halbe» (meio litro). Clara ou escura? Conforme a opinião do povo, a cerveija escura é mais gostosa. No entanto, cada vez mais gente prefere a cerveja clara e a «Pilsen». Ou, que tal uma Weissbier (cerveija branca), altamente fermentada, feita de trigo? Ou então uma «Märzen» e uma «Bock» (cerveijas fortes)? Seja qual fo a sua escolha, sempre sera gostosa. Especialmente, se tomada com um «Radi» (rábano) bem salgado, que dá mais sede ainda. Ou com um dos tipos de pão especial, como a «Brezn», o «Remische», o «Salzstangerl», o «Loawen» ou o «Mohnzöpferl». O melhor é deixarse inspirar pelo «roteiro culinário» de uma cervejaria. Tambem não devemos esquecer o cardápio cada vez maior de pratos internacionais, sem o qual a lista de especialidades ficaria bem incompleta. Se prende fazer uma viagem culinária em volta ao mundo, não precisa ir longe: encontra aqui as delicias das cozinhas italiana, francésa, húngara, russa, iugoslava, mexicana, espanhola, austriaca grega, suiça, tcheco-eslovaca, e até chinesa, japonesa e indonesia.

These features provide the text with a jovial and amusing touch, which compensates for the strictly informative character of some passages. They should be regarded merely a means to this end with no value of their own. This is why the translators may feel free to use any other device provided by the target languages or cultures, as long as it helps them achieve the same end. They need not bother to search for a translation of the saying or of *Gemütlichkeit* (untranslatable as a word), but may use other, specifically target-cultural devices to keep the reader happy (despite all the unpronounceable German words). However, whenever a conflict arises between the informative and the appellative function of the text, the informative function must take priority.

5.3.4. Translation criticism

In accordance with the procedure of ST analysis I shall now analyse the English (ET, 1984, transl. by Michael Orloff), French (FT, 1983, transl. by Jaques P. Evin), Italian (IT, 1985, transl. by Giuseppina Petan), Spanish (SpT, 1981, translator unknown), and Portuguese (PT, 1978, transl. by Maria Clara Maucher) versions of the text, concentrating on the problems deriving from the factors of text function and audience orientation. There will be no overall evaluation of the translated texts.

a. Subject matter

We found that the heading of the ST met the requirements of a heading for this particular text type. The same cannot be said of the headings of the translations. Seen in the context of a combination of texts on various subjects (see above), the literal translations of *Spezialitäten* by *Specialities* (ET), *Specialità* (IT) and *Especialidades* (SpT and PT) are not an accurate description of the subject matter dealt with in the text. The meaning of these words is more general than that of the German word *Spezialitäten* (cf. OED 1961, Felice & Duro 1976, VOX 1979, and Aulete 1958). In a more specific context (e.g. on a menu) they would certainly be understood as a reference to food and drink or cooking. But since a title or heading is without context, the reference in the sample texts is not clear (despite the photograph). The reader might come to the conclusion that the text is about Munich specialities in general (and not only culinary ones).

For the same reason, these headings do not correspond to the headings in the rest of the folder, which describe other "specialities" worth seeing or visiting in the town. A specification such as *culinary* or *gastronomic* would serve to make the reference inambiguous (cf. Felice & Duro 1976: *specialità culinarie*). On the other hand, such a solution might be too long for one line (→ NON-VERBAL ELEMENTS) or it might destroy the formal analogy with the other titles, which all consist of a single word. Both problems seem to be solved elegantly by the French version. The title *Gastronomie* gives the reader a clear hint as to what to expect in the text and fits perfectly into the layout of the page (cf. GLLF 1973).

b. Content

Moving on now to the factor of content, I shall consider whether or not the information presented in the translations will mean anything to the respective receivers. This largely depends on the explanations accompanying the Bavarian proper names.

English:
ET explains *Schmankerl, Leberkäs, Knödl, Schweinswürstl, Weissbier, Märzen, Bock,* and *Radi.* However, the explanation that "Leberkäs, despite its name, has nothing to do with liver or cheese" does not make any sense to a reader who does not know that *Leber* means "liver" and that *Käs(e)* is the German word for cheese. Instead of going into the many varieties of bread and rolls, the English translator uses an ingenious compensatory device. *Dampfnudel, Rohrnudel,* and *Schmalznudel* (which are not mentioned in the ST) are similar to a doughnut and at the same time illustrate variety in a field in which the target reader knows only one sort. So the reader gets a rough idea of what to expect.
The problem of any presupposed knowledge about beer specialities is solved by a **change of content**. ET explains that the preference for light beer is a question of time, whereas the source text implies that the reason why people in Munich prefer the light and bitter *Helle* or *Pils* to the sweeter and stronger dark beer is a question of taste. But this slight change in no way interferes with the function of the text and is preferable to non-coherence.
The translation of *Liter* by "quart" and *½ Liter* by "pint" is **not adequate**, since the measures are not equivalent. Moreover typically British measures will seem odd to American readers.
ET omits the German (or rather Bavarian) names for *sauerkraut, light* ("pale" is neither English nor German), and *dark,* which means that the reader will be unable to order these specialities in a restaurant. Additional explanations would have been useful for the *-wurst* part of *Weisswurst* ("mixture" is not sufficiently clear) and for the *Leber-* part of *Leberknödl.*

French:
FT explains *Leber, Knödel, Schweinswürstl, eine Mass* ("un litre bien tassée" might not give a true picture of reality, though!), *eine Halbe, Weissbier, Märzen* and *Bock* giving the French equivalent in brackets after the German name, except for *blanche (Weissbier),* where the order is changed. That more people

prefer light beer in spite of the more alcoholizing effect of the dark beer (*passe pour plus capiteuse*) does not seem convincing, but this does not interfere seriously with the function of the text.

FT omits the German or Bavarian names of *saucisse blanches, brune, blonde,* and *radis*; it explains neither the word *Schmankerl* (the reader is not informed that the word appears on the menu) nor the different kinds of bread and rolls. The description of the ingredients of the *Weisswurst* omits the parsley, and that of *Leberkäs* and *Schweinswürstl* lacks the information about how they are prepared (baked and grilled, respectively). The explanation of the German name *Leberkäs* is made comprehensible by the addition of the French equivalents of *Leber* and *Käse* in parenthesis; however, it still sounds rather superfluous since the French reader without a knowledge of German would never have expected *foie* or *fromage* in something called *Leberkäs*. The translation of *Kraut* by *aux fines herbes* is a **serious error** which gives the reader a false piece of information.

Italian:
IT explains *Schmankerl, Leberkäs* (using the same procedure as FT), *Leberknödel, Schweinswürstl mit Kraut, eine Mass, eine Halbe, das Dunkle, das Helle,* and even *das Pils* (Italian: *la Pils*), *Weissbier, Bock, Radi.* The addition of the standard German word for *Radi* (*Rettich*) seems superfluous since it is usually not found on Bavarian menu cards. The remark on the difference between light and dark beer is comprehensible if *più amabile* is interpreted as a description of taste.
IT omits the information about the *Märzen* beer. The omission, possibly due to lack of space, does not interfere with the function of the text.
The German name is missing in the case of the *salsiccia bianca*. There is no explanation about the Munich bread specialities.

Spanish:
SpT explains *Schmankerl, Leberknödel, eine Mass, eine Halbe, Weissbier, Märzen, Bock,* and *Leberkäse.* A literal translation of the German name seems to justify the explanation, but it is doubtful whether a Spanish reader has any idea of what *queso de higado* ("liver cheese") would taste like even if it is not made of a combination of liver and cheese.
SpT omits the German or Bavarian names for *salchicha blanca, salchicas* [sic] *de cerdo con chucrut, negra* and *rubia, rábanos salados.* There is no explanation about the bread varieties. The reader is given no information about the preparation of *Leberkäs.*
The remark that, "although people think that dark beer is more 'drinkable', more and more people prefer light beer" lacks coherence and is **incomprehensible**. It does not contribute to the understanding of German culture.

Portuguese:
PT explains *Leberkäs* (in the same way as FT and IT), *Schweinsbratwürstl* and *Sauerkraut* (which will not be found under this name on Bavarian menus), *eine Mass, eine Halbe, Weissbier, Märzen, Bock,* and *Radi.*
PT omits the explanations about *Leberknödel* and *Knödel* and the bread specialities. The explanation of *Schmankerl* is confusing; moreover, the accumu-

lation of three untranslated German words (scarcely pronounceable for Portuguese tongues!) seems a tough nut for the reader to crack.

The German name is missing in the case of *salsicha branca* (the translator forgot to mention the pepper as well), *clara*, and *escura*. Like the Spanish and the Italian readers, the Portuguese visitors will be puzzled by the information that Germans prefer light beer although the dark tastes better.

The mere enumeration of good, bad, and acceptable solutions clearly indicates that none of the translations presents a consistent translation strategy which could have been derived from the analysis of the source text and the translation skopos.

c. Composition

In their macrostructure, all the target texts are constructed according to the model of the source text. Since the ST has a functional structure which is not bound to SC conventions, this seems to be an adequate solution. However, where the microstructures are concerned, there are some smaller deviations in connection with the information on ethnic restaurants in Munich.

English:
Starting with the European countries and Mexico, ET puts the Asian countries, with the addition of Vietnam, into one separate sentence. This may be due to the orientation towards an American readership; in this case, we find a discrepancy with other elements which seem to point to an orientation towards the British reader (e.g. *pint*).

French and Spanish:
FT and SpT follow exactly the order of the ST.

Italian:
IT mentions Japan along with the other Asian countries at the end of the enumeration, adding a reference to Rumanian and Russian restaurants.

Portuguese:
PT adds a reference to Russian cooking between the information on Hungarian and Yugoslavian restaurants and mentions Japan along with the Asian countries as well.

The variations might be due to the difference in time of publication, but this cannot be proved by the dates given in the imprints of the texts. If the added information is correct there is no objection. Changes of microstructure which are due to audience orientation or to factual (in this case: geographic) reasons, must be accepted. But there cannot be any objection to the reproduction of the ST order either since the order in which the countries are mentioned is not a feature that is relevant to text function.

d. Presuppositions
The problem of presuppositions is solved satisfactorily in those passages where the explanations are sufficient and allow a comparison
with target-cultural realities (such as the explanation of *Knödel* in ET,
FT, IT, and SpT, even if *dumplings*, *albóndigas*, or *gnocchi* cannot be
regarded as an equivalent of *Knödel*). The addition of *sparkling* to
Weissbier in ET is a good means of compensating for the TT reader's
lack of experience with German beer.

The problem is not solved satisfactorily in all those cases where
the explanations are missing or where they are false or confusing (cf.
CONTENT).

Names like *Mohnzöpferl* or *Salzstangerl* contain linguistic presuppositions: The German reader gets a certain idea of the object by
merely analysing the name (*Mohn* refers to poppy seeds, *zopf* to a kind
of bread in form of a plait, *-erl* is the Bavarian diminutive suffix),
whereas for the target receivers these names are meaningless chains of
phonemes or graphemes. These linguistic presuppositions have not
been taken into account in an adequate way in the translations, except
for ET, which has solved the problem by means of a compensation (cf.
CONTENT).

A similar case of linguistic presuppositions is presented by the
play on the name *Leberkäse* (Bavarian: *Leberkäs*). The author presupposes that the reader would expect *Leberkäse* to be a composition of
Leber ("liver") and *Käse* ("cheese") and anticipates this wrong association by his remark. However, since nowadays most Germans from
all parts of the country know *Leberkäse*, this may also be a pseudo-
presupposition. In this case, the "explanation" must be regarded as a
humourous play on words. But this play on words can only work if the
receivers know the meaning of the lexical elements. If they do not,
Leberkäs is for them just another label for an unknown reality, which
needs not be explained.

e. Non-verbal elements
In spite of the numerous expansions, all target versions present the
same layout as the source text. FT separates the structural units (cf.
COMPOSITION) by dashes which add to the clarity of the text.

The characterization of the exotisms (i.e. German or Bavarian
proper names) by quotation marks is not stringent in ET, FT, and PT.
The explanations are usually put in brackets, whereas in SpT the

characterization of both exotisms and explanations by quotation marks has a rather confusing effect.

For the same reason, the use of quotation marks as a stylistic means of emphasis should be avoided (e g. IT: «misto», FT: un voyage «culinaire»). It is not a very good idea in the ST either.

Another problem is the orthography of those German words containing the grapheme *ß*. The readers of FT and IT may find it difficult to pronounce this letter which their languages do not have. ET, SpT, and PT have consistently replaced it by *ss*.

The significance of the photograph has already been mentioned in connection with the subject matter.

f. Lexis

One of the difficulties arising in the field of lexis is the proverb used as an introduction of the text. *Liebe geht durch den Magen* (literal translation: "Love passes through the stomach") sounds odd, or even incomprehensible, to other people who do not know such a proverb (PT), saying (ET, IT), or "phrase" (SpT), even if it is referred to as a German proverb (FT). If the target culture has a similar proverb or saying emphasizing the importance of good eating and drinking for the wellbeing of people (not only of men, as ET seems to suggest!), the translator could use a substitution. But for the function of the text it is not necessary to find a proverb or saying. Any form of (factual, humourous, literary or even poetic!) introduction into the subject would do better than a translation which is liable to create a cultural misunderstanding.

Along with *Weltanschauung* and *Kindergarten*, the German word *Gemütlichkeit* is, in fact, "often quoted" (as the ST says), but usually as an example of untranslatability. In our context it does not present any difficulty to the translator since it means nothing but "inviting atmosphere", as SpT (*acogedora atmósfera*) and PT (*bem-estar*) paraphrase it. In a text which is already larded with (necessary) German words, the target readers should not be bothered with another one which they would certainly never find on a menu card or notice board in Germany. ET and FT simply avoid it, while IT slightly changes the meaning translating it by *giovialità*.

The stylistic features intended to influence the readers' attitude towards the subject matter are reproduced in different quality and quantity in the target texts, such as "Munich has been styled the unofficial beer capital of the world", "Bavaria's answer to the dough-

nut" (ET), "un vrai régal", "laissez vous donc tenter par l'offre alléchante d'un restaurant....!" (FT), "..una squisitezza", "un gusto delizioso", "un viaggio nel mondo culinario"... (IT), "delicioso manjar",
"deliciosos bocados", "las delicias que ofrecen al paladar..." (SpT
could have done with a little more variation in lexis), "uma viagem
culinaria em volta ao mundo", "as delicias das cozinhas...!", "roteiro
culinário" (PT).

5.3.5. Conclusions

The analysis of the five translations shows that none of them meets the
requirements set by text function and audience orientation. Although
all the translators seem to have at their disposal the linguistic means
which are necessary for the production of a functional target text, they
evidently have not been able to use these means in a consistent and
adequate manner. The defects and imperfections discovered in the
translations could have been avoided by a translation-oriented text
analysis.

Text analysis would have been helpful, above all, for the solution of the following translation problems: translation of the proverb
Liebe geht durch den Magen, of "intranslatable" words (*Gemütlichkeit*), of polysemous SL words (*süffig*), of names of SC realities (*Knödel*) and of metaphors (*Magenfahrplan*). The analysis of text function
has made clear that audience orientation is the fundamental factor for
the translation of this text. Accordingly, a consistent translation strategy for the whole text has to take this into account. Translation criticism reveals that the inadequacies of ET, FT, IT, SpT, and PT are not
due to a lack of linguistic competence on the part of the translators,
but that these were not able to overcome the difficulties presented by
the translation task.

On the other hand, the analysis of the sample text shows that the
translation problems presented by this text are not specifically linked
to a specific target language or language pair but to the text type. The
systematization of those problems which arise in the process of translation of a certain text type or genre would have been a valuable tool
for the translators.

III. FINAL CONSIDERATIONS

This book is an introduction to the theory, methodology and teaching of translation-oriented source-text analysis, completed by an application of the model to several sample texts. In conclusion, I should like to restate some fundamental aspects of the study.

a. Theoretical aspects
The theoretical principles of the model of text analysis are based on an action-oriented concept of textuality, on the one hand, and a functional concept of translation, on the other. Both concepts are closely linked with each other.

From an action-oriented viewpoint, the text is regarded as an element of a communicative interaction which takes place in a situation. The communicative situation (including the participants in the communicative act) becomes then the centre of attention, while the linguistic structure of the text body, which can be analysed by textlinguistic methods, is of secondary importance.

It is on the basis of an action-oriented concept of textuality that we may regard the translation of a text as an "action" which makes it possible that a text fulfils certain functions for other participants in a new situation. From this point of view there cannot be a doubt that translation is more than replacing certain linguistic elements of the source language by certain (equivalent, synonymous, etc.) linguistic elements of the target language. As we have stated above, translation is the production of a functional target text maintaining a relationship with a given source text that is specified according to the translation skopos (see ch. 2.4.1.)

It is the specification of the function of the source text or its elements that permits the translator to decide whether or not these elements (elements of content or effect, non-verbal elements, structural elements, etc.) are an appropriate means of achieving the intended function of the target text. It is clear that such a specification of function or functions can only be realized on the basis of a thorough analysis of the source text and its elements.

In this book, the main focus of attention is centred on the translation of written texts which can be analysed in detail according to the looping model. Due to the short-lived character of the spoken word, the procedures of analysis will be different in the simultaneous translation of spoken texts, where part of the ST analysis usually coincides with the TT production. But in principle, the factors of analysis stated for our model are applicable to the process of interpreting as well. The analysis of extratextual and intratextual factors may be realized in separated phases in interpreting. Since the interpreter participates in the situation of ST production, s/he is able to analyse the extratextual factors "on sight", observing the speaker's non-verbal behaviour, the listeners and their reactions to the text, the specific conditions of time and place, etc. The interpreter may even have the chance to get into contact with the participants (e.g. in consecutive or conversational interpreting, during the briefing before the actual interpretation). On the other hand, the analysis of intratextual factors has to be realized under extreme pressure unless the interpreter has a written documentation at her or his disposal beforehand. Nevertheless, I claim that my model of translation-oriented text analysis is principally valid for both written and oral translation, although its application may be different in translating and interpreting.

Considering the specific conditions of the process of intercultural communication, there is no alternative to the concept of ST analysis, as is shown by the numerous contributions on translation-oriented text analysis on which we have based our theoretical considerations. It is uncontested that the process of translation should be guided by means of a source-text analysis, but so far nobody has presented a consistent model of procedure which is integrated into a global concept of translation. Most of the existing approaches are based on either linguistic or literary viewpoints, and only some of them have integrated pragmatic and action-oriented aspects in the last few years.

We have to mention another approach to translation which has been neglected until now. The empirical psycholinguistic approach tries to find out the conditions of the process of translating by means of Thinking Aloud Protocols (TAP) (cf. Krings 1986). The TAP method promises to throw some light on the famous black box of the translator and reveal "what is going on in the translator's mind". In the long run, the collection of empirical data on the psychological processes in translation activities might lead to the development of strategies how to influence the translator's mental processes in the sense of "what should be going on in the translator's mind". However, in the short run, i.e. as long as we do not have these data at our disposal, the analysis of text, situation and translation skopos seems to be the only practicable way of controlling the translation process. Influenced by foreign language classes (including latin) at school, by the reception of translated texts, etc. the students have a certain idea of what translation is or should be, which, although it does not correspond to the requirements of professional translation, widely determines their translation activities. This unreflected, mostly equivalence-based concept of translation must be replaced by a stringent frame of reference which tells the (future) translators what they have to do in a particular translating task under particular conditions (of source text, translation skopos, linguistic and other competence, etc.). Such a frame of reference is offered in this book.

b. Methodological aspects
According to the fundamental theoretical principle of the text as a communicative act or action, the method has to include the analysis of both extratextual and intratextual factors, giving priority to the extratextual or situational factors, which, therefore, are analysed first. Based on the New Rhetoric-formula, the chain of WH-questions includes all the relevant extratextual factors, offering the advantage of a practical formula which is easy to be remembered and can be used as a checklist in text analysis.

The intratextual factors have been selected from a sender perspective. Out of the variety of possible factors I have selected those which in a transfer situation are liable to cause specific translation problems, either pragmatic (e.g. presuppositions) or linguistic and conventional (e.g. lexis, sentence structure, suprasegmental features).

The model can be called translation-oriented because it serves not only for a (retrospective) analysis of the source text-in-situation, but also for a (prospective) analysis of the target text-in-situation defined by the translation brief. Thus, the result of the ST analysis can be immediately contrasted with the result of the analysis of the TT skopos. Comparing both results, the translator is able to decide whether and in what respect the ST has to be adjusted to the TT situation and what procedures of adaptation will produce an adequate target text.

I have attributed great importance to the fact that the model is applicable to source texts of any language and any text type and to translations from and into any language and culture. After analysing the intended or required function(s) of the target text and the "material" provided by the given source text, the translator elicits the language-dependent translation problems arising in a particular translation task, which are then specified with regard to the target culture and the target language. The practical application of the model (e.g

Sample Text 3, chapter 5.3.) shows that there are, in fact, translation problems which are specifically linked to a particular text type or a particular translation task.

c. Pedagogical aspects

The model for text analysis is not meant primarily for the professional translator. Intended to guide the fundamental steps of the translation process, it points to the essential competences required of a translator (competence of text reception and analysis, research competence, transfer competence, competence of text production, competence of translation quality assessment, and, of course, linguistic and cultural competence both on the source and the target side, which is the main prerequisite of translation activity).

All these competences have to be developed in the course of a training programme for professional translators and interpreters. If we want to give a logical structure to such a training programme, we have to develop the competence components up to a certain level in specific classes, practising, at the same time (but possibly not in the same type of class), their combined application. This means that the traditional practical translation class, in which the theoretical knowledge of methods and procedures is applied to the translation of complete (authentic) texts is by no means obsolete. It would be sensible, however, to systematize the teaching aims and bring them into a progression which allows a reasonable and fair control of learning progress.

This is where the model developed in the present book may prove useful. Since it comprises the essential factors and dimensions of the translation process, it seems appropriate to find out the priorities of a particular translation task, thus allowing a systematical approach for both teachers and students. Moreover, the distinction between general, i.e. language-pair independent, translation problems, and language or culture-pair specific translation problems might lead to a more efficient organization of translator training. If general problems are dealt with in a combined programme outside the language departments (e.g. in lectures open to all students), translation classes might concentrate on those translation problems which are really bound to a particular pair of languages or cultures and on the development of linguistic and cultural competence. Such an integrated training programme requires a great deal of constructive cooperation on all levels, but I feel that it would be worth the effort.

d. The sample texts

There are several aspects that have guided the selection of the sample texts. On the one hand, in order to prove the translation-relevant character of the model, it was necessary to find texts in which a great number of the discussed factors of analysis would come into play. On the other hand, the sample texts had to be complete and yet short enough to demonstrate a consistent process of analysis. Therefore, I have chosen two texts which, although part of a text combination, are complete units (Sample Texts 1 and 3). Being the first paragraph of a novel, Sample Text 2 is only a text segment, but nevertheless it is suitable to show exemplarily the importance of a single factor of analysis for the interpretation of a whole text.

Moreover, I intended to show that particular source texts and translation skopoi may require the priority of specific dimensions, allowing the restriction of the analysis to certain factors, without jeopardizing the validity of its results. Therefore, the spectrum of aspects had to be as broad as possible in spite of the reduced number of texts. This is why the selected sample texts represent, as it were, some extreme positions.

The tourist information text *Spezialitäten* (5.3.) is a non-literary text, whose translation is expected to be a functional and acceptable communicative instrument for the target receiver. Since the translation procedures must be oriented towards the aim of producing a functional TL tourist information text (= equifunctional instrumental translation), the ST analysis may be restricted to those ST elements which are relevant to this function.

The text by Unamuno (5.2.) is a fragment of a literary text, whose translation, according to the norms and conventions of literary translation, is ST-oriented. This means that the specific ST features of subject matter and effect have to be reproduced in the target text (= documentary, exoticizing translation). The analysis of the paragraph shows that, in this case, irony, as a specific effect-producing device, is bound to structural features of the text, most of which seem to be language-independent and can be transferred into the respective target languages. Without the analysis, however, function and effect of the TT structures will be purely accidental, as shown by the published translations of the text.

The text by Alejo Carpentier (5.1.) represents a kind of intermediate position between ST-oriented and TT-oriented translation. Mixing the functional styles of scientific and literary texts, the author expresses a specific intention which is the element that has to be transferred in this case (ST orientation). But functional styles are culture-specific and therefore the translator has to take into account the genre conventions of the target culture (TT orientation). Combining both perspectives, the translator has to produce a coherent and functional target text corresponding to the author's intention. Again, the translation type is instrumental and equifunctional.

One last aspect for the selection of the sample texts was the variety of languages and cultures involved. By including as many language and culture pairs as possible I tried to illustrate the interdependence of general and specific translation problems. The three sample texts cover the following directions of translation: Spanish-German, Spanish-English, Spanish-Dutch, German-English, German-French, German-Italian, German-Spanish, and German-Portuguese, although the language-specific problems have not always been dealt with in detail. The translations of Sample Text 3 will provide the interested reader with a lot of material for individual analysis and translation criticism in this respect.

In any case, it is an important aim of this book to add fuel to the discussion about the theoretical, methodological, and pedagogical questions brought up in the study, which I feel have not been treated with sufficient energy and commitment up to now. If these considerations, which in the views of many a reader may differ considerably from the conventional concept of translation and interpreting, provoke disagreement and concrete contra-suggestions which, in the long run, lead to a broad consensus on the needs and concepts of teaching programmes, both translation and translator training – and it is this I actually care about – will have gained a lot.

IV. INDEX OF TRANSLATION PROBLEMS

Anaphora – Ex. 3.3./2
Asyndeton – Ex. 5.1.6./16
Change of text function – Ex. 2.2.3./1
Coherence – Ex. 5.1.6./3
Comparison – Ex. 3.2.6./6
Connotation – Ex. 3.2.2./5, 5.1.6./14
Contrastive stress – Ex. 5.1.6./4
Culture-specific perspective – Ex. 3.1.5./2
Culture-specific realities – Ex. 2.1.2./2, 3.2.2./5, 3.2.3./1
Deixis – Ex. 3.1.4./1, Ex. 3.1.5./3
Embedded texts – Ex. 3.1.0./1, cf. Examples
Epoch-specific lexis – Ex. 3.2.6./7
Examples – Ex. 3.2.4./3
Faulty texts – Ex. 2.1.3./1, 4.4.2./1
Focus – Ex. 5.1.5./1, 5.1.5./2, 5.1.6./4, 5.1.6./5
Headings cf. Titles
Hypotaxe – Ex. 5.1.6./17
In-texts cf. Embedded texts
Inclusion – Ex. 5.1.6./18, 5.1.6./19
Information units – Ex. 3.2.2./1, 3.2.4./5
Internal sender – Ex. 3.2.0./1
Internal situation – Ex. 3.2.2./6
Intonation patterns – Ex. 3.1.2./3, Ex. 3.2.8./2
Isotopic chain – Ex. 3.2.1./3, 5.1.6./6-7
Language varieties – Ex. 3.1.1./3a,b, 3.1.5./1
Metalanguage – Ex. 3.2.6./8
Newspaper language – Ex. 3.2.6./5
Parallelism – Ex. 3.3./2
Paraphrase – Ex. 3.2.2./2, 3.2.2./3
Presuppositions – Ex. 3.1.1./4, 3.1.6./2, 3.2.3./1
Pronominal substitution – Ex. 3.2.2./1
Proper names – Ex. 3.2.3./2
Quotation – Ex. 3.2.4./2, 5.1.6./11, 5.1.6./12
Quotation marks – Ex. 3.2.8./1
Reading-incentive – Ex. 3.1.3./2
Reference to intention – Ex. 3.1.2./3
Reference to sender – Ex. 3.2.6./1, 3.2.6./2, 5.1.6./8
Relative clause – Ex. 5.1.6./5
Sender orientation – Ex. 3.1.1./3
Sender's intention – Ex. 3.1.1./2
Social dialect – Ex. 3.1.3./2
Source of reference – Ex. 3.1.3./1, 5.1.6./13
Stream of consciousness – Ex. 3.2.8./1
Technical terms – Ex. 5.1.6./9, 5.1.6./10
Temporal deixis – Ex. 3.1.6./3
Text-type conventions – Ex. 1.2.3./1, 2.1.2./1, 2.1.2./3, 3.1.2./1, 3.1.3./6, 3.3./3, 3.1.6/1, 3.2.0./1, 3.2.1./1
Titles – Ex. 3.1.3./4, Ex. 3.1.7./1, 3.2.1./2, 3.2.4./4, 5.1.6./3
Topicality – Ex. 3.1.3./4

V. INDEX OF EXAMPLES

Example 1.1.1./1, p. 6
Example 1.1.1./2, p. 7
Example 1.1.1./3, p. 7
Example 1.1.1./4, p. 8
Example 1.1.2./1, p. 9
Example 1.1.2./2, p. 11
Example 1.2.1./1, p. 14
Example 1.2.1./2, p. 14
Example 1.2.1./3, p. 14
Example 1.2.3./1, p. 21
Example 2.1.2./1, p. 28
Example 2.1.2./2, p. 29
Example 2.1.2./3, p. 30
Example 2.1.3./1, p. 30
Example 2.2.3./1, p. 37
Example 3.1.0./1, p. 45
Example 3.1.1./1, p. 48
Example 3.1.1./2, p. 49
Example 3.1.1./3, p. 50
Example 3.1.1./4, p. 51
Example 3.1.2./1, p. 54
Example 3.1.2./2, p. 56
Example 3.1.2./3, p. 56
Example 3.1.3./1, p. 57
Example 3.1.3./2, p. 58
Example 3.1.3./3, p. 59
Example 3.1.3./4, p. 60
Example 3.1.3./5, p. 60
Example 3.1.3./6, p. 61
Example 3.1.4./1, p. 63
Example 3.1.4./2, p. 65
Example 3.1.5./1, p. 68
Example 3.1.5./2, p. 68
Example 3.1.5./3, p. 69
Example 3.1.6./1, p. 70
Example 3.1.6./2, p. 71
Example 3.1.6./3, p. 71
Example 3.1.6./4, p. 71
Example 3.1.6./5, p. 72
Example 3.1.7./1, p. 76
Example 3.1.9./1, p. 83
Example 3.2.0./1, p. 90
Example 3.2.1./1, p. 95

Example 3.2.1./2, p. 95
Example 3.2.1./3, p. 95
Example 3.2.2./1, p. 100
Example 3.2.2./2, p. 101
Example 3.2.2./3, p. 101
Example 3.2.2./4, p. 102
Example 3.2.2./5, p. 103
Example 3.2.2./6, p. 104
Example 3.2.3./1, p. 106
Example 3.2.3./2, p. 109
Example 3.2.3./3, p. 110
Example 3.2.4./1, p. 111
Example 3.2.4./2, p. 112
Example 3.2.4./3, p. 113
Example 3.2.4./4, p. 113
Example 3.2.4./5, p. 115
Example 3.2.5./1, p. 118
Example 3.2.6./1, p. 124
Example 3.2.6./2, p. 124
Example 3.2.6./3, p. 125
Example 3.2.6./4, p. 126
Example 3.2.6./5, p. 126
Example 3.2 6./6, p. 127
Example 3.2.6./7, p. 127
Example 3.2.6./8, p. 127
Example 3.2.6./9, p. 128
Example 3.2.7./1, p. 131
Example 3.2.8./1, p. 137
Example 3.2.8./2, p. 138
Example 3.2.9./1, p. 139
Example 3.3./1, p. 146
Example 3.3./2, p. 148
Example 3.3./3, p. 152
Example 4.0./1, p. 157
Example 4.0./2a, p. 159
Example 4.0./2b, p. 159
Example 4.1.1./1, p. 163
Example 4.4.2./1, p. 182
Example 5.1.6./1, p. 203
Example 5.1.6./2, p. 203
Example 5.1.6./3, p. 203
Example 5.1.6./4, p. 204
Example 5.1.6./5, p. 204

Example 5.1.6./6, p. 205
Example 5.1.6./7, p. 206
Example 5.1.6./8, p. 207
Example 5.1.6./9, p. 208
Example 5.1.6./10, p. 208
Example 5.1.6./11, p. 208
Example 5.1.6./12, p. 209
Example 5.1.6./13, p. 210
Example 5.1.6./14, p. 211
Example 5.1.6./15, p. 211
Example 5.1.6./16, p. 212
Example 5.1.6./17, p. 214
Example 5.1.6./18, p. 216
Example 5.1.6./19, p. 217

VI. REFERENCES

Allemann, B. (^{2}1969): *Ironie und Dichtung*, Pfullingen.

Alonso, M. (^{6}1979): *Diccionario del español moderno*, Madrid.

Antón Andrés, A. (1961): *Geschichte der spanischen Literatur (Vom 18. Jahrhundert bis zur Gegenwart)*, Munich.

Arcaini, E. (1984): L'auxiliaire comme problème de traduction, in Wilss & Thome 1984, 9-19.

Arntz, R. (1982): Methoden der fachsprachlichen Übersetzerausbildung im Sprachenpaar Spanisch-Deutsch, in Rodríguez Richart, J. & Thome, G. & Wilss, W. (eds.) (1982): *Fremdsprachenforschung und -lehre. Schwerpunkt Spanisch, Internationales Kolloquium an der Universität des Saarlandes*, Saarbrücken 1980, Tübingen, 109-122.

Arntz, R. (1984): Das Problem der Textauswahl in der fachsprachlichen Übersetzungsdidaktik, in Wilss & Thome 1984, 204-211.

Aulete, C. (1958): *Dicionário contemporâneo da língua portuguésa*, 3 vols., Rio de Janeiro.

Balcerzan, E. (1970): La traduction, art d'interpreter, in Holmes 1970, 3-22.

Barral, C. (1980): De raíz americana y formación europea, *La Vanguardia Española*, 26-4-1980, 45.

Bassnett-McGuire, S. (1978): Translating spatial poetry: an examination of theatre texts in performance, in Holmes et al. 1978, 161-176.

Bastian, S. (1979): Die Rolle der Präinformation bei der Analyse und Übersetzung von Texten, in Kade 1979, 90-133.

Bausch, K.-R. & Weller, F.-R. (eds.) (1981): *Übersetzen und Fremdsprachenunterricht*, Frankfurt.

Bausch, K.-R. (ed.) (1979): *Beiträge zur Didaktischen Grammatik. Probleme, Beispiele, Perspektiven*, Königstein/Ts.

Beck, G. (1973): Textsorten und Soziolekte, in Sitta & Brinker 1973, 73-112.

Beer, R. (1982): Nachwort, in Pantschatantra (^{2}1982): *Die fünf Bücher der Weisheit*, transl. from Sanscrit by T. Benfey (1859), revised by K. Fitzenreiter, with a postscript by K. Beer, Berlin, 387-420.

Behrmann, A. (^{5}1982): *Einführung in die Analyse von Prosatexten*, Stuttgart.

Benjamin, W. (1972): Die Aufgabe des Übersetzers, in *Gesammelte Schriften*, ed. by T. Rexroth, Bd. IV.1, Frankfurt/M., 82-96.

Berger, K. (1977): *Exegese des Neuen Testaments*, Heidelberg.

Black, M. (1973): Presupposition and implication, in Petöfi, J. S. & Franck, D. (eds.) (1973): *Präsuppositionen in Philosophie und Linguistik /Presuppositions in Philosophy and Linguistics*, Frankfurt/M., 55-70.

Blanzat, J. (1985): Vorwort, in Carpentier 1985, 9-16.

Brockhaus, Der Neue (^{5}1973): *Lexikon und Wörterbuch in fünf Bänden und einem Atlas*, Wiesbaden.

Brown, G. & Yule, G. (1987): *Discourse Analysis*, Cambridge.

Bühler, H. (1982): General Theory of Terminology and Translation Studies, in *Meta* 27 (1982), 4, 425-431.

Bühler, H. (1984): Textlinguistische Aspekte der Ubersetzungsdidaktik, in Wilss & Thome 1984, 250-259.

Bühler, K. (1934): *Sprachtheorie*, Jena.

Bussmann, H. (1983): *Lexikon der Sprachwissenschaft*, Stuttgart.

Carpentier, A. (1963): *Explosion in a Cathedral*, transl. by V. Gollancz, Harmondsworth.

Carpentier, A. (1964): *Explosion in der Kathedrale*, transl. by H. Stiehl, Frankfurt/M.

Carpentier, A. (1985): *Le siècle des lumières*, transl. by R. L.-F. Durand, Paris.

Carpentier, A. (^{2}1965): *El siglo de las luces*, Barcelona.

Cartellieri, C. (1979): Zur Analyse des Ausgangstextes beim Übersetzen, in Kade 1979, 9-45.

Cherubim, D. (1980): Abweichung und Sprachwandel, in Cherubim, D. (ed.) (1980): *Fehlerlinguistik. Beiträge zum Problem der sprachlichen Abweichung*, Tübingen, 124-152.

Clark, H. H. & Lucy, P. (1975): Understanding what is meant from what is said: a study in conversationally conveyed requests, in *Journal of Verbal Learning and Verbal Behavior* 14 (1975), 56-27.

Crystal, D. & Davy, D. (1969): *Investigating English Style*, London.

Crystal, D. & Quirk, R. (1964): *Systems of Prosodic and Paralinguistic Features in English*, London-The Hague-Paris.

Daneš, F. (1978): Zur linguistischen Analyse der Textstruktur, in Dressler, W. (ed.) (1978): *Textlinguistik*, Darmstadt, 181-192.

de Beaugrande, R. & Dressler, W. (1981): *Introduction to Text Linguistics*, London-New York.

de Beaugrande, R. (1980): *Text, Discourse and Process. Towards a Multidisciplinary Science of Texts*, Norwood/N.J.

DEA (1999): *Diccionario del español actual*, by Manuel Seco Reymundo & Olimpia Andrés Puente & Abino Ramón González, Madrid: Santillana.

Dressler, W. (1975): Textgrammatische Invarianz in Übersetzungen?, in Gülich & Raible 1975, 98-112.

Dressler, W. (^{2}1973): *Einführung in die Textlinguistik*, Tübingen.

DUW (1983): *DUDEN Deutsches Universal-Wörterbuch*, Mannheim.

Ehlich, K. & Rehbein, J. (1972): Erwarten, in Wunderlich, D. (ed.) (1972): *Linguistische Pragmatik*, Wiesbaden., 99-115.

Essen, O. von (^{5}1979): *Allgemeine und angewandte Phonetik*, Berlin.

Ettinger, S. (1977): Inwieweit ist die Übersetzung lehr- und lernbar?, *Linguistische Berichte* 49 (1977), 63-78.

Felice, E. de & Duro, A. (1976): *Dizionario della lingua e della civiltà italiana contemporanea*, Florence.

Fourquet, J. (1973): Der Text und sein beiderseitiges Hinterland, in Sitta & Brinker 1973, 113-121.

Fröland, R. (1978): Einige Gesichtspunkte zur Übersetzungsproblematik anhand von fünf Übersetzungen von Günter Grass' 'Aus dem Tagebuch einer Schnecke', in Grähs, L. & Korlén, G. & Malmberg, B. (eds.) (1978): *Theory and Practice of Translation*, Nobel Symposium, Bern-Frankfurt/M.-Las Vegas, 255-280.

Gadamer, H. G. (^{3}1972): *Wahrheit und Methode*, Tübingen.

García López, J. (^{12}1968): *Historia de la literatura española*, Barcelona.

Garner, J. (1971): 'Presupposition' in Philosophy and Linguistics, in Fillmore, C. J. & Langendolm, G. T. (eds.): *Studies in Linguistic Semantics*, New York 1971.

Gerzymisch-Arbogast, H. (1987): *Zur Thema-Rhema-Gliederung in amerikanischen Wirtschaftsfachtexten*, Tübingen.

Gili y Gaya, S. (^{9}1967): *Curso superior de sintaxis española*, Barcelona.

Gleason, H. A. (1969): *An Introduction to Descriptive Linguistics*, London-New York-Sydney-Toronto.

GLLF (1973): *Grand Larousse de la langue française*, ed. by L. Guilbert, R. Lagane & G. Niobey, Paris.

Grabes, H. (1977): Fiktion – Realismus – Ästhetik. Woran erkennt der Leser Literatur?, in Grabes, H. (ed.) (1977): *Text   Leser   Bedeutung. Untersuchungen zur Interaktion von Text und Leser*, Grossen-Linden, 6l-81.

Graustein, G. & Thiele, W. (1981): Principles of Text Analysis, *Linguistische Arbeitsberichte* 31 (1981), 3-29.

Gregory, M. (1967): Aspects of varieties differentiation, *Journal of Linguistics* 3 (1967), 177-198.

Groeben, N. & Scheele, B. (1984): *Produktion und Rezeption von Ironie*, vol. I, Tübingen.

Gülich, E. & Heger, K. & Raible, W. (²1979): *Linguistische Textanalyse*, Hamburg.

Gülich, E. & Raible, W. (1977): *Linguistische Textmodelle*, Munich.

Gülich, E. & Raible, W. (eds.) (²1975): *Textsorten*, Wiesbaden.

Gutknecht, C. & Mackiewitz, W. (1977): Prosodische, paralinguistische und intonatorische Phänomene im Englischen, in Gutknecht, C. (ed.) (1977): *Grundbegriffe und Hauptströmungen der Linguistik*, Hamburg, 95-132.

Halliday, M. A. K. & Hasan, R. (1976): *Cohesion in English*, London.

Hartmann, P. (1970): Semantische Textanalyse, in Schmidt 1970, 15-42.

Harweg, R. (1974): Textlinguistik, in Koch 1974, 88-116.

Hatim, B. & Mason, I. (1992): *Discourse and the Translator*, London-New York: Longman.

Helbig, G. (1980): Zur Stellung und zu Problemen der Textlinguistik, *Deutsch als Fremdsprache* 17 (1980), 5, 257-266.

Holmes, J. S. & Lambert, J. & van den Broeck, R. (eds.) (1978): *Literature and Translation*, Leuven.

Holmes, J. S. (ed.) (1970): *The Nature of Translation*, The Hague.

Holz-Mänttäri, J. (1984a): *Translatorisches Handeln, Theorie und Methode*, Helsinki.

Holz-Mänttäri, J. (1984b): Sichtbarmachung und Beurteilung translatorischer Leistungen bei der Ausbildung von Berufstranslatoren, in Wilss & Thome 1984, 176-185.

Hönig, H. G. & Kußmaul, P. (1982): *Strategie der Übersetzung*, Tübingen.

Hönig, H. G. (1986): Übersetzen zwischen Reflex und Reflexion ein Modell der übersetzungsrelevanten Textanalyse, in Snell-Hornby 1986, 230-252.

House, J. (1981b): Ein Modell zur Durchführung und Bewertung von Übersetzungen in der sprachpraktischen Ausbildung an der Hochschule, in Bausch & Weller 1981, 192-202.

House, J. (²1981a): *A Model for Translation Quality Assessment*, Tübingen.

Jakobson, R. (1960): Linguistics and Poetics, Closing Statement in *Style in Language*, ed. by T. A. Sebeok, Cambridge/Mass., 350-377.

Japp, U. (1983): *Theorie der Ironie*, Frankfurt/M.

Kade, O. (ed.) (1977): *Vermittelte Kommunikation, Sprachmittlung, Translation*, Leipzig.

Kade, O. (ed.) (1979): *Sprachliches und Außersprachliches in der Kommunikation*, Leipzig.

Kayser, W. (⁸1962): *Das sprachliche Kunstwerk*, Bern.

Keller, R. (1980): Zum Begriff des Fehlers im muttersprachlichen Unterricht, in Cherubim 1980, 23-42.

Kerrigan, A. (1976): Introduction, in Unamuno 1976, vii-xxxiv.

Kloepfer, R. (1967): *Die Theorie der literarischen Übersetzung*, Munich.

Kloepfer, R. (1984): Intra- and Intercultural Translation, *Parallèles* 7 (1985/86), 37-43.

Koller, W. (1979): *Einführung in die Übersetzungswissenschaft*, Heidelberg.

Koller, W. (1995): The Concept of Equivalence, *Target* 7(2): 191-222.

Kommissarov, V. N. (1977): Zur Theorie der linguistischen Übersetzungsanalyse, in Kade 1977, 44-51.

Königs, F. G. (1981): Zur Frage der Übersetzungseinheit und ihre Relevanz für den Fremdsprachenunterricht, *Linguistische Berichte* 74 (1981), 82-103.

Königs, F. G. (1983): Zentrale Begriffe aus der wissenschaftlichen Beschäftigung mit Übersetzen, *Lebende Sprachen* 1/1983, 6-8 (1983a) and 4/1983, 154-156 (1983b).

Königs, F. G. (1986): Der Vorgang des Übersetzens: Theoretische Modelle und praktischer Vollzug. Zum Verhältnis von Theorie und Praxis in der Übersetzungswissenschaft, *Lebende Sprachen* 1/1986, 5-12.

Krings, H. P. (1986): *Was in den Köpfen von Übersetzern vorgeht*, Tübingen.

Kühlwein, W. & Raasch, A. (eds.) (1980): *Angewandte Linguistik*, Tübingen.

Kühlwein, W. & Thome, G. & Wilss, W. (eds.) (1981): *Kontrastive Linguistik und Übersetzungswissenschaft*, Munich.

Kupsch-Losereit, S. (1986): Scheint eine schöne Sonne? oder: Was ist ein Übersetzungsfehler?, in *Lebende Sprachen* 1/1986, 12-16.

Kußmaul, P. (1995): *Training the Translator*, Amsterdam-Philadelphia.

Lausberg, H. (^{4}1971): *Elemente der literarischen Rhetorik*, Munich.

Leonhard, K. (1976): *Der menschliche Ausdruck in Mimik, Gestik und Phonik*, Leipzig.

Levý, J. (1967): Translation as a Decision Process, in *To Honor Roman Jakobson. Essays on the Occasion of his 70th Birthday*, vol. II, The Hague, 1171-1182.

Levý, J. (1969): *Die literarische Übersetzung*, Frankfurt/M.-Bonn.

Lüger, H.-H. (1977): *Journalistische Darstellungsformen aus linguistischer Sicht*, Freiburg.

Lux, F. (1981): *Text, Situation, Textsorte*, Tübingen.

Marco, J. (1980): La magia del mestizaje, *La Vanguardia Española*, 26-04-1980, 45.

Martinet, A. (ed.) (1973): *Linguistik*, Stuttgart.

Matt, P. & Thiel, G. & Thome, G. & Wilss, W. (1978): Übersetzungsrelevante Typologie deutscher und französischer Texte, *Zeitschrift für Germanistische Linguistik* 6 (1978), 189-233.

Matute, A. M. (1967): *Erste Erinnerung*, transl. by D. Deinhard, Munich.

Matute, A. M. (1979): *Primera memoria*, Barcelona.

Mentrup, W. (1982): Gebrauchsinformation sorgfältig lesen! Die Packungsbeilage von Medikamenten im Schaltkreis medizinischer Kommunikation: Handlungsausschnitt, in Grosse, S. & Mentrup, W. (eds.) (1982): *Anweisungstexte*, Tübingen., 9-55.

Mikes, G. (1984): How to Be an Alien, in G. Mikes, *How to Be a Brit*, London 1984, 20-94.

Moliner, M. (1975): *Diccionario de uso del español*, Madrid.

Morgenstern, C. & Knight/M. (1975): *Galgenlieder   Gallows Songs*, Munich.

Mudersbach, K. & Gerzymisch-Arbogast, H. (1989): Isotopy and Translation, in Krawutschke, P. W. (ed.) (1989): *Translator and Interpreter Training and Foreign Language Pedagogy*, American Translators Association Scholarly Monograph Series, Vol. III, New York.

Neubert, A. (1968): Pragmatische Aspekte der Übersetzung, in Wilss 1981, 60-75.

Neubert, A. (1984): Text-bound Translation Training, in Wilss & Thome 1984, 61-79.
Neubert, A. (1986): Translatorische Relativität, in Snell-Hornby 1986, 85-105.
Newmark, P. (1980): Teaching specialized translation, in Poulsen & Wilss 1980, 127-148.
Newmark, P. (1981): *Approaches to Translation*, Oxford-Frankfurt/M.
Nickel, G. & Raasch, A. (eds.) (1975): *Kongreßbericht der 6. Jahrestagung der GAL, vol. I: Übersetzungswissenschaft*, Heidelberg.
Nida, E. A. (1964): *Towards a Science of Translating*, Leiden.
Nida, E. A. (1975): The Nature of Translating, in *Language Structure and Translation. Essays by E. A. Nida*, ed. by A. D. Dil, Stanford, 79-101.
Nida, E. A. (1976): A Framework for the Analysis and Evaluation of Theories of Translation, in Brislin, R. W. (ed.) (1976): *Translation: Applications and Research*, New York., 47-91.
Nord, C. (1986a): 'Treue', 'Freiheit', 'Äquivalenz' – oder: Wozu brauchen wir den Übersetzungsauftrag?, *TextconText* 1/1986, 30-47.
Nord, C. (1986b): 'Nación', 'pueblo', 'raza' bei Ortega y Gasset – nicht nur ein Übersetzungsproblem, *TextconText* 3/1986, 151-170.
Nord, C. (1987a): Übersetzungsprobleme – Übersetzungsschwierigkeiten. Was in den Köpfen von Übersetzern vorgehen sollte..., *Mitteilungsblatt für Dolmetscher und Übersetzer* 2/1987, 5-8.
Nord, C. (1987b): Textanalyse im Übersetzungsunterricht? Überlegungen zur Verhältnismäßigkeit der Mittel: Verhindert die Textanalyse im Übersetzungsunterricht dessen eigentliches Ziel, das Übersetzenlernen?, *TextconText* 1/1987, 42-61.
Nord, C. (1987c): Zehn Thesen zum Thema 'Übersetzungslehrbuch', in Königs, F. G. (ed.) (1987): *Übersetzen lehren und lernen mit Büchern. Möglichkeiten und Grenzen der Erstellung und des Einsatzes von Übersetzungslehrbüchern*, Bochum, 65-82.
Nord, C. (1988a): *Textanalyse und Übersetzen. Theoretische Grundlagen, Methode und didaktische Anwendung einer übersetzungsrelevanten Textanalyse*. Heidelberg, 2nd ed. 1991.
Nord, C. (1988b): Übersetzungshandwerk - Übersetzungskunst. Was bringt die Translationstheorie für das literarische Übersetzen?, *Lebende Sprachen* 2/1988, 51-57.
Nord, C. (1989): Loyalität statt Treue. Vorschläge zu einer funktionalen Übersetzungstypologie, *Lebende Sprachen* 3/1989, 100-105.
Nord, C. (1990a): Neue Federn am fremden Hut. Der Umgang mit Zitaten beim Übersetzen, *Der Deutschunterricht* 1/1990, 36-42.
Nord, C. (1990b): Funcionalismo y lealtad: algunas consideraciones en torno a la traducción de títulos, in Raders, M. & Conesa, J. (eds.): *II Encuentros Complutenses en torno a la Traducción*, Madrid 1990, 153-162.
Nord, C. (1991): Scopos, Loyalty and Translational Conventions, *Target* 3:1 (1991), 91-109.
Nord, C. (1992a): Text Analysis in Translator Training, in Dollerup, C. & Loddegaard, A. (eds.) (1992): *Teaching Translation and Interpreting. Training, Talent and Experience. Papers from the First Language International Conference* 31 May - 2 June 1991 (= Copenhagen Studies in Translation), Amsterdam/Philadelphia, 39-48.
Nord, C. (1992b): The Relationship between Text Function and Meaning in Translation, in Lewandowska-Tomaszyk, B. & Thelen, M. (eds.) (1992): *Translation and Meaning, Part 2: Proceedings of the Lódz Session of the 1990 Maastricht-Lodz*

Duo Colloquium on Translation and Meaning , Maastricht: Rijkshogeschool Maastricht Faculty of Translation and Interpreting, 91-96.

Nord, C. (1993): *Einführung in das funktionale Übersetzen. Am Beispiel von Titeln und Überschriften*, Tübingen: Francke.

Nord, C. (1995): Text-functions in translation. Titles and Headings as a Case in Point, *Target* 7:2 (1995), 261-284.

Nord, C. (1997a): *Translation as a purposeful activity. Functionalist approaches explained*, Manchester: St. Jerome.

Nord, C. (1997b): Alice abroad. Translating paralanguage in fictional texts, in Poyatos, F. (ed.): *Nonverbal Communication and Translation*, Amsterdam/Philadelphia: John Benjamins 1997 (= Benjamins Translation Library, 17), 107-129.

Nord, C. (1997c): A Functional Typology of Translations, in Trosborg, A. (ed.), *Text Typology and Translation*, Amsterdam/Philadelphia: John Benjamins 1997, 43-66.

Nord, C. (1997d): Leicht - mittelschwer – (zu) schwer. Zur Bestimmung des Schwierigkeitsgrades von Übersetzungsaufgaben, in Fleischmann, E. et al. (eds.): *Translationsdidaktik. Beiträge der VI. Internationalen Konferenz zur Grundfragen der Übersetzungswissenschaft*, Tübingen: Narr 1997, 92-102.

Nord, C. (1997e): Functional Units in Translation, in Mauranen, A. & Puurtinen, T. (eds.): *Translation - Acquisition - Use*, AFinLa Yearbook 1997, Jyväskylä: University Press (= Publications de l'Association Finlandaise de Linguistique Appliquée, 55), 41-50.

Nord, C. (1997f): El texto buscado. Los textos auxiliares en la enseñanza de traducción, *TradTerm* (São Paulo, Brazil) 1997, 101-124.

Nord, C. (1997g): Defining Translation Functions. The translation brief as a guideline for the trainee translator, *Ilha do Desterro* (Florianopolis, Brazil), Special Issue: *Translation Studies in Germany*, ed. by W. Lörscher, 2.1997, 39-53.

Nord, C. (2000): What do we know about the target-text receiver? in Beeby, A. et al. (eds.): *Investigating Translation*, Amsterdam/Philadelphia 2000, 197-214.

Nord, C. (2001a): Loyalty Revisited, in Pym, A. (ed.): *The Return to Ethics*, Special Issue of *The Translator*, Manchester, 185-202.

Nord, C. (2001b): Das hinkende Beispiel und andere Merk-Würdigkeiten. Metakommunikation in deutschen, spanischen und französischen Lehrbuchtexten, in Wotjak, G. (ed.): *Studien zum romanisch-deutschen und innerromanischen Sprachvergleich*, Frankfurt/M. etc., 329-340.

Nord, C. (2001c): Dealing with Purposes in Intercultural Communication: Some Methodological Considerations, *Revista Alicantina de Estudios Ingleses* 14 (2001): 151-166.

Nord, C. (2001d): *Lernziel: Professionelles Übersetzen Spanisch-Deutsch*, Wilhelmsfeld: Gottfried Egert Verlag.

Nord, C. (2002): Function and Loyalty in Bible Translation, in Calzada Pérez, M. (ed.): *Apropos of Ideology. Translation Studies on Ideology Ideologies in Translation Studies*, Manchester: St. Jerome 2002, 89-112.

Nord, C. (2003): *Kommunikativ handeln auf Spanisch und Deutsch. Ein übersetzungsorientierter funktionaler Sprach- und Stilvergleich*, Wilhelmsfeld: Gottfried Egert Verlag.

Nord, C. (2005): Training functional translators, in Tennent, M. (ed.): *Training for the New Millenium*, Asterdam/Philadelphia: Benjamins, 209-223.

OALD (^{2}1963, ^{3}1974, ^{4}1989): *Oxford Advanced Learner s Dictionary of Current English*, ed. by A. S. Hornby et al., London.

OED (1961): *The Oxford English Dictionary*, London.

Oomen, U. (1983): Ironische Äußerungen: Syntax Semantik Pragmatik, *Zeitschrift für Germanistische Linguistik* 11 (1983), 22-38.

OUD (^{3}1970): *The Oxford Universal Dictionary Illustrated*, 2 vols., ed. by C. T. Onions, London.

Pabón, J. (1971): *La subversión contemporánea y otros estudios*, Madrid.

Paepcke, F. (1974): Georges Pompidou und die Sprache der Macht. Analyse eines Textes vom 10. November 1970, in Wilss & Thome 1974, II, 82-103.

Penkova, M. (1982): Die Präinformation bei der Analyse und Übersetzung von Texten, *Linguistische Arbeitsberichte* 37 (1982), 56-66.

Pequeño Larousse (1970): *Pequeño Larousse Ilustrado*, ed. by M. de Toro y Gisbert, Paris.

Plett, H. F. (^{2}1979) : *Textwissenschaft und Textanalyse*, Heidelberg.

Popovič, A. (1977): Übersetzung als Kommunikation, transl. by K. H. Freigang, in Wilss 1981, 92-111, .

Poulsen, S.-O. & Wilss, W. (eds.) (1980): *Angewandte Übersetzungswissenschaft*, Aarhus.

Poulsen, S.-O. (1981): Textlinguistik und Übersetzungskritik, in Kühlwein & Thome & Wilss 1981, 300-310.

Poulsen, S.-O. (1984): Der Gebrauch des Konjunktiv I als Übersetzungsproblem, in Wilss & Thome 1984, 71-79.

Presch, G. (1980): Über schwierigkeiten zu bestimmen, was als fehler gelten soll, in Cherubim, D. (ed.) (1980): *Fehlerlinguistik. Beiträge zum Problem der sprachlichen Abweichung*, Tübingen, 224-252.

Quirk, R. & Greenbaum, S. & Leech, G. & Svartvik, J. (1973): *A Grammar of Contemporary English*, London.

Raabe, H. (1979): Didaktische Translationsgrammatik, in Bausch 1979, 239-256.

Reiss, K. & Vermeer, H. J.(1984): *Grundlagen einer allgemeinen Translationstheorie*, Tübingen.

Reiss, K. (1971): *Möglichkeiten und Grenzen der Übersetzungskritik*, Munich; English translation by Erroll F. Rhodes (2000): *Translation Criticism The Potentials & Limitations*, Manchester: St. Jerome.

Reiss, K. (1974a): Ist Übersetzen lehrbar?, in *Kongreßbericht der 4. Jahrestagung der GAL, IRAL-Sonderband, Heidelberg*, 69-82.

Reiss, K. (1974b): Zur Bestimmung des Schwierigkeitsgrades von Übersetzungen, *Mitteilungsblatt für Dolmetscher und Übersetzer* 20 (1974), 3, 1-6.

Reiss, K. (1974c): Didaktik des Übersetzens. Probleme und Perspektiven, *Le Langage et L Homme* 1974, 32-40.

Reiss, K. (1975): Zur Bestimmung des Schwierigkeitsgrades von Übersetzungen aus didaktischer Sicht, *Le Langage et L Homme* 1975, 37-48.

Reiss, K. (1976a): *Texttyp und Übersetzungsmethode: Der operative Text*, Kronberg/Ts.

Reiss, K. (1976b): Didaktik des Übersetzens: Integration der Sprachwissenschaft in den Übersetzungsunterricht, in Bausch & Weller 1981, 127-144.

Reiss, K. (1977): Übersetzen und Übersetzung im Hochschulbereich, *Die Neueren Sprachen* 26 (1977), 535-548.

272 Text Analysis in Translation

Reiss, K. (1980a): Zeichen oder Anzeichen. Probleme der AS-Textanalyse im Blick auf die Übersetzung, in Wilss 1980, 63-72.

Reiss, K. (1980b): Der Übersetzungsvergleich als didaktisches Instrument im Übersetzungsunterricht, in Poulsen & Wilss 1980, 149-164.

Reiss, K. (1981a): Der Übersetzungsvergleich. Formen – Funktionen – Anwendbarkeit, in Kühlwein & Thome & Wilss 1981, 311-319.

Reiss, K. (1984): Methodische Fragen der übersetzungsrelevanten Textanalyse, *Lebende Sprachen* 1/1984, 7-10.

Reiss, K. (1985): Paraphrase und Übersetzung. Versuch einer Klärung, in Gnilka, J. & Rüger, H. P. (eds.) (1985): *Die Übersetzung der Bibel   Aufgabe der Theologie*, Bielefeld, 272-287.

Reiss, K. (1986): Übersetzungstheorien und ihre Relevanz für die Praxis, *Lebende Sprachen* 1/1986, 1-5.

RHD (1968): *The Random House Dictionary of the English Language*, College edition, ed. by L. Urdang, New York.

Roloff, J. (1981): *Die Apostelgeschichte*, NTD vol. 5, Göttingen.

Saile, G. (1982): Wie montiert man einen Fleischwolf? Linguistische Analyse einer Anleitung, in Grosse, S. & Mentrup, W. (eds.) (1982): *Anweisungstexte*, Tübingen, 134-158.

Sandig, B. (ed.) (1981): *Stilistik, vol. I: Probleme der Stilistik, Germanistische Linguistik* (1981), 3/4.

Scherner, M. (1984): *Sprache als Text*, Tübingen.

Schmidt, S. J. (1970): Text und Bedeutung, in Schmidt, S. J. (ed.) (^{2}1970): *Text, Bedeutung, Ästhetik*, Munich, 43-79.

Schmidt, S. J. (1971): 'Text' und 'Geschichte' als Fundierungskategorien, in Stempel, W.-D. (ed.) (1971): *Beiträge zur Textlinguistik*, Munich, 31-52.

Schmidt, S. J. (^{2}1976): *Texttheorie*, Munich.

Selinker, L. (1972): Interlanguage, *IRAL* 10 (1972), 209-230.

Sitta, H. & Brinker, K. (eds.) (1973): *Studien zur Texttheorie und zur deutschen Grammatik*, Düsseldorf.

Snell-Hornby, M. (1986a): Übersetzen, Sprache, Kultur, Introduction to Snell-Hornby 1986, 9-29.

Snell-Hornby, M. (ed.) (1986): *Übersetzungswissenschaft. Eine Neurientierung*, Tübingen.

Sowinski, B. (1973): *Deutsche Stilistik,* Frankfurt/M.

Stackelberg, J. (1978): *Weltliteratur in deutscher Übersetzung*, Munich.

Stempel, W.-D. (1971): Möglichkeiten einer Darstellung der Diachronie in narrativen Texten, in Stempel, W.-D. (ed.) (1971): *Beiträge zur Textlinguistik*, Munich, 53-78.

Stenzel, J. (1966): *Zeichensetzung*, Göttingen.

Stevens, H. S. & Gullón, R. (1979): Introducción, in Unamuno 1979, 7-46.

Stolt, B. (1978): Die Relevanz stilistischer Faktoren für die Übersetzung, *Jahrbuch für Internationale Germanistik* 10 (1978), 2, 34-54.

Strausfeld, M. (ed.) (1976): *Materialien zur lateinamerikanischen Literatur*, Frankfurt/M.

Swift, J. (1983): *A Voyage to Lilliput/Gullivers Reisen nach Lilliput*, transl. and with a postscript by Dieter Mehl, Munich 1983.

Thiel, G. (1974a): Ansätze zu einer Methodologie der übersetzungsrelevanten Textanalyse, in Kapp, V. (ed.) (1974): *Übersetzer und Dolmetscher*, Heidelberg, 174-
185.

Thiel, G. (1974b): Methodische Probleme einer übersetzungsunterrichtlich relevanten
Textanalyse, in Wilss & Thome 1974, II, 64-81.

Thiel, G. (1978a): Führt die Anwendung linguistischer Analysemodelle zu einer
Übersetzungsdidaktisch relevanten Textanalyse?, in Gomard, K. & Poulsen, S.-O.
(eds.) (1978): *Stand und Möglichkeiten der Übersetzungswissenschaft*, Aarhus,
37-54.

Thiel, G. (1978b): Überlegungen zur übersetzungsrelevanten Textanalyse, in Wilss
1981, 367-383.

Thiel, G. (1980): Vergleichende Textanalyse als Basis für die Entwicklung einer
Übersetzungsmethodik, dargestellt anhand der Textsorte Resolution, in Wilss
1980, 87-98.

Thürmann, E. (1977): Die Phonetischen Wissenschaften. Trends und Entwicklungen,
in Gutknecht, C. (ed.) (1977): *Grundbegriffe und Hauptströmungen der Linguistik*, Hamburg, 19-52.

Titzmann, M. (1977): *Strukturale Textanalyse*, Munich.

Tophoven, E. (1979): Möglichkeiten literarischer Übersetzung zwischen Intuition und
Formalisierung, in Peisl, A. & Mohler, A. (eds.) (1979): *Der Mensch und seine
Sprache*, Frankfurt-Berlin-Vienna, 125-144.

Toury, G. (1978): Interlanguage and its manifestations in translation, in Toury 1980,
S.71-78.

Toury, G. (1983): Sharing relevant features. An exercise in optimal translating, *META*
28 (1983), 2, 116-129.

Unamuno, M. de (1968): *Nebel*, transl. by O. Buek and revised by D. Deinhard, Munich.

Unamuno, M. de (1976): Mist, in *Novela/Nivola*, transl. and with an Introduction by
A. Kerrigan, Princeton.

Unamuno, M. de ([7]1979): *Niebla*, Madrid.

van den Broeck, R. (1978): The Concept of Equivalence in Translation Theory: Some
Critical Reflections, in Holmes et al. 1978, 29-47.

Vanguardia (1980): Un gran escritor del Caribe, in *La Vanguardia Española*, 26-04-
1980, 45.

Vermeer, H. J. (1970): Generative Transformationsgrammatik, Sprachvergleich und
Sprachtypologie, *Zeitschrift für Phonetik, Sprachwissenschaft und Kommunikationsforschung* 23 (1970), 385-404.

Vermeer, H. J. (1972): *Allgemeine Sprachwissenschaft*, Freiburg.

Vermeer, H. J. (1974a): zur beschreibung des übersetzungsvorgangs, in Vermeer
1983, 1-11.

Vermeer, H. J. (1974b): interaktionsdeterminanten- ein versuch zwischen pragma-
und sociolinguistik, in Vermeer 1983, 12-32.

Vermeer, H. J. (1978): ein rahmen für eine allgemeine translationstheorie, in Vermeer
1983, 48-61.

Vermeer, H. J. (1979): vom 'richtigen' übersetzen, in Vermeer 1983, 62-88.

Vermeer, H. J. (1981): übersetzen und verständnis, in Vermeer 1983, 89-130.

Vermeer, H. J. (1983): *Aufsätze zur Translationstheorie*, Heidelberg.

VOX ([4]1979): *VOX Diccionario general ilustrado de la lengua española*, ed. by S.
Gili y Gaya, Barcelona.

Warning, R. (1976): Ironiesignale und ironische Solidarisierung, in Preisendanz, W. & Warning, R. (eds.) (1976): *Das Komische, Poetik und Hermeneutik 7*, Munich, 416-423.

Weinrich, H. (1966): *Linguistik der Lüge*, Heidelberg.

Willer, B. & Groeben, N. (1980): Sprachliche Hinweise auf ironische Kooperation: das Konzept der Ironiesignale unter sprechakttheoretischer Perspektive re-konstruiert, *Zeitschrift für Germanistische Linguistik* 8 (1980), 3, 290-313.

Wilss, W. & Thome, G. (eds.) (1974): *Aspekte der theoretischen, sprachenpaarbezogenen und angewandten Sprachwissenschaft*, vol. I: Saarbrücken, vol. II: Heidelberg.

Wilss, W. & Thome, G. (eds.) (1984): *Die Theorie des Übersetzens und ihr Aufschlußwert für die Übersetzungs- und Dolmetschdidaktik*, Tübingen.

Wilss, W. (1977): Textanalyse und Übersetzen, in Bender, K. H. & Berger, K. & Wandruszca, M. (eds.) (1977): *Imago Linguae, Beiträge zu Sprache, Deutung und Übersetzen, Festschrift zum 60. Geburtstag von Fritz Paepcke*, Munich, 625-651.

Wilss, W. (1980a): Semiotik und Übersetzungswissenschaft, in Wilss 1980, 9-22.

Wilss, W. (1980b): Übersetzungswissenschaft, in Kühlwein & Raasch 1980, 67-76.

Wilss, W. (1982): *The Science of Translation. Problems and Methods*, Tübingen.

Wilss, W. (ed.) (1980): *Semiotik und Übersetzen*, Tübingen.

Wilss, W. (ed.) (1981): *Übersetzungswissenschaft*, Darmstadt.

Wittgenstein, L. (1955): *Tractatus logico-philosophicus*, with an introduction by Bertrand Russell, London.

Wittich, U. (1979): Texttypologie unter funktionalstilistischer Sicht, *Zeitschrift für Phonetik, Sprachwissenschaft und Kommunikationsforschung* 32 (1979) 6, 764-769.

Wittschier, W. (1982): *Geschichte der spanischen Literatur vom Kubakrieg bis zu Francos Tod* (1898-1975), Rheinfelden.

Zalán, P. (1984): Didaktik der Übersetzerausbildung auf Konfliktkurs oder sind Katastrophen auf der einen Seite und Resignieren auf der anderen vermeidbar?, in Wilss & Thome 1984, 196-203.

Zimnjaja, I. A. (1977): Die psychologische Analyse der Translation als Art der Redetätigkeit, in Kade 1977, 66-77.